FILM LIBRARY TECHNIQUES

FILM LIBRARY TECHNIQUES

Helen P. Harrison

Introduction by
Dr. A. William Bluem

FOCAL PRESS
London and New York

©1973 *FOCAL PRESS LIMITED*

ISBN 0 240 50820 3

Printed by Biddles Ltd., Guildford, Surrey
Bound by The Pitman Press, Bath

CONTENTS

Introduction by Dr. A. William Bluem   11

1. Function of Film Libraries   13

Purpose of film libraries   13
Reuse of film   14
Users of library film   17
How film is used   18
Nature of film   18

2. History and Development of Film Libraries   20

Growth of national collections   20
Types of film library   21
Distribution libraries   22
Documentary production libraries   23
Feature production libraries   23
Government libraries   24
Government libraries: research   25
National archives   25
Newsreel libraries   26
Television libraries   29
Education libraries   29

3. Selection Principles and Techniques   31

Haphazard selection   31
Principles of selection   32
Responsibility for selection   43
Timing of selection   44
Practical example of selection procedure   47
Selection from offcuts for stockshots   48
Technique of selecting stockshots   49

4. Film Handling and Retrieval   50

Types of film material   50
Types of copy   53
Differences in composition   54
Accession and recording   55
Temporary storage of film   56
Permanent storage   58
Other storage systems   59
Handling and storage equipment   60
Retrieval of film from storage   62
Film movement records   63
Viewing procedures   64
Viewing machines   65
Scratch prints   66
Preparation for laboratories   67
Laboratory printing   67
Breakdown on return   70
Examination before refiling   70
Refiling   72

5. Shotlisting or Sequence Listing   73

Principles of shotlisting   73
How to shotlist   74
Viewing machines for shotlisting   75
Essential features of shotlists   76
Film title and number   77
Treatment of credits   77
Recording footage   78
Indicating types of shot   79
Description of shot   81
Dealing with sound content   83
Additional information   85
Standard shotlisting abbreviations   86
Types of shotlist   86
Layout of shotlists   87
Instant cataloguing   89

6. Documentation and Storage of Documents   90

Production records   90
Shotlists   91
Storage equipment   93
Photocopying methods and requirements   95

Applications of microfilm 96
Combining records 99
Types of reference material for shotlisting 100

7. Cataloguing 106

Choice of main heading 106
Form of heading 109
Descriptive cataloguing 110
Use of secondary sources 111
Perfect copies 112
Cataloguing procedures 113
Accessions numbers 114
Numbering methods 115
Combining records in the main catalogue 118
Filing order 118
Form of entry 119
Type of entry 125
Types of catalogue 129
Standardisation 131
Codes of practice 134
Authority file 146
User's guide 147
Staff manual 148

8. Information retrieval 149

What to index 150
Index according to needs of user 151
Attributes of efficient indexing systems 152
Indexes for feature and documentary film libraries 153
Indexes for distribution film libraries 154
Indexes for educational film libraries, national and other 154
catalogues
Indexes for newsfilm libraries 155
Name indexes 157
Filing and reference in alphabetical indexes 159
Types and aims of subject indexing 162
Classified subject indexes 163
Dictionary-style subject index 168
Alphabetico classed subject index 168
Machine based retrieval systems 174
Systems in use 176

9. Storage and Preservation   177

Storage principles   178
Construction and use of vaults   179
Storage conditions   181
Storage equipment   183
Film preservation and maintenance   186
Problem awareness   188
Company preservation policies   189
Co-operative schemes   192

10. Staffing   193

Administrative staff   193
Clerical staff   194
Technical and professional staff   195
Professional and non-professional staff   200
Flexibility of staff   201
Size of staff   202
Salaries   203
Working conditions   205
Union agreements   206
Staff training   207

11. Layout and Planning   211

Responsibility for planning decisions   211
Planning for the future   212
Site planning   213
Relationship between units   215
Space requirements   218

12. Economics   224

Film acquisition costs   224
Expenditure on staff salaries   225
Laboratory costs   225
Maintenance costs   225
Cost of site facilities and equipment   226
Sources of income   226
Analysis of processing charges   227
Royalty payments   230
Calculation of royalty charges   231
Revision of royalty charges   234
Search fees   235

13. Copyright 236

Restrictions on usage 236
How rights are obtained 237
Enforcement of rights 239
Material not library copyright 240
Contracts between owner and purchaser 241
Contractual details 242
Investigating new customers 244
Progress of production 245
Recording contracts and sales 245

14. Future Developments 248

Developments in film material 248
Video recording methods 251
Electronic video recording (EVR) 253
Developments in handling techniques 254
Developments in dissemination of information 257
Developments in standardisation 260
Developments in national and international co-operation 263
Conclusion 264

Bibliography 267

Index 272

INTRODUCTION

I T IS heartening to note that practitioners of the archival and library sciences are bringing their skills to bear upon the heavy task of identifying and organizing the immense outpouring of the non-print media in this century. Those who have interest in the destiny of "electric man" now recognize that posterity will never fully understand what we were or what we aspired to without full access to the sight-sound records created during a century in which film and electronic communication have ranged over the face of the earth.

The effort to identify, catalogue, preserve and make available this vivid record of humanity requires a truly international thrust. Indeed, world-wide cooperation and exchange of intelligence has long been essential to the evolution of print-media archival and library organization. In addition, major programs in motion picture preservation are in a state of full international development. Still to be solved are complex problems of selection and retention as well as a host of technological difficulties which are inherent to preservation of the output of the electronic media, but this work is also under way.

As the burgeoning of information technology enables archivists and librarians to deal with problems of collection fragmentation, the easy exchange of films, tapes, discs and print information related to such materials will become commonplace. And as common modes and standards of description are universally adopted, major difficulties in classification and control will also be resolved.

There is great value, then, in encouraging various production and programming sources, as well as educational institutions, to establish sight-sound libraries which serve not only their immediate internal needs, but the interests of the scholarly community — and posterity — as well. For this reason, those with interest in non-print media will welcome the addition of Helen Harrison's useful volume dealing with film library organization and administration. Her observations and recommendations reflect standard and accepted international practice, and will therefore be of particular value to all concerned archivists and librarians.

A. William Bluem, Ph.D.
Professor of Media Studies
Syracuse University
(Syracuse, New York)

I

FUNCTION OF FILM LIBRARIES

ALTHOUGH general principles are common to all film librarianship, there are many types of library with different aims and methods of work. The major difference between film libraries exists in the reuse of their material. Many deal with complete films and distribute or sell them for showing in their entirety. Others deal with film for reuse in shorter sequences; they usually sell material to be included in new films or as illustrative material for special situations, such as lectures, theatrical productions, and television compilations. Some libraries do not sell film or distribute it, for example the research libraries attached to particular organisations or departments where film is used as an integral part of current research work. Nevertheless these libraries do encounter problems of administration, storage and retrieval similar to those of any other film library.

This book concentrates on the field of film librarianship in which the problems are most pronounced. General principles can be extracted from this commercial field and applied to other types of film library, but the type of library does highlight the difficulties special to film librarians and serves as a basis for some solutions to these difficulties.

PURPOSE OF FILM LIBRARIES

Film libraries exist to collect, organise and utilise motion pictures. Although they have grown with the film industry for more than 70 years, their growth has not been a steady progression from first principles, but rather an adaptive process which used the more established techniques of book librarianship or improvised on these techniques to cope with the medium itself. As with any other collection, before it can be organised account has to be taken of the special nature and characteristics of the material to be organised.

The application of library science can be extended to media other than books. Library science exists to lay down principles of

13

good practice which can be applied to all media requiring collection and organisation to enhance their usefulness. Most of the problems presented by film can be approached from principles of librarianship and logical solutions found. By applying library principles to film libraries, standardisation should be achieved and a more rational approach can be made to the special problems.

REUSE OF FILM

Film is expensive to produce and in the production context should be kept and reshown in order to pay for itself. It must be carefully stored and organised for easy retrieval and the library is the most obvious department to perform these functions. The job of a production unit is to make new films, not to be diverted into exploiting those already completed. The film can be reused in its entirety, or in selected pieces. Generally feature films are reshown complete for entertainment or because they have been designed as a creative whole to be reviewed in this way, but many types of film can be cut or re-edited into new compilations. Several libraries are based on this premise, i.e. to sell sections of films for reuse.

There are five main reasons for reusing film:
1. Entertainment
2. Historical purposes
3. Where reshooting is impossible
4. To avoid repetitious shooting
5. As illustration

Reissues for entertainment. Entertainment is the most obvious of film. As it is so expensive to make there would be little point in making a film for one showing only. Films can be reshown for entertainment purposes in several contexts, in cinemas where the popularity of revivals is clear, on television, to film societies and as light relief for conferences. Feature films and documentaries are the most popular films for this type of usage.

Historical records. Film can be kept as a history of the art itself. Feature films, for example, are retained for reshowing at a later date to demonstrate the development of the art of film-making, and as examples of the work of particular artists, such as directors, cameramen, actors etc. Documentary film is also retained for historical purposes; many documentaries show life or customs of a particular people at a particular time, such as a tribe or community which may have become extinct or so altered its way of life in the intervening years that only the filmed record is left to show what their life was like. Research film may be kept and reshown for historical purposes only, to show the steps taken in the development of a product or machine.

Many types of film therefore serve as historical records either of the cinema as art, documentary record, scientific experiment or newsfilm which provides a major example of an historical record showing the events and personalities of the past 70-80 years. Without a film library, film and events which were produced or occurred 10, 20 or 50 years ago cannot be shown visually. Verbal descriptions cannot replace the filmed record, and although the memoirs of people connected with events are of importance, an extra dimension is added if the events are seen and the personalities involved are shown as they reacted at the time rather than how they think they reacted in retrospect. Political figures can be shown in public office and the progression of their careers can often be traced on film. Events which were recorded on film can be reshown as they occurred, but if the event itself is not on film it can be illustrated by showing related scenes. These scenes are in historical perspective, that is they concern the same people and are set in the same place and period to convey the atmosphere of the time.

Unfortunately many 'events' have been faked using this technique, a practice which has resulted in some serious errors. Once a fake has been passed off, the error moves into fact until it is discovered. One event may be substituted for another, as when films purporting to show the sinking of the *Titanic* actually contained shots of the *Lusitania* and *Mauritania*. In some cases film used for propaganda purposes may inadvertently come to be treated as genuine. This sort of error easily occurs and sets many problems both for the libraries and their users. Distortion of fact in the reuse of film can range from mild to blatant, but where the film is being used for information or education care has to be taken to ensure authenticity.

This raises the question of control by libraries over the reuse of their material. A library *can* place some restrictions on the use of its material, although often these restrictions are imposed by the original supplier of the film and passed on to the customers of the library. In general, ethical questions of what to use and how to use it are left to the producer of the particular project that purchases the film. The undiscriminating audience that treats fact and fiction on the same level is not the concern of the library. The library's concern is to provide the producer with the sort of material he is looking for.

Gradually, historians are becoming interested in the potentialities of film as source material, but they are finding that they have to study the history of the film making industry as well as the facts or fictions presented in the films before they can sort out the authentic material. In particular historians have trouble with newsfilm, which is often edited at the time of showing for a particular purpose. Commentaries are misleading, film may purport to be from a particular place, but on examination prove to be used even then as illustration and have come from an entirely different place. If it contained shots to show the type of action required, the film was used for want of any other, regardless of where the film may have been taken. However, once authenticity is established, film can be a useful visual record of events.

Educational usage of film is a subdivision of historical. Film is used for educational purposes in the same way as for historical purposes whether the film is educational in the limited or more general sense.

Substitute for reshooting. Closely allied to the reuse of film to show historical events is the reuse of film which it would be impossible or inconvenient to reshoot. One cannot reshoot historical events; they happen only once and if film is not obtained at the time, dramatic reconstruction gives an impression of a 'live' event. People who made news may no longer be alive. Buildings may have been demolished, damaged or altered out of recognition, take the Reichstag before the fire, or Hyde Park before the underpass. Film provides records of all these. Other techniques such as artists' impressions or photographs exist, but these may not be satisfactory for inclusion in a film. A more obvious impossibility for reshooting is when the season is wrong, e.g. trying to shoot snow scenes in summer, or rain or fog on bright summer days. In these circumstances it is useful to have a collection of film shot in all seasons ready for use.

As well as being impossible to reshoot, some places may be inaccessible, or it may be inconvenient to reshoot the scene. Foreign policies can be such that certain locations are no longer available. For all these reasons library film may have to be reused rather than reshoot the scene.

Avoiding uneconomic reshooting. Repetitious shooting of the same or similar scenes is uneconomic. It is expensive to use a full crew to shoot material for short scenes and inconvenient to have to hold up a production crew until the right conditions are reached, when film could as easily be held in a film library as a stockshot. A comprehensive film library becomes an invaluable asset in these circumstances.

Illustrative uses. The reuse of library film is also valuable in television journalism when an important news story breaks and there is no time to shoot new film, send it from source to laboratories, develop and then transmit. In these cases library film can be used to set the scene while a newsreader comments on the new incident over the film.

USERS OF LIBRARY FILM

The most frequent user of film today is television. Television stations throughout the world are constantly looking for material to illustrate their news and documentary programmes. Television also uses library material for establishing shots, stockshots or backdrops for entertainment and other programmes.

Advertising media both inside and outside television use library film. Usage here is intensive and repetitive rather than extensive.

Cinema uses library film although to a lesser extent than television. A piece of actuality material may be used for effect in a feature film. In documentaries, actuality material is more essential. The film *To Die in Madrid,* for example, was about the Spanish Civil War and consisted entirely of newsfilm collected from all over the world and welded into a very successful whole.

The theatre can use film for back projection or reference. Film was used in a recent production of *The Representative* by Rolf Hochhuth, where the queues waiting for transportation or the gas ovens served as backdrops to the arguments being presented on stage. In this way the audience was receiving information on two levels through two media. This usage of film is strictly limited in order to preserve the difference between the theatrical and the cinematic media.

Education makes use of library film. New educational films are made from library material either to illustrate current affairs or to indicate progress in science, geography and other research topics. Universities have also become interested in the possibilities of using film as source material. Film is becoming increasingly useful in the study of current affairs or the history of modern times as more recent history is committed to a filmed record and newsfilm as a chronicle of the twentieth century is recognised as a major source of material.

Another use for film is in reference work, when the film is not transmitted, but is studied for details of historical importance it may contain, such as style of dress or form of ritual. Sets can be rebuilt using film as a reference point.

There are other more incidental uses for film. Stills taken from

the film can be used by newspapers or magazines, although the
quality of a 'blow-up' from 16mm newsfilm is not good. In some
cases only film exists of a particular incident when no still
photographer was present.

HOW FILM IS USED

Film is not necessarily reused for its original purpose. This is
especially so with stockshots and newsfilm, which are reused in
documentary for television or cinema, as stockshot or backdrop,
for reference etc. The use of library film does not follow output
distinctions. At BBC it is estimated that 75 per cent of the news
output is reused for purposes other than news. Newsfilm,
documentary, stockshots are all used together in making up a new
production.

Nor is film always reused in its entirety. Film can be fully
retransmitted if it forms complete programmes or films. Several
pieces of library film can be intercut to form longer pieces, but
only the relevant sequences from each piece are used. When short
film is used in its entirety it is usually an interview where the
speaker is developing an argument or discussing a single topic. The
film editor can use several sequences to make a coherent film, an
establishing shot to show locale, the actual incident reported,
shots of personalities involved, any special features and a good end
piece to finish the film off logically. In reusing this library film the
new editor has a new purpose and may require only one of the
sequences included in the original story.

NATURE OF FILM

The nature of film determines many of the policies in the
libraries devoted to the medium. By comparison with other
materials film can be relatively unstable chemically, difficult and
dangerous to store, awkward to handle, fragile and easy to
damage, difficult to replace and presents many problems in
indexing.

When collected even in small numbers (ten half hour
documentaries or information films can contain a large amount of
data), films have to be organised for easy location and identification. Accuracy of indexing is needed to pinpoint certain items.
While one can search a book for the information it contains,
searching film without the aid of comprehensive indexes is more
difficult. A viewing machine has to intervene between user and
information and this machine takes time to prepare. Also it is time

consuming to view a thirty minute film for a thirty second sequence without accurate location. With detailed indexing and adequate written information in the form of shotlists much of this difficulty can be alleviated. Cataloguing principles can be adopted from general library science with due consideration for the special nature of film.

One further problem emerges in the conflict between the fact that the film is an art form or piece of information in itself and therefore needs to be viewed to convey the full impression or complete data and the opposing fact that each viewing of a film will inevitably damage it to an extent. This conflict is not peculiar to film; any heavily used information carrier is subject to deterioration, but film is one of the more obvious examples.

2

HISTORY AND DEVELOPMENT OF
FILM LIBRARIES

FILM LIBRARIES began with small trading companies who issued catalogues or published lists of the film they made up. Film distribution became an essential complement to production and the libraries rented out film nationally and internationally. They began to buy up distribution rights in films and included them in their own catalogues. Gradually the libraries accumulated film and expanded, storing complete film for distribution and selecting and storing surplus material against future use in productions.

An important distinction grew up between the distribution and the production libraries. Distribution libraries deal with complete films ready for projection and exploitation, while production libraries hold master copies and maintain stocks of filmed material for use in other productions. Newsfilm libraries are a special type of production library. They need a constant supply of current news to maintain their rate of development and help to cover their overheads. Therefore they became closely allied to those companies producing newsreels rather than buying up the rights in considerable stocks of newsreel and acting as distribution agents for the several companies involved.

GROWTH OF NATIONAL COLLECTIONS

As far back as 1899 the annual of *The Magic Lantern Journal* called for some form of central collection of current events, but it was not until 1919 that action was taken to preserve a national or central collection. In that year it was decided to preserve all the official war film at the War Office. This became the nucleus of the present Imperial War Museum's collection. Even so this catered for only a small number of films on a specialised subject.

In 1933 the British Film Institute was established with a list of ten objectives, including the establishment of a national repository of film of permanent value. The formation of national archives and museums really began in 1935 when the need to preserve material became apparent. In June 1935 the National Film Library of the British Film Institute was formed and its title was changed in 1955 to the National Film Archive. The aim of the Archive is to preserve all those films, including television films, which have been shown in the United Kingdom and which are considered to be of value and of future historical interest.

Another small archival collection was also established with the Kodak Museum of Photography in 1927. Film archives were set up in other countries during the 1930's, including the Museum of Modern Art film library in New York, the Cinematheque Francaise in Paris and the Film Library of Belgium. In 1938 an international body was set up to deal with the common aims and problems of the national film archives. The International Federation of Film Archives deals with all questions relating to the collection, preservation, classification and circulation of film, co-ordinates research on the history of the cinema, facilitates and controls loan and exchange of films and documents among members and establishes rules for its members in the control and organisation of film. At present cataloguing rules are being debated, and in 1965 a valuable report on film preservation was issued for the use of members.

The formation of the national film archives and the International Federation helped to promote film as a source of serious study. Film libraries of all types continued to progress, and with the advent of television special libraries were set up by television organisation and ancillary suppliers.

One of the landmarks in the growth of British film libraries was a paper given by Sir Arthur Elton at the Aslib (Association of Special Libraries and Information Bureaux) Annual Conference in 1955, 'The Film as Source Material for History'. From this paper new interest emerged and Aslib set up a Film Production Librarians group who have been active in the professional interest of film librarians.

TYPES OF FILM LIBRARY

Several types of film library have emerged and eight of them are listed in the Aslib rules: distribution, documentary production, feature production, government, government research, national archives, newsreel, and television. To these can be added the educational film libraries. There is considerable interrelationship between all film libraries. It will therefore help to mention each type, its aims, policy and contents for later reference.

The differences between film libraries are not always well

defined; one library may carry out several functions, but the primary factor in distinguishing one library from another is the intent.

DISTRIBUTION LIBRARIES

The main function of distribution libraries is to distribute and exploit complete films suitable for projection. They are not necessarily attached to any production unit but buy up the film and its copyright or obtain distribution rights over it for a stated period. With short films the distributor may buy the film and its copyright outright, but in other cases a distribution contract with the production company allows them to exploit and use the film to best advantage. The distribution contract usually stipulates a number of years' clearance of copyright after which time copyright reverts to the original owners. Distribution libraries are sometimes more appropriately known as film renters.

The film goes into the central library of the distributing agency, which deals mainly with show copies, that is prints from originals ready for projection and use. The distribution company decides on the number of prints to be struck according to its general policy, and handles the film's publicity. The necessary number of copies including dubbed and subtitled copies for overseas are ordered and dispatched by the central library. Once used they are returned and checked to ensure that they are ready for recirculation and any repairs are effected. Extensive bookkeeping routines are necessary in this type of library together with minute checking procedures.

Much non-theatrical distribution is also carried out by these libraries to educational organisations, industrial firms and embassies. This is especially developed in the USA where film circuits are set up to supply public libraries, schools and universities, making use of film and other audio visual aids.

The normal routine in a distribution library involves:
1. Intake
2. Viewing
3. Boxing-up and numbering
4. Reserve prints in store, prints for lending to circulation stocks
5. Registration and dealing with requests
6. Prints dispatched
7. Returned to second intake
8. Examination and back to store.

The most general way of indexing distribution copies is to list the cans the library contains together with the individual contents, and a card index system is used to book films in and out, one card for each print of a film, or each film, containing information on the usage of the film, location, inspection details, any damage found and repair effected.

DOCUMENTARY PRODUCTION LIBRARIES

A documentary film is usually defined as a 35mm factual film of under 3000ft in length. By definition it is a film using actual or reconstructed film drawn from real life and based on a sociological reference. Many short films do not match this definition, but the producers are still known as documentary film producers and registered as such with the Association of Specialised Film Producers. The libraries of these units hold the original material and show copies for sale and distribution. In addition substantial collections of stockshots and good quality material not used in the production are built up for future use.

The main operations in handling material in such a library are: sorting, viewing, assembling, cataloguing, storage control, classifying. Of these operations the one peculiar to this type of library is 'assembling'. This involves joining related film together for printing in larger rolls in subject or stockshot sequence.

Indexing is an important part of documentary production library work. The film held is complex and indexing is often detailed to cope with the subject matter and the stockshots in particular. A stockshot needs minute description to save searching time in locating angles or types of shot. Detailed description can be extended from shotlists to index headings, and the use of form headings as in UDC is helpful in the library catalogues.

Film Centre Production library is one of the largest in the UK having more than 6,000,000ft of documentary and scientific material taken from productions of ten major industrial and business concerns. Documentary production libraries may also act as agents for overseas firms and others doing research work and gathering material for use in productions other than those of the owning company. Rayant Pictures do this work as well as maintaining a wide selection of film in their own library.

FEATURE PRODUCTION LIBRARIES

A feature is defined as the principal 35mm film or films used in a cinema programme and over 3000ft in length. The libraries attached to production companies exist principally to serve these companies. Associated British Picture Corporation and Twentieth Century Fox are important feature production libraries. They retain originals, show copies, studio tests and other material useful in the progress of production as well as stock material. Features themselves are sold or hired complete, but the libraries are also concerned with stock material for supply to their own company productions and to outside customers. The stock material is more flexible in use and can be more easily reduced to its components. The library breaks down the spare film material physically into small exact categories for each roll of film. Indexing is usually done on a shot by shot basis for greater detail. Use is made of apertures in the catalogue cards. This speeds location of exact shot when the user can see a sample frame and judge the focal length of shot, direction, and surrounding detail, but cataloguing a library in this way can become very laborious if not well controlled.

Other material held by these libraries includes sound effects and music stocks. Different principles of handling have to be applied to these and separate libraries or separate departments are often set up to cope with material other than film. Music in particular with its complex copyright problems needs a specialist sound librarian.

GOVERNMENT LIBRARIES

These libraries are attached to government departments or to a film unit operating for such departments. For example, British Transport, National Coal Board, The Admiralty and The Central Office of Information. The last of these produces British news for overseas distribution, maintains a large collection of COI and MOI film for distribution and makes up special films for theatrical and non-theatrical exhibition. COI also produces film for television including a weekly newsreel *Television News from London* and a service of 6 to 10 weekly news items of 1-2 minutes duration for inclusion in overseas television news programmes.

The library includes show copies ready for distribution, originals and stock material for use by other organisations and their own productions. COI also acquires film from other units for inclusion in their newsreels and complete films for distribution abroad.

Government libraries have several functions in production and distribution, and the procedures used relate to the function of the individual library. Their distinguishing feature is the relationship to a government department, rather than the type of material they contain.

GOVERNMENT LIBRARIES : RESEARCH

This includes the more specialised government library units designed to cater for research and record experimental work, trials and routine testing and equipment. The filming itself is a specialised task designed to fit in with the progress on particular projects. The libraries provide film for the use of technical staff and lecturers, but exist primarily to preserve selected material for use within their departments. Distribution is not normally undertaken. Indexing is highly specialised and many special schemes have been designed to deal with technical subject matter. The Royal Aircraft Establishment in Farnborough is one of the most important and most widely known of the libraries in this category. Considerable footage is held in the libraries of government departments. In 1954 the Grigg Committee quoted some 40,000,000ft of master material alone.

NATIONAL ARCHIVES

As well as the specialised national collections already mentioned there are the National Film Archives. Film libraries attached to production units developed naturally with the industry itself, but the need for preserving film in the long term as a serious medium of communication and as a source of history and information was only gradually realised. This situation was indicated in discussing the setting up of the British Film Institute. It is possible for the owning companies to preserve their film but they seldom operate permanent preservation policies. Their main business is to distribute and exploit the film, not to preserve it beyond the time it will serve these ends. It will be preserved only as long as it is economically viable to the company. Also there is no guarantee that a production company will last for ever. An organisation with some assurance of permanence is needed to preserve film in the national interest.

Archives are organised differently from other film libraries. Their acquisition policies are different and more active, while indexing, storage and reuse procedures are all more detailed because of the aims of the archives. They work closely with the whole of the film industry. They also need sufficient resources to obtain, organise and preserve the film, which usually means government support in addition to support from the film industry.

As yet there are no deposit laws for film and archives have to depend on bequests, voluntary deposits and direct purchase of films. Archive resources are never sufficient and many films are being lost through lack of funds to buy or make preservation copies.

Selection plays an important part in the acquisition policy of the National Film Archive. Selection committees are formed and make recommendations on films for acquisition. Film is retained for two reasons, the subject matter and its importance in the history of film art.

The film is acquired and preserved by the archive, but copyright remains vested in the owning company, and this company is entitled to receive royalties on public exhibition of the films. The archive has to make special provisions for notifying the user of copyright ownership, and a special index of distributors is included in archive catalogues to cope with these problems.

Cataloguing and classification are of importance in national film archives and the systems used in the archives are often amended and developed to form standard systems for other film libraries. For example UDC is widely used by FIAF members as a classification scheme, and special schemes based on UDC are used for several other large film libraries, e.g. BBC, Film Centre International, Royal Aircraft Establishment, Farnborough.

NEWSREEL LIBRARIES

The newsreel and newsfilm libraries are another important store of history on film, or source material. The newsreel libraries retain complete items — newsreels, news stories or magazine programmes — and stock material taken from offcuts or purposely produced. The increase of television news coverage has meant that cinema newsreels have lost much of their importance as a source of current news and there are comparatively few newsreel libraries left. Those which exist in their own right today cater for the cinema trade with news magazines, and send newsreels to overseas countries without television. In the UK, only British Movietonews continues to function as a newsreel library, and COI issues a newsreel for overseas. Pathe News has closed down although the library continues to supply material for reuse. Many newsreel companies ceased production in the late 1950's and were transferred to agencies such as Visnews Ltd. These newsfilm agencies supply the older newsreel material and issue their own current news items. They are able to offer a wide coverage of newsfilm taken over the past 70 years.

Newsfilm libraries normally exist to serve a parent organisation, and this relationship is usually for mutual benefit. The parent organisation may be a news producing agency, or may be attached to a large production company, or they may be associated with television newsfilm agencies.

Newsfilm agencies provide short clips of particular news items as and when they arise. The agencies depend on the demand for this type of film and their job is to obtain it or have it specially shot, edited into usable form and reshipped to customers. The aim of a newsfilm agency is to cover as wide an area in the world as possible and to obtain film of all important events in the fastest possible time. Television stations are the most frequent users of the newsfilm agencies for current newsfilm, because few television stations have the necessary staff of reporters and cameramen to cover all areas in the world and obtain film. The libraries connected with the agencies acquire all the film shot by the agency, and supply it to the parent company for reuse as and when required as well as to its own set of customers.

Newsreel and newsfilm are the two major types of visual news available, and they complement one another. Newsreel libraries grew up with the cinema industry and contain film from 1900 to date. Newsfilm libraries are more closely allied with television and if dependent on television film alone would be restricted to news events dating from 1954. Newsfilm libraries have extended their range by purchase or transfer, obtaining the older newsreel collections as these stopped production.

The main characteristics of newsreels have been listed by Baechlin and Muller Strauss in the Unesco booklet *Newsreels across the world*, 1952, and the following features are included:

Frequency. Newsreels appear regularly and at relatively short intervals, e.g. twice a week. Many companies are now ceasing production of this type of newsreel film because the material is no longer news when it reaches the cinema screen.

Structure. Each newsreel issue includes several topics that are not directly related. This distinguishes the newsreel from today's newsfilm and from the news magazine which concentrates on a single topic. The television bulletin has similar characteristics, a selection of news arranged in a certain order to try to maintain the viewer's interest, and to emphasise the more important stories.

Length. Although the number of items varied in a newsreel the overall length remained constant. The length was limited for technical reasons and convenience of exhibition and handling. Programme planning was easier with a set length, cutting and printing in a fixed time framework were simplified and many shipping problems eliminated by restricting the newsreel to one reel.

Content. Each topic related to current events of general interest at the time of presentation.

Style. Presentation is straightforward, not interpretative or didactic. Material is edited to reconstruct a sequence of events and focus the viewer's attention.

Newsfilm differs from newsreel material in that it is normally concerned with only one topic at a time and is designed to be shown separately. Several individual films are offered to the television stations who make their own selection and are free to re-edit the material as required. As the material is meant to be re-edited a sound commentary is seldom provided. Material is exhibited daily in short sequences of 1-2 minutes duration. However editing is still essential to news if it is not to become boring and the presentation of items must be objective and straightforward as in newsreels. The object of fiction film is to entertain or tell a story, that of documentary and non-fiction to educate or inform. The aim of newsfilm is to disseminate objective information about current affairs and events.

The newsfilm libraries, because they are dealing with material which loses its currency so fast and because they have to serve customers with recent news as well as older material, need very fast retrieval systems. It may be thought that computer retrieval would help the newsfilm agencies, but such has not proved to be the case. The material has to be catalogued as soon as it comes into the library, often within hours of the event being filmed and once in the library has to be available for immediate retrieval from the catalogue. Because of the amount of material coming into the library on all sorts of topics and the number of enquiries received, the catalogue is the only place to find the information — staff memory cannot be relied on, especially as the agencies work extended hours and stagger shifts so that the person who indexes the material initially may no longer be on duty when it is required by a user. Subject indexing assumes great importance in a newsfilm library, because this film does not have titles, and the reuse of newsfilm is by subject, and even then not necessarily the subject of the whole film, but only a small part. Analytical entries are used a great deal in the catalogues.

Selection is also important, so that the vast number of pieces of film pouring into the library does not cause any one item to be swamped by others, and so that the limited storage space is used only for those films which have reuse potential.

Much technical work has to be carried out in libraries attached to newsfilm agencies. Film handling, customer viewing and preparation for laboratories all require technical staff.

TELEVISION LIBRARIES

Television film libraries are a comparatively new development and are attached to television companies all over the world. Television companies are the largest producers of film today and their libraries have to cope with an ever growing amount of film. Like the national film archives these libraries hold all types of film; fiction, non-fiction, news and educational material. Earlier the figure of 40,000,000ft was given as the stock held in government departments, but when this is compared with 150,000,000ft of material estimated in the BBC film library in 1965, the special problems of television libraries become more apparent. Selection for permanent retention is a major task and requires a large staff working to careful policies to sort through the material. Information and film retrieval methods need to be advanced and well run. A large enquiry staff is also needed, often working on a shift system to fit in with the extended hours of television.

Not all the material dealt with by television libraries is on film; much is now being recorded on magnetic or video tape. Granada TV in Manchester has the greater proportion of its output on tape. Because video tape had certain peculiarities and disadvantages in its developmental stages, programmes selected for permanent storage in BBC and ITN are currently transferred to film, but the libraries will come to consider videotape and adjust their procedures to cope. As videotape produces a visual image akin to film and can be used with it, the film libraries will probably expand their activities to include it rather than set up separate departments to deal with the storage and exploitation of video-tape.

EDUCATION LIBRARIES

This is not a distinct type of library and it can overlap with several of the others. The education film library can either be attached to a production unit or it can exist as a repository for the productions of several organisations, such as schools, colleges and universities. In this way it may retain experimental film as well as the completed productions and offer the functions of a research library. It has a major function as a distribution library and hires film to member institutions. Other films may be purchased from outside sources and distributed on a similar basis. ILEA, the Inner London Education Authority, purchases film for retention in the library which it then loans out to member institutions at special

rates. Other material may be purchased for possible recutting into
new productions, although this is usually done at the time the new
film is to be made, rather than purchasing film on the offchance.
However if film clips are bought for these reasons the library
becomes a source of stockshots and sequences and may be
organised along these lines. Television is playing an increasing part
in education today and a lot of material may be recorded 'off air'
on to videotape for reuse by member institutions. In this case
some of the techniques used in television libraries will apply to the
educational libraries.

The major functions of an education film library are not very
different from those of other libraries although the emphasis is on
different aspects. For example, education film libraries concentrate on pre-selection of material, previewing, acquisition and
evaluation. They are in general not commercial libraries in that
they do not sell film in entirety or in short sequences for reuse in
different contexts, but normally exist to service a particular set of
users, either intra-organisation or inter-organisation, i.e. the
school, college or university where the library is situated or a
group of schools and colleges, an admixture of all educational
institutions, or in the case of the educational hire libraries, any
user who becomes a member of the library. The educational hire
libraries are closely allied to the distribution libraries who acquire
film and rent it out to members and others on a hire-charge basis
per viewing. Distribution libraries are of course by no means
restricted to educational film, although some do specialise in
education and it is these which are being discussed here.

3

SELECTION PRINCIPLES AND TECHNIQUES

SELECTION is an essential part of film librarianship as it is of any other type. It requires constant and precise policies and the librarian is constantly making decisions on what to keep and what to throw away. The high cost of maintaining and exploiting a film library means that a firm policy of selection has to be adopted. If a film library becomes a repository and simply collects all material, it will soon have no space left and a great deal of unused material which it cannot exploit effectively. This is as true of an archive, as it is of a production company, and newsfilm libraries serve as a classic example. Without a policy of selection, unusable films are kept and take up space in the vaults and misuse staff time and effort in handling it. Commercial film libraries cannot afford to keep film on this basis and others are unwise to do so.

Material coming into a film library includes edited and unedited film, offcuts, duplicates, telerecordings and original film, video recordings, separate sound tracks, colour and black and white coverage. Unless some controls are put on a collection any amount of space will quickly be used up. Large and small libraries are alike in the need for these controls. The BBC film library, which copes with some 2,000,000ft of film a month, and a large newsfilm agency with some 1,250,000ft a year have the same problems of finding space for the film and selecting only the material which will benefit the library concerned.

HAPHAZARD SELECTION

Selection should be done according to set principles, for haphazard selection can be as harmful as no selection at all. Newsreel companies unable to foresee the demands and the growth of the film as a means of communication and illustration threw out the contents of entire vaults regardless of film content when space became short. Vaults of uncut material for which there was no immediate use would be 'junked', without checking to see if a cut story was available or had been made from any particular film. Too often the libraries were administered by a producer or editor with no understanding of library requirements or the basic principles of a librarian's work. Present day librarians suffering from these policies have to make do with a few over-exposed pieces, or attempt to remedy by purchase some of the mistakes, while they must concentrate on their own current collections, work systematically and endeavour to leave a more representative collection than they inherited. A great deal of material does of course remain, more by accident than design, when a collection has never been subjected to junking. Even recently there have been cases of arbitrary junking. A large television company in the United States disposed of all its black and white stock on the introduction of colour, apparently oblivious to the fact that black and white film is a valuable source of film history as well as twentieth century history and achievement. It is needed as an authentic illustration of the past 70-80 years.

The main aims of selection are to provide for foreseeable demands and ensure that a balanced coverage is maintained. In order to anticipate future demands, past demands have to be studied and rationalised into principles for selecting current stock. The more the library tries to anticipate user's requirements, the more successful it is likely to be and the only way to do this is to gain experience in operating a particular collection and make some study of the actual stories issued to customers, using a film movement catalogue, library sales and orders, and enquiry sheets.

PRINCIPLES OF SELECTION

Selection principles are based mainly on the quality of the film and its relevance to the collections as it already stands. These are the most important principles, but cost and copyright with its attendant restrictions also need to be considered. The principles can be applied to both current and older film material.

CONSIDERATIONS OF QUALITY

By 'quality', we mean the technical quality of the film, not its content. The film can be technically unusable, usable but poor quality, duplicated and in various stages of completeness. Each of these can be considered separately.

Technically unusable film may be very badly scratched, fogged or out of focus, in which case it cannot be used again. Other technical trouble include deterioration, especially of nitrate film. In many cases this film can be saved by duping, but in others the deterioration will have gone too far for remedy. If the film is technically no good it is impossible to reuse and should be thrown away immediately. It can also be in a dangerous state and likely to affect the rest of the collection.

Apart from the technically unusable film some may be of poor quality but reusable, such as film shot in varying degrees of under or overexposure and many telerecordings and satellite recordings with 'snowstorm' effects on the picture. Considerations other than those of quality are included in the decision to retain and the decision is frequently a compromise.

A film may be unique, or difficult to repeat and as this factor increases in importance so the standard of selection is lowered and the film retained as the only available material. The space and moon shots resulted in some interesting pictures from the modules and the moon surface. The earlier attempts are relatively poor in quality, but film of a particular mission is unrepeatable and although it is poor quality it has been retained for its content. Other poor quality film is retained for its rarity, such as film from Eastern European countries available only in positive print form in the UK.

The film library, especially a commercial newsfilm agency library which is expected to supply world wide coverage has to be as self contained as possible, and if there is any difficulty in obtaining better quality prints or covering similar events again the library has to retain some material despite the inferior technical quality. When material is selected for these reasons a note should be made on the catalogue cards and shotlists as a guide to users, pointing out the poor quality and reasons for retention. If the user is forewarned in this way he will understand the reasons for the poor quality and this will improve future relations with the library.

Telerecordings and video recordings have to be considered by some libraries in selecting material for permanent preservation. Film libraries are geared to cope with film and it is more convenient to transfer videotapes to film for storage and utilisation. Mixing film and videotape causes confusion and damage to both media.

There are certain disadvantages in the use of videotape at present. The equipment is bulky and requires a mobile power supply. The resulting image cannot be seen for quick checking and a complicated machine has to intervene before any knowledge of the content can be implied. It is also less easy to cut and edit from videotape than film, or even to select sequences. The principal users of video recording at present are the newsfilm and television agencies closely followed by the closed circuit television users. A newsfilm or television agency with bases all over the world, and moving into difficult territory needs highly mobile cameramen to obtain film in the fastest time possible. The cameramen use film cameras as the lightest, most convenient form of visual recording available today.

Telerecordings and satellite recordings sometimes resolve selection policies into a choice of content against quality. With advances in the techniques of telerecording, the quality of the film is gradually being improved, but it is still inadequate for many library purposes. In addition another printing stage has to be made from the telerecording before the film reaches the customer. This reduces the quality further and it becomes almost unusable. Satellite recordings are the poorest quality, but neither type should be the aim of the film librarian.

Telerecording techniques have been developed to enable viewers to see what is happening in the world with as little time lag as possible. The agencies and television stations work on the basis that fast coverage, first shots, 'scoops' make good copy or news, but the library works on an entirely different basis. Days, months and years after an event, the library is called on for coverage. To produce only blurred, poor quality prints of an event at this remove shows a lack of initiative and interest in the quality of the library service. A library needs the best quality film available to store and preserve. If a tele- or satellite recording is relevant to the collection and it is possible to obtain a copy from the original film this should be done and the telerecording thrown away. The aim is to store as few poor quality films as possible.

Original film can be cut to match the telerecording and the shotlists already available can be retained. If the original adds something useful to the telerecording it can be left intact and a new shotlist made. This depends on the policy of the library and the availability of staff. A time lag between the telerecording entering the library and the original or copy arriving is not always important. The library can afford to wait for quality.

Throwing away telerecordings for which replacements are available introduces another principle of quality selection: duplication.

If only to prevent the misuse of valuable space, duplication should be avoided. But there are some forms of duplication that are not necessarily wasteful. Positive and negative forms of the same story, for example, can have equal value for different uses. If a 35mm fine grain print and a 16mm dupe negative taken from this print are both available, they can serve two different purposes.

The library needs best quality for reproduction and printing, but many customers require only 16mm black and white prints. Printing these from the 16mm dupe negative saves the customer reduction printing costs and gives the best quality available. The 35mm 'original' is retained to make further dupe negatives if necessary, either for customer orders or library replacements.

Some libraries retain serviced stories in both negative and master positive form, using whichever is appropriate when printing and passing through as few stages as possible. (For unserviced stories only one version is usually available). Ordinary black and white prints are not kept when the negative or fine grain positive is also available. As a general rule of thumb the material closest to the camera original, or the nearest fine grain material to the camera original should always be retained. Rush prints and non fine grain material should be junked. Some libraries retain several copies of film as a matter of policy, e.g. the loan collection and distribution libraries.

Sometimes, there is a choice between colour and black and white coverage of the same story. The colour and black and white coverage could have been shot by two different cameras, or with two different raw stocks, or a black and white copy may have been taken from the colour story. Technically there may be no difference between the separate black and white colour coverage. The librarian can then decide which version is of most use. A black and white version of the story could always be made from the colour coverage, but the quality of a black and white dupe negative from colour is not as good as separate black and white coverage. If most of the library's customers take only black and white they will require monochrome of a high quality and both versions are kept. It is also normal practice to retain both colour and the black and white dupe negative from colour for future printing. Requests for black and white coverage can then be filled without resort to easily damaged colour material. This is the same principle as retaining a negative and master positive on black and white stories.

If a choice has to be made between colour and black and white coverage and other technical factors are equal, the colour version is to be preferred on aesthetic grounds rather than technical quality. Current news and information stories, especially in the early days of colour coverage, have greater impact, and it is not likely that there will be a general return to black and white. It is of course still used to good effect, but colour is predominant in the industry today.

The completeness of the film available for retention is only a marginally technical choice. There may be both an uncut and an edited version of a film available. If the uncut version of an information film adds nothing to the edited one, or if only the best material has been used in the edited version and the rest is technically no good, then the uncut can be junked immediately. Shooting ratios vary with types of film; feature film may have a very high ratio, but once selection is made from the rushes the rest of the material is not much use except in the case of stockshot selection.

Documentary film may also have a high shooting ratio and here more of the material may be retained as useful. The shooting ratio for newsfilm is usually very low — about 2:1 — and what is left after editing may not be of any future use. The library may be offered the edited story and the unjoined cuts, which are retained for a short period and then junked. Some stories need to be retained in their most complete form, such as speeches by well known personalities. The editorial staff may have picked out certain passages of a speech to illustrate a current topic of interest. Other passages may become important at a later date. The uncut and edited speeches can both be retained in these cases or it may be decided to retain only the uncut version and print out sections as required.

The length of a shot also determines its usefulness. If sequences of film are reused more than stills the very short shot will not be required for reuse and can be junked unless unique. The viewer must have time to assimilate the image on the screen. Shots of less than 5 ft can be considered for junking. This will allow for editing the material.

Stockshot selection is also based on technical considerations to a large extent. The aim is to retain only those stockshots of the best possible quality which can be transferred to large projection screens without detriment or deterioration in sharpness of image, colour imposition and value. Quality considerations determine the junking of unusable material, but when the quality is poor but usable other non-technical criteria have to be considered before a decision is taken.

RELEVANCE TO OTHER ITEMS

This principle concerns the relevance of a film to the collection as it stands, and to the maintenance of a balanced collection. It is the most complex and also the most important of the factors guiding the selection of material. It is also the one in which the librarian's experience and knowledge of the collection and the uses to be made of it will be of the most assistance.

The most important criteria is whether the film will be needed again. This is not to be interpreted as 'it might come in useful some day'. This negative approach shelves the responsibility of the librarian, whereas the decisions should be taken positively and with prior knowledge. It should always be possible to say why a particular piece of film has been selected for the library. It must relate to the type of material held in the collection already and to the type of service offered.

Selection in a feature library is frequently a question of stockshot selection from rushes and offcuts for use in other features or documentaries. Whole films are also kept in the most complete and technically usable form, negatives and showprints. Educational libraries select material for inclusion on the basis of its educational value and its relevance to customer requirements. Film material may go out of date quickly in this type of library and other films have to be brought in to maintain the collection on the same level and with teaching objectives similar to those of the educational system it is trying to serve.

A newsfilm library attempts to retain newsworthy events of interest now and in the foreseeable future. It works rather like a news agency retaining press cuttings for reuse and reference. The library has to incorporate all significant events in international affairs, politics, economics and finance, technical and industrial achievements, sporting events, items on prominent and not so prominent personalities in all fields and countries, stockshot material or background establishers, social and religious events and, to maintain a balance, a good sprinkling of the unusual, oddities, stunts and mass manias.

The type of service offered and to whom it is offered influence selection to an extent, but an adequate all round collection is more useful than one which caters for a particular group of users. The library will long outlast the present users and the requests of the users will change with the years. If a library is set up simply to serve one group of users, however thoroughly, it may have too narrow an interest to outlive this group, and will either be absorbed into a larger unit or diffused into other units and no longer have a function of its own.

Most film libraries, although set up originally to serve a parent organisation, extend their activities and serve outside customers as well. This is a useful source of revenue, reduces the risk of monopoly by one or two agencies, and therefore adds to the useful film material available to the general user. The principles in this type of selection are most marked when considering the commercial agencies which deal with short films or stockshots and they can best be shown by considering selection in a newsfilm agency.

Newsfilm libraries cater for two major types of interest, the long term, retrospective programmes and illustration for a fast news service. With a wide basis for selection the library should cope adequately with topics investigated in depth and also illustrate the news story which breaks overnight.

Four major indexes serve to answer many questions in a news library:

1. Date of event
2. Location
3. Subject
4. Personality involved

These represent the main areas of interest in news information and consideration of each will illustrate how the principles can be applied to the general process of selection.

The date has little relevance to selection processes on its own, but when considered as part of another index the date of filming becomes important. Once it has been decided to keep material on a particular topic, it is important to retain authentic material. Often in visual news the camera only records aftermath and the actual event is not on film. The date of event and date of filming supply a guide to the authenticity of the material and at what stage in the news story the film was taken. The closer the date of filming to the date of event, the more useful that film will be in trying to reconstruct actual events.

Locations are retained for their value as stockshots, or as background to an event. When the film is retained for stockshot purposes, a clear indication should be made on the catalogue card. Relatively few pieces need to be kept for stockshot reasons — enough to illustrate the location from different angles: a skyline view, an aerial view and a full general view may suffice. Film of locations in different seasons is useful to add variety and avoid showing a blanket of snow in midsummer. However, stockshots can be used too liberally. The cameraman can often as easily take an establishing shot at the same time as the story. This establishing shot will add an authenticity to the film which a stockshot cannot.

Selection aims for a wide general coverage as well as specific events. All sorts of *subjects* make the news, but some subjects are more newsworthy than others and often the amount of film available is in inverse proportion to the interest of the story. People remember the extraordinary events, which have the greater impact on the viewer, but a library that concentrated on the sensational or unusual would not reflect general current affairs. The extraordinary material can be retained but not to the detriment of the normal event.

Examples of different subjects and the factors governing their retention will help to clarify the issue. Political events may be difficult to film interestingly. Conferences become a group of faces around a table, major political discussions the comings and goings at set locations. Statements made to the press and public by the personalities involved relieve the monotony and an item illustrating the general setting and attendance at the event may be enough. Much film shot on these occasions is too general for future use because it does not refer specifically to the event. For technical, scientific and medical news topics, one or two pieces on the actual process and a number of pieces on the application of these processes are retained. Some of these films also have monotonous content. Medical discoveries and operative measures can become a series of medical bulletins of no lasting interest when events are concluded. These interim pieces can be junked unless they contain something of future use such as a discussion of the process involved.

Only a selection of the best available copies of annual events need be retained. Normal correctly performed ceremonies can be kept and any in which important deviations are made, or the main participants change. National customs can be treated in the same way. A representative selection can miss a few years, especially with religious festivals where personalities are not particularly important. Annual sporting items on the other hand might all have to be retained, as personalities or teams change each year and these become more important than the actual events. This is true for example of the FA Cup Final, Boat Race, major athletic meetings, annual motor races or horse races. Other sporting items are subject to more stringent selection, especially if they are restricted by the authorities concerned and are not freely available for reuse, as when time restrictions are put on the reshowing of material which reduces its value as a record of any game. Other sporting items can be shown in their entirety within the time restrictions and this may influence their selection. Unusual sports should be represented in the collection to illustrate the sport. As a general rule with sporting items, it is advisable to retain only the more important or spectacular items where difficulties of copyright are encountered.

Disasters make news but it is difficult to obtain continually interesting film about them. The disaster itself has probably occurred before anyone is alerted and only aftermath scenes are

available. Too much coverage of too many disasters will unbalance
the collection, but any major disasters or large scale relief
operations have to have a representative coverage. Much
repetitious news coverage is expended on riots and demonstrations. Alternatively riots are becoming progressively more violent
and library film may be used to illustrate this trend with a
selection of riots over a period of years. Only the more
representative demonstrations need to be retained, and a mixture
of violent and 'peaceful' demonstrations should be kept in
balance.

Many military operations and activities have to be retained to
show different military, air force and naval personnel, such as
guards, marines, paratroops etc; new equipment such as tanks or
guns, new areas of operation, peaceful defence measures;
offensives and war scenes. The policy may be to retain as much as
possible for a short period, and defer selection to a later date when
the war or military operation is over. War footage is repetitious,
but it is also in demand and does move into different areas which
look different and where the strategy changes. Any number of
factors have to be considered in selecting war footage, a battle
may be fought over the same ground, but won by different sides
on the two occasions, new weapons may be used and so on.

Programmes are continually being made about wars or battles
and with a large stock of material there will be less danger of
repetition for the viewer. Film in which the cameraman shows
surrounding terrain and fighting scenes is more valuable for reuse
than one which concentrates only on the fighting. As with many
other subject topics, the more endless the material appears, the
less likely it is to be used again. The producer will concentrate on
the few well known pieces of film as 'instant' scene setters and the
vast amount of footage is left to moulder in the vaults, obscured
by the blanket coverage.

Subjects with many different aspects or types, such as aircraft,
ships, missiles will be retained in the various aspects. This builds
up large collections of film under general headings. The library
may have a great deal on aircraft, for example, but only half a
dozen good pieces on the VC 10. Representative pieces on all
ships, aircraft and missiles available should be retained. It is much
better to be able to show the actual ship one is talking about than
one of the same type. In the same way enough material of the
space programme has to be kept to show all stages of each
different programme so that the user can trace developments and
compare achievements and improvements in techniques.

Stunts and odd events can also be retained but again repetition should be avoided. National and world wide crazes have a lot of coverage spent on them while in vogue, but are forgotten in a short time. One or two good illustrations of these is enough.

The aim in retaining shots of *people* is to build up a comprehensive picture of their activities and contribution to events as well as their personalities. Film of people at important conferences, on tours and missions, making speeches and carrying on their normal working lives is needed. Unfortunately the cameraman often has to illustrate international and political affairs by arrivals and departures at airports or conference buildings. These endless pieces seldom illustrate the event but are kept because they are good quality shots of the personality doing something which identifies him with an event. If one personality meets another, for example, the film may show where the meeting took place and its significance. Film of personalities is collected with a view to reuse in a compilation or profile. The library retains films of people at various stages in their lives. With political or international figures this means retaining important events in their career, the various posts they have held, on missions and any important speeches in as full a form as possible. Additionally if film of the lighter side of a personality is available it should be retained. This gives a personal touch to any profile and provides a balance for more serious topics.

COPYRIGHT AND SELECTION

Normally a commercial film library holds copyright in its own films, but in some cases copyright or usage restrictions arise. They arise particularly in educational libraries which retain film from several sources in distribution or hire libraries and in archives. Educational libraries have to consider how they will be able to use the material, if they can lend to all their borrowers, if they can charge for hire or are restricted in any way. Similarly hire libraries have to consider if it is worthwhile distributing film with restrictive exhibition, or if their users are being served by such film. Archives are in a different position in the way they are retaining material and the reasons for retaining it, but they still sell footage for reuse and need to take copyright into account when deciding to acquire or reject.

Any copyright restrictions and the ease of clearance or gaining usage should be considered in the selection process. If material is exclusive or difficult to repeat copyright difficulties may be worth overcoming. If material is available elsewhere and similarly restricted the library can keep a copy for its intrinsic value and clear copyright when needed. If the material is available elsewhere and not restricted the library will probably not retain its own copy. The user can go to the other source where he will not incur additional copyright expense.

Some copyright material is easier to clear than others, and this influences the selection. Olympic material cannot be supplied more than one month after the event without application to the Olympic committee for clearance. This is normally left to the customer and is not difficult to negotiate so that the film is reused. In these cases the library is justified in retaining it.

Another consideration refers to the length of time the film is restricted by copyright. If it is a short period the film can be retained unused during the copyright period for reuse later. However the copyright may run out after a period of time only to be taken up again by a new company. If the copyright restrictions are severe the library should seriously consider rejecting the film rather than keep it unused indefinitely.

Sometimes the owning company may obtain rights on film for service purposes only, not for library use. It will be confusing to retain the film in the library for a long period, but it will have to be kept for a short time in order that service customers can acquire additional or replacement prints. Restrictions on international usage by the library or service departments also arise. Films made in the USA and supplied by libraries in the UK are restricted. The original film remains in the USA and the resale of other prints is not allowed. The films can be kept in the UK libraries for supply to other customers, but a note is made of the restricted area of supply. Finally in newsfilm libraries certain restrictions are placed on satellite and Eurovision coverages. These are restricted to reuse on television, but may have to be kept as the only record of an event available. The restriction is mainly one of quality. Wherever possible replacements should be obtained for these satellited films.

MATTERS OF COST

In this context, cost means the direct costs incurred by the library for film rather than the indirect costs tied to copyright. When the library has a budget allowance it can obtain additional film. Many film libraries have so many other drains on their finances that it is usual to reject film which will be charged to library. In commercial film libraries attached to a parent company most film is deposited free, by that company, but sometimes a cameraman sends in unassigned material. If the cameraman is freelance and the library retains the film he will be paid a fee and expenses for the story. If the library already has an adequate coverage the film can be rejected. Film can also be obtained on exchange from foreign companies and the librarian should be aware of any agreements and how they operate when selecting the film. A list of sources should be available to show which require payment, which offer material on an exchange basis and how much footage is involved in each agreement, and which sources have no payments on supply.

RESPONSIBILITY FOR SELECTION

The librarian should be responsible for selection. He is responsible for maintaining and exploiting the collection and should have the necessary authority over its contents. Other staff members can recommend the retention or junking of material, but the final decision should rest with the library staff.

There are several methods of recommendation for final selection. The national archives use committees of experts in the fields covered. The National Film Archive in the UK has four expert committees whose brief is to consider all films released in the UK whether fact or fiction and whatever the country of origin of the film. The committees meet about once a month and either view material or take notice of suitable material already viewed by the acquisition officers of the Archive. If material is selected, the acquisitions officers follow up the decisions and obtain the film. The four committees are:
1. General, for fiction and entertainment films.
2. Television, for programmes shown on all British channels.
3. Science.
4. History.
The last two are principally concerned with documentary film.

Apart from film brought to the attention of the committee by the acquisitions officers, they work from offers made to the archives, film deposited and recommendations from others, such as librarians and producers. The Archive depends largely on donation and voluntary deposit, but may also have to purchase material. The system of using committees ensures that several points of view are taken into account, and informed recommendations can be taken on films to be preserved for reference and reuse. In the same way some television companies with large selection staff use subject specialists to cope with the amount and variety of material. All the film is viewed by selection staff and complete programmes may be broken down to keep only relevant sections. In smaller television library units, such as those which deal only with newsfilm, the number of staff is reduced and subject specialists are not used. ITN staff do selection as part of their normal work of viewing, shotlisting and cataloguing.

In other film libraries there may be only one person, usually the librarian in charge, doing the selection, either on his own initiative or based on recommendations by other members of staff. Normal daily selection is done by the librarian, and periodical conferences can be held for long term selection, attended by the selection librarian and members of the editorial and cutting room staff.

If a list is prepared of the material selected or rejected each day, it can be used within the library for cataloguing purposes to indicate the material which requires indexing. The list can also be used by the accounts department to sort out payments and check against invoices from cameramen.

TIMING OF SELECTION

Selection can be current or retrospective. Current selection can be done on a day to day basis, selecting uncut or unedited material. Edited film can be reviewed currently after allowing a short period for the collection to settle down and before the final canning-up of the film. After final canning-up, one advantage of selection is lost in many film libraries, that of saving storage spece. When several films are filed in one can and a weeding process begins material withdrawn from the cans is not necessarily replaced. This causes confusion in the actual canning up procedure and loses valuable space in the can and vault. This does not apply to feature libraries and those holding complete films of any length. Here complete cans are removed after selection, but even so vaults may need changing round.

Day to day selection may be necessary when the question of payment follows on the rejection or retention of the film. This concerns unedited film as payment is made for all used, edited or serviced material. The unedited film may add to the serviced story, or be better quality, in which case it is retained. For these immediate decisions the librarian either has to view the film or use a number of the syndication staff as his eyes and take recommendations on quality and content of the film. It may prove impossible for the library staff to view all incoming film. Film comes in to some libraries 24 hours a day, but library staff do not work 24 hours a day. If there is any doubt about the selection of unedited film the librarian should view it before a decision is made. Syndication staff working 24 hours a day on a shift basis see the film, know what has been used in service and can recommend retention or junking on the basis of quality and relevance to the current output. The librarian, using comments from production sheets or editorial information, makes his final decision about the usefulness of the material to the collection as a whole.

Some libraries do not operate selection procedures. Decisions of retention or rejection are taken by editing or cutting room staff before the film ever reaches the library. This method is not recommended for newsfilm libraries where control of stock should be in the hands of the librarian.

Selection decisions are not always immediate. With some film it is possible to wait for up to three months before deciding to junk. Selection in these cases has to be balanced against necessary work already carried out on the film. A piece of film which has to be accessioned, viewed, shotlisted, catalogued and stored represents a considerable amount of work by several members of staff, and selection decisions can be taken quickly before many of the processes are carried out. The position is sometimes different, as with material or newsfilm which has been selected for inclusion in the library by other departments. Many of the processes may then have been carried out before the film reaches the library. In newsfilm libraries, for example, accessioning, viewing and shotlisting may be complete for serviced film. The library has to catalogue and store the material. In such cases material should be available to customers for two or three months in case they require replacements or additional copies.

In a newsfilm library the heaviest demand for film relates to events of the previous six months, with a sharp reduction in demand beyond this period. Serviced news film is retained for at least one month before considering junking in favour of other pieces. The cataloguing has to be withdrawn on junking the film, but this is not a major chore and it will probably have been used in the interim period. In practice not many serviced films are rejected. They are more likely to be replaced for quality reasons, as when serviced telerecordings are replaced by original film for library retention.

Some film libraries have different periods of retention for their material. The shooting ratio at the BBC for example is low (3:1) and the spare takes are usually technically no good. Selection staff attend rushes and select library material for retention before it is edited. The decision has to be taken early and the film sent to the laboratories for fine grain printing before editing the negative. Newsfilm libraries on the other hand select after service use because of the tight schedules. Film is edited and shown on television screens without delay and no time can be allowed for taking fine grain prints before service. Instead offcuts have to be searched for additional material.

The other selection procedures carried out at the BBC are done at more leisure after transmission and concern whole programmes rather than stockshots. Because of the type of selection carried out and when it is done, decisions can be made to retain film for a three-month period, for 12 months or in a permanent retention section. This allows selection staff a leeway to make further decisions on retention in the light of experience, usage and demands. Three months' retention may not prove long enough for some film and it will be reconsidered and put into a longer period. Additionally the permanent library is subject to annual review to ensure that a balanced coverage is maintained and storage space is not wasted.

In some libraries material is selected for inclusion in an archive before work is carried out on the film or even before it is ever acquired for the archive. Recommendations for acquisition are made by the selection committees.

Distribution and hire libraries have acquisition policies, but again decisions are taken before the material enters the library.

Selection is not a once for all procedure. After a few years, further selection in overloaded sections of the collections may be necessary. In a film library which contains current affairs, ongoing events make it difficult to select material except on a qualitative basis, as with wars or military operations. Each piece of film has value on service and will probably be in demand for some time after, but after a few years one battle looks much like another. Material goes on accumulating until the index section becomes large and unwieldy and only the most recent film is cited in the face of so much. Some films stand out from the rest, but they do not always give a true picture of the action. However, the weeding process should not be too drastic; someone may want to make an extended study of the subject. Recently a choice has arisen between black and white and colour coverage for ongoing events. Colour has more impact and is selected rather than black and white when there is such a choice. Distribution libraries also weed out their collections according to how much return or usage they are still getting on individual films. Information film may be updated or outdated and it is not the function of a commercial hire library to keep film which is no longer being used or serving a useful purpose. Film movement records can indicate where film has not been called on for a considerable time and a decision to remove the film from the hire service can then be taken.

Selection decisions are also necessary for older film; when it begins to deteriorate, is it worth duping or should it be re-edited in a shorter version and duped or can it be junked? Similar principles can be applied to older film and current material for building up a representative collection of history on film. The physical quality of the film may prompt retrospective selection, but the content is still the most important factor.

PRACTICAL EXAMPLE OF SELECTION PROCEDURE

An illustration of selection in a particular organisation will help to clarify some of the points already made. Most of the principles apply particularly to commercial libraries and a newsfilm collection serves as a good example.

In a newsfilm agency with an intake of 12,000 items a year, the selection is done by the librarian in charge of the cataloguing section. *Day by day* selection of unserviced material is made from production records. This gives the production number, the source of the material, details of stock and footage, title of film and any editorial recommendations for retention. Shotlists and information about the film are attached to the production sheets. Using this information and recommendations plus a knowledge of the collection and the foregoing principles the librarian decides on retention or junking. The film may have to be viewed before a decision can be taken if there is a lack of information. A selection list is made out giving number and title of film selected and rejected. This is circulated to the editorial staff, cataloguing staff and accounts department for appropriate action.

The selection of serviced film occurs after a settling down period of two months. The selection librarian compares the lists of unserviced and serviced film already available and rejects some serviced film or weeds out telerecordings for which original replacements have been obtained. Once again a list of films selected for junking is compiled and sent to editorial staff, or a conference is called for final decisions to be taken. Once the list is approved it is circulated to the canning-up assistant who throws the unwanted film away, to the library clerk who removes all related dopesheets and shotlists, and to the cataloguing staff who withdraw indexing records.

Selection of older material is continually being carried out as the film is viewed for shotlisting or is found to be deteriorating by the film preservation officer.

SELECTION FROM OFFCUTS
FOR STOCKSHOTS

The preceding points have referred to complete films, the selection of which can often be carried out without the film itself, although viewing is always desirable. Another field of selection concerns selecting from offcuts for stockshots — special high quality shots of locations, types of scenes, subjects or people. In a film library, stockshots should be long enough to allow for reuse as film sequences, not stills. They are selected offcuts of original material. Fine grain prints or duplicates are used for intercutting with new material and the original is kept for further duping when this fine grain material is used.

When a film is made a greater amount of footage is exposed than is used in the final production. This is known as the shooting ratio, that is the amount of film exposed to the amount of film used. Much of the film left over is of use for other productions. Material which is likely to be of value can be selected as a stockshot, processed and indexed. The shooting ratio can vary from 2 : 1 for newsfilm to 20 : 1 for feature work and the higher the ratio the more likely it is that useful material will be left over from the production.

The low ratio in newsfilm work reflects the cameraman's brief which is designed to make the service viable. When editing newsfilm a lot of establishing shots are used, but the news cameraman does not dwell on establishing shots unless specifically asked to do so. Newsfilm libraries keep small collections of establishing shots of much used materials, such as shots of towns, buildings, etc. These establishing films can of course be shot on request and edited. Fine grain prints can be filed and used and the original film kept for further printing.

If the offcuts are found to be a useful source of establishing and stockshots they can be searched and a collection built up for the benefit of the parent organisation. This type of collection will probably be in addition to the ordinary collection covered by the organisation, and not a stockshot library as such. The reasons for setting up any collection of establishing material including stockshots include the waste of stock, cameraman's time and the money involved in reshooting the same basic material several times over. Also on occasions it may not be possible to shoot a scene when it is needed because of weather conditions eg. snow in summer. One cannot film a building or landscape which has been demolished or changed. Access to a collection of stockshots is useful for these purposes.

TECHNIQUE OF SELECTING STOCKSHOTS

Actual selection for a stockshot library has to be carefully controlled. The film has to be viewed on a full size projection screen. The slightest loss of quality will be magnified and a proper evaluation of the material can be carried out. Standards for stockshot material are very high, although occasionally this standard is lowered if the particular shots are unrepeatable. Emphasis is however placed on quality selection principles.

Selection work is done with positive film rather than risk original negative. Key numbers of the film stock are printed through or marked on all film taken from the negative for easy identification. Sorting and selection is done from the positive prints and key numbers are transferred to these. Material for selection is preferably assembled by the director or editor of the original film who can identify shots quickly. It is then handed over for selection.

Useless or technically poor film is sorted out and discarded, by both the director and the selection staff. Short shots can also be eliminated at this stage. The material is viewed by selection staff in a full size projection theatre. When the final selection is made the key numbers on the positive are used to locate the corresponding negative. Negative material is stored in individual sequences for easier retrieval and less damage in handling, but positive material is stored in reels of 1000-1500ft.

After final selection the positive material has to be assembled for retention and use in the library. The positive material is joined together first under subject heading and then within the subject by key numbers.

Catalogue entries are made out for each shot or sequence giving the edge number, location and description of the shot. In many cases a frame print is attached to the catalogue card to assist identification.

4

FILM HANDLING AND RETRIEVAL

BEFORE GOING on to discuss the handling of film in the library it will be useful to establish the sort of material a library can be expected to handle.

TYPES OF FILM MATERIAL

As well as differences in subject content there are physical differences in the film contained in libraries. A wide range of film has been used to record visual images and there may be a conscious selection or preference in the type handled, or the library may adapt to deal with several types.

The most commonly used gauge in the production and feature film industry used to be 35mm. It was the first commercially used gauge of film and is used for cinema projection because of its quality. However the equipment to produce and project 35mm is bulky and weighty and later developments concentrated on narrower film in the so-called sub-standard gauges, resulting in the widespread adoption of 16mm. Sound was introduced on to 16mm in 1939 and this helped to establish it as an alternative professional medium. It is well suited to films for smaller audiences than the cinema screening and is now used as the standard gauge for educational films and for industrial applications and productions. Television also makes wide use of 16mm and it proved to be a boon to the newsreel cameraman who had to take equipment into dangerous terrain. The lighter 16mm cameras increased the mobility of the news cameraman. The smaller gauges of 8mm and Super 8mm are now being developed, especially in education, and are ideal for cassetting, but they do not as yet produce film of sufficient standard for television or professional screening.

Wide gauge film may also be encountered in the feature and production libraries, the accepted standard width being 70mm.

Feature libraries probably hold 70mm, 35mm and possibly some 16mm although this is unlikely. Distribution libraries may hold 35mm and 16mm depending on whether they are distributing to cinemas or other organisations. Newsfilm libraries hold both 35mm and 16mm, 35mm for the older cinema newsreels and 16mm for more recent film. Some 8mm may be held but it is usually converted to 16mm before inclusion in the library. Educational libraries hold 16mm and 8mm in cassette and open reel form. Most educational establishments have 16mm projectors whereas 35mm projection is rare and an expensive investment for any educational institution. Therefore the libraries serving the education field make 16mm film available. This gives better quality than 8mm open reel for larger audiences, but 8mm is normally adequate for individual or small group viewing by up to 10 people. Eight-millimetre film is also more awkward to handle and use in open reel form especially for the non-educational libraries such as television and newsfilm.

Videotape is being used extensively in television and education and will have to be allowed for in the future design of 'film' libraries. The cost of using videotape is less than film when the tape can be wiped and reused. Initial cost is high, but reuse reduces it. This is a considerable advantage to television companies who can record long films of entire ceremonies or full sporting fixtures. The video can be edited down and rerecorded and the rest of the tape wiped and reused. The disadvantages include lack of mobility, because at present the video camera has to be attached to a power supply vehicle and is very large and conspicuous. The resulting tape needs careful storage to prevent spontaneous wiping by coming into a magnetic field. It has to be viewed to determine if anything has been recorded on it and the content of that record, and is more awkward to edit into short coherent clips than film. If a videotape story is selected for preservation in television libraries at present it is transferred to film for incorporation in the main collection. This situation may change rapidly in the next few years and video libraries become as important as film libraries today.

Another physical difference in the film kept by libraries is the base of the stock. Early film material was recorded on a nitrate base which has certain properties that eventually make it unstable and deteriorate rapidly until the film explodes or burns spontaneously. Long before this stage is reached however the film becomes irretrievable. Nitrate film has to be stored separately from acetate as the two interact to mutual detriment. Also because of its combustibility nitrate has to be stored in small capacity, closed vaults, while acetate can be stored adequately on open racking. These factors affect the design and work policy of a library holding the two types of film. Vaults are designed for storing the two types and a special preservation section has to be set up to examine the nitrate film for signs of deterioration so that it can be transferred to acetate stock. A library which holds only 16mm and 8mm stock does not have these problems, because all such stock is acetate based. But any film library containing 35mm film shot before approximately 1950 will contain some nitrate film.

Colour film has existed commercially since the 1930's but many film organisations were prevented by expense from producing material in colour until a much later date. Until 1968 or 1969 television libraries in the United Kingdom were concerned with black and white film only, while others including the newsreel libraries dealt in both colour and black and white. Now however most film libraries are faced with the additional problems of colour film. Film libraries still have an obligation to provide black and white footage, but television and newsfilm libraries shoot most of their original material on colour stock, duping to monochrome for those customers who transmit in black and white. The libraries are therefore retaining colour and black and white versions of the same stories for customer use. One advantage to the library which does not have a policy of making show copies is that the black and white duplicate print can be treated as a show copy and the colour version used only for printing. This helps to preserve the more easily damaged colour material. Colour is more expensive to shoot, process, store and handle, but with greater usage, costs should fall within a few years. Colour prints may eventually become economically possible as show copies. Any long standing film library will have considerable stocks of black and white footage and additional storage facilities may have to be found to keep colour and black and white footage separate. Colour film needs lower temperatures than monochrome and even more care in handling. The emulsion is softer and subject to greater variation than black and white.

Sound on film is normally recorded on an optical track or magnetic stripe laid on the picture track. It can be recorded on to a separate optical track or magnetic tape. Film which is sent around the country on a hire basis is normally sent on a combined picture and track, either COMOPT or COMMAG. These are technical abbreviations denoting combined optical (COMOPT) or combined magnetic (COMMAG) film, i.e. the picture and sound track are combined on to the one strip of film. The optical track is printed on to the side of the film and the magnetic track is laid on the side of the film on a magnetic strip. The combined film is used for sending to customers for cost reasons, but the libraries may retain the original sound separate from the picture. The only problem is making sure that the sound and picture on a particular story, even if recorded separately are available for combining when necessary. The sound is an essential part of most stories and to lose either sound or picture on a combined story renders the other part ineffectual. The only point to consider in storing magnetic tape is to keep it away from magnetic fields to prevent wiping the record from the tape.

Film, especially if it is obtained from outside sources, is not always stored in negative form. Distribution libraries nearly always operate with multiple prints and have to request the production company for additional prints when those in hand are damaged. Other libraries may have to take prints several stages away from the original. Positive and negative film is often stored separately but this is more for convenience sake than for any technical reasons. The different film does not require different storage conditions, but it may be easier to handle and quicker to locate if all the negative material is in one store and the positive in another. Additionally if positives and negatives are stored separately and one store is accidentally damaged by fire or flood, or is allowed to become too hot or too dry, there is greater insurance against irretrievable loss by having another copy of the film in a separate store.

TYPES OF COPY

A show copy is the complete film suitable for projection and a library show copy is a reference print of the complete film kept for exhibition. These are kept by libraries and are usually stored separately for ease of location and to ensure that originals are not damaged by constant viewing. In many film libraries with a large intake of original film, such as the television or newsfilm libraries, show copies are not made, because of the expenditure involved and lack of storage space for double the amount of film. On the other hand a newsfilm library may obtain a negative and print of stories serviced to customers, and this print can be used for viewing and the negative for printing. These are not show copies as such, but acquire the function of show copies when opportunity arises. The libraries with large supplies of show copies are those who hire or preview film produced by one or several companies, such as distribution libraries who have multiple copies made of the feature production for distribution to cinemas, hire libraries who may hold up to six prints of a film for exhibition in situations other than cinema showings, and feature production libraries who may hold at least one show copy for internal use and viewing by potential customers.

Review copies are similar to show copies but are used primarily by companies who also sell film prints to customers. The production company shows the film in a preview theatre or sends it out on loan for previewing by a customer before purchase. It is similar to a show copy, but used for more restricted purposes by the production company.

There may be several spare prints left over from a newsfilm service or any other agency selling film. These are in addition to the original negative and library positive normally retained by the film library. They are not show copies as such, just additional copies which have been printed due to planning mistakes. It is useful to retain these spare prints for immediate supply to customers. They are not usually booked in to the library, but can be stored with the rest of the film until permanent canning-up is done.

DIFFERENCES IN COMPOSITION

Apart from the physical differences there are differences in the composition or degree of editing of film held in a library. The film may be uncut, that is developed, but in exactly the same sequence and length as it was shot in the camera. Sometimes it may be a cut story or cutting copy roughly assembled for use or polished up into a complete film. Feature and production libraries may keep several versions of the film for varying periods of time in case it becomes necessary to change the original selection of sequences and so on. Rushes are usually kept until the production is complete and may be made available to the librarian for the selection of stockshots before or after production is complete. BBC Library staff see the rushes before the final cutting copy is edited and can then arrange to have sections printed for stock material. Other libraries view the rushes after the final copy is edited.

Rushes and unedited material are seldom retained for any length of time, although newsreel libraries may keep uncut stories that are not topical when they first arrive, or arrive in the news agency too late, or are superseded by a more up to date or important story. These reasons do not preclude reuse of the material at a later date for purposes other than news.

Cuts, trims or offcuts are bits of film left over from cutting or editing the material. They may be retained for a period of time for selection for stock and establishing material. Cuts are usually wound in with each other in disorder and cannot be located accurately on a reel. They are seldom kept in this form for long as they take up a great deal of space, are difficult to handle and in libraries with low shooting ratios seldom contain useful material as all the good shots are included in the edited items. If cuts are retained they will be joined together in related sequences and given a separate location mark. In addition each sequence will have its own identification. Cuts are usually treated and stored separately from other film material in a library.

Another difference in composition occurs as a result of a library's policy in regard to the retention of newsreel, television news bulletins or magazine type compilations. These films are made up of several unrelated items and the main decision for a library to take is whether to retain the complete reel or break it into items. In reuse, the subject matter of the individual items is often of more importance than the compilation of the complete reel, so the reels are usually broken down.

ACCESSION AND RECORDING

Every film is given a number on or before receipt into the library. This is usually a running number and may be the date of transmission in a television library, an acquisition number, number of issue, story number or film number (see page 114). Normally all film in a library is accessioned whether it is to be kept or not. In this way film can be traced through its various stages in the organisation and it can be filed in one sequence while awaiting decisions on permanent retention or junking.

When the film is taken into the library, each can is checked and examined. This is an important part of the library function. Identifying film correctly at this stage avoids errors which become increasingly difficult to rectify the more stages the film passes through.

The film number is recorded on the production record together with other relevant details of library intake, i.e. negative, positive stock received, colour and type, any cuts, separate tracks or special types of film such as library positives, fine grain prints etc. The production record should be designed to show what film came into the organisation, how and if it was cut and what form and footage remain for retention and reuse.

As many housekeeping purposes as possible should be served by this one record and any department which has a concern with the physical property of the film and its origin will need access to its own copy of the record. A general record which can be used by each department can be devised. This record can be printed on a multiple copy form which includes information common to each department. As the form moves through the interested departments particular records can be added within a department which will then detach its own copy of the record before passing film and record to the next stage. Each department will then have a record of the essential details as well as those particular to it.

A typical production sheet for a commercial or syndicating organisation can be made up into six or seven copies. All copies have production number, details of stock received, time of receipt and where the film came from, whether sound or silent, colour and type of colour. The traffic department retain this record of film received filed according to the country, agent or cameraman the film came from. The film passes on to syndication who add details of customers serviced with the film and retain a copy of the record. Laboratories retain a copy giving the number of prints required and stock received. The accounts department use a copy for checking payments to the supplier of the film and customer payments. Film library retains a copy to which it adds material finally received and whether it was retained permanently or junked. A copy of the production record is often sent back to the cameraman with a report on the technical quality of the film received and the use made of it.

TEMPORARY STORAGE OF FILM

After the film is accessioned and recorded into the library it is prepared for temporary storage. This temporary store is useful and even essential to allow time for the collection to accumulate and settle down into its most complete form.

The film has to be identified in some way in storage, either by title in feature film, or by date of transmission and production number in television and newsfilm. The best way to ensure that the production number is associated with the film is to scribe the number on to the film stock itself as close to the picture as possible. The number can be written on the film with a felt pen if preferred but this is less permanent than a scribe. It tends to rub off the original film, although any prints taken from this film will have the number permanently printed. With some types of stock and printing the number written in felt pen will not print through whereas a scribed number will. The number needs to be close to the picture so that when laboratories print up the film it will remain associated with it and not be removed with the spare leader. When laboratories are running considerable quantities of film they remove most of the leader to avoid printing blank film. If the leader immediately precedes the film the number will be scribed close to the join between them. If blank film precedes the picture the number can be scribed on this.

The film should be scribed on receipt so that it is identified as soon as possible. A large amount of inscribed or unnumbered film will cause confusion and possible loss.

Film can be held in temporary storage in individual cans or boxes for the shorter film. Boxes are cheaper, easier to mark clearly, disposable and take up less space than cans.

When film is stored according to date of transmission, cans are normally used and these will be retained for later permanent storage if labelled with the date. One or more cans are used for each date, signalled according to whether negative, positive, colour, cuts or tracks, etc.

When short film is stored by production number, boxes can be used more easily. One box is used for each piece of film. The films in a newsfilm library for example are normally short and can be fitted into small boxes approximately 4in square and 1in deep. The film is checked, scribed, leadered at head and end and put into the boxes. The film may be wound on to plastic bobbins for convenience of handling, but this is not essential. The boxes are edge-labelled with the production number and stock contained inside. This means the box can seldom be reused and should be cheap and easily disposed of. Boxes are stored in blocks of numbers (9150 — 9159/70, for example), all negatives, positives, cut and uncut film, colour film and tracks being filed together. Groups of ten numbers are probably not too large to exclude easy filing and withdrawal. An attempt to regulate storage too rigidly in racks at this stage will make it difficult to effect quick withdrawal and addition to existing film.

Cuts, unless they are to be used for stockshots, are best stored separately because they are the items most likely to be withdrawn and will probably not be held in the same way as the edited stories. Cuts can be retained in separate cans for examination by the selection staff, and labelled with the date of syndication or transmission or production title. If the cuts are separated they can easily be sorted and junked if necessary without interfering with the main system. If there is considerable selection from cuts they can be joined together on intake for ease of handling, otherwise they can be left as cuts and joined only when necessary.

Spare prints due to overprinting for service requirements can be retained in many libraries in temporary storage for immediate supply to customers. These are in addition to the multiple copies needed in distribution or hire libraries. They can be stored in individual boxes labelled with the production number and clearly marked as spares. They can be withdrawn from temporary storage without interfering with the system, but should not be retained in permanent storage as spare prints. If they are canned up and then withdrawn the space left in the can will not be filled by other film and valuable storage space is lost. Adding film to completed cans uses considerable time and necessitates alteration of records. There is also the uncertainty of whether it is a real gap or film out being processed.

During this temporary storage period, cataloguing and selection procedures are carried out on the film.

PERMANENT STORAGE

After a period of time the collection will be ready for more permanent storage and preservation. Although the system described is useful for its purpose it consumes a lot of space and becomes untidy and difficult to control over long periods. Where there is a large intake of 1000 films a month it is probably feasible to store in this way for a maximum period of six weeks.

After the period of temporary storage the film has to be withdrawn from the vaults, gathered together and checked against the production record. The production record will have been amended according to the decisions taken by the selection staff and any film it has been decided to junk, together with unwanted duplicate material and spare prints can be junked at this stage. The remainder is prepared for permanent storage. The film is wound through and the story rechecked, head and end leaders are replaced if they have been lost and the number or scribe on the film is rechecked.

Film is best stored permanently on a central core or bobbin and, if these bobbins are of wood, information can be written on the core, to assist in quick search and identification. However, film which is constantly in use in hire libraries can be wound on spools to facilitate handling and loan procedures. In these cases the labels are attached to the cans and the film. When film is wound on to the wood bobbin, the bobbin is labelled with the production number and stock. The can number can also be written on the reverse side of the bobbin, enabling the film to be refilled correctly after use without reference to further records. The film itself can be secured with white tape to prevent unwinding, and the production number can be written on to the tape or better still on to the outside of the leader to emphasise identification. Film libraries which do not use wood bobbins as central cores use these methods instead. The film is then placed in cans in one or two layers depending on the depth of the can, the size of the film reel and the likely usage. Full use should be made of the space available in the can in libraries which do not lend or hire film, but the film should never be pushed in tightly or it will be damaged. If the film is put into the cans with the production number and stock visible on the top of the bobbin search is facilitated and film need not be disturbed unnecessarily.

The production record should be marked according to what is done with the film at this stage. This means either putting the can number on for reference, or marking the records of the material which has been junked or canned-up.

Numerical labelling of cans is the easiest and most flexible method. Production number order is not necessarily consecutive within the cans and all available pieces of film on one production number may not fit into the same can. However a separate record should be made for use in transferring location numbers to other records. A list of can numbers' and the contents of each can is sufficient. The information can then be transferred to shotlists or catalogue cards by the documentation staff.

When film is placed in the vaults for final storage it may be convenient to separate some stock into separate vaults. This is to be recommended wherever feasible, especially the separation of colour and black and white. Wherever it occurs signalling has to be introduced into the retrieval mechanisms to show exactly what stock is available and where. The prefix X can be used for colour rather than C which could easily be confused with the numbering system for the film. Other libraries use K for colour. N is an adequate symbol for negative or P for positive. Other signals may be colour cards, colour strips on cards and so on. Where colour cards are used, other reinforcing signals must be employed if any retrieval system cannot cope with coloured strips or if cards are to be copied on a non-colour copier.

OTHER STORAGE SYSTEMS

Other systems of storage include filing alphabetically on shelves by title or by the date of transmission. Film inside these cans is given an individual number for retrieval, and the labelling of the film is similar to that already described. All film may be filed in the same can or one can may be used for master copies and another for spares and tracks. Cuts and unused material are viewed and selected and may then be filed in a special sequence under subject or personality. ITN, for example, have a sequence of cans filed in wide subject areas and a parallel file of dopesheets and shotlists corresponding to the material in the cans.

Some libraries put film into plastic bags before filing in cans. This has the advantage of protecting the film against constant handling within the cans when a search is being made and prevents incidental damage to the film when it rubs up against the sides of the can or other film. The bags are airtight and help to prevent damage from moisture and dust. However, film filed in this way is usually 35mm and in larger rolls than a 16mm newsfilm library's stock; storage in bags is not recommended for the more numerous 16mm stock. Additionally plastic tends to sweat and may eventually damage the film. It should never be used with nitrate film.

Other libraries file alphabetically by title. Production libraries may sometimes file in this way where all film connected with a particular production is labelled with the title and a distinguishing code put on the cans to indicate if the material is positive, original or duplicate negative, fine grain, show print, colour internegative or positive, etc. Distribution and hire libraries normally hold prints of the material and each film is given a location or library catalogue code number. This is usually the number used to file the film. File number, title, duration, number of reels and copy number are all put on a top label on the can. The can edge label may contain only the catalogue number or in some cases an abbreviated title as well. Archive film is normally filed by location and vault number edge marked on the can, with the film title etc. on the top label.

HANDLING AND STORAGE EQUIPMENT

Film handling equipment used at this stage includes waste bins, joiners, film cement, leader, bobbins, cans. The waste bins are needed for getting rid of unwanted film and if both nitrate and acetate are being handled in the library the two types should be kept separate to avoid accident when disposing of the waste. These bins should be cleared regularly and, to reduce accident risk, should never be allowed to overfill.

Joiners or splicers are needed for joining broken film, or leader to film. Joiners can be automatic or fixed to a power supply for the necessary heat. An adequate supply of film cement is also needed. This should be stored in large containers, but used in small containers. Being acetone it congeals if constantly subjected to the open air. Small bottles with applicators incorporated containing a day's supply should be on all winding benches.

Leader is used for protection and as an indication of the type of film attached, so that different types of leader are necessary according to the film handled, such as sound or silent. The leader indicates to the projectionist or user the type of film and how to lace it up on viewing machines. It is also helpful to use different coloured leader for negative or positive, black and white or colour film. The rolls of leader can be racked in several devices for ease of use. One neat solution is to have ordinary cans filled with leader with a small piece cut out of the side of the can through which leader feeds ready for use. The cans are then racked above the winding bench.

Bobbins are needed in large supply. For normal purposes of projection an ordinary plastic bobbin meets most needs in a library, and these bobbins should have a smooth surface and not be subject to changes in atmosphere. They should also fit the viewing machines in use in the library and organisation. For storage a bobbin which can be written on for quick identification and location is the most satisfactory, and wood is the most satisfactory substance for this. Other libraries need to spool the film and therefore need spools, preferably plastic, of varying sizes. Split spools are useful to any library which has projectors as well as viewing machines and may store film on bobbins. In order to put the film on a projector a spool is necessary and split spools save a great deal of time in this instance.

Cans of different sizes are needed, either round for transport or holding large reels, or square or rectangular according to storage racks provided. When handling and storing small reels of film a square can is more space saving than a round one. The same amount of storage space is used up, but the corners will provide additional room for film. 16mm film is normally filed in double layers in the cans thus allowing more compact storage and less movement of film within the cans.

The quality of the can is also important. Cans are used in large quantity, but cheap ones are a false economy in storage because they are not rustproof and rust damages can and contents very quickly. Plastic cans are useful for any library which stores larger reels of film or sends much film off the premises. The plastic can is lighter and often pleasanter to handle than the metal can. It is also much easier to open.

A felt pen and stencil forms for the numbers is often the most effective way of labelling cans. Dymo type labels could be used, although they are often too small. Special strip labels could be printed and signalled with prefixes or colour to denote type of content in the can, i.e. negative, positive or colour. Cans should be edge numbered for quick identification and may also have top labels specially designed with more details included as to the contents. Felt pen does not take well on plastic and edge labels have to be used for these cans.

Film has constantly to be examined during its time in the library, but whenever it is removed from the vaults it has to be rewound for examination or preparation and to remove the bobbin carrying the production and location numbers. This work is most effectively carried out on a winding bench rather than a viewing machine. Winding benches fitted with rewinders, measuring instruments and underlights should be available to accommodate all members of staff who will need to use them. Other work carried out on the winding benches includes intake, examination, repair and breaking down reels of material from the laboratories. The rewinding equipment should also be fitted with interchangeable central spindles so that 35mm and 16mm and any other width used can be rewound on the same bench. Upright rewinders should also be available, especially for measuring film. They take up less space because they can be mounted on narrower benches, but are not recommended for all rewinding jobs. Automatic rewind is useful for non-technical staff.

Protection for film and staff is essential. Film has to be protected against dirt, moisture and the stickiness of finger marks. Dust may be wound into the film and cause scratches, and sticky finger marks, apart from showing up as dirt in projection, will eventually attack the emulsion. It is essential that staff handling film wear gloves. This prevents the transfer of dirt and finger marks on to the film emulsion and also protects the wearer from any residue chemicals or other damage to the hands as well as ingrained dirt. Forms of industrial dermatitis are frequently found in people handling film and gloves afford some protection from this. The gloves should be cotton which will not deposit fluff on the film. Cotton is better than nylon which, besides causing overheating of the hands creates friction on the film and sets up a static charge which attracts dust and dirt.

Overalls are also necessary for vault assistants and others working continuously with film. Despite efforts to keep film clean, cans become dusty and chemicals spread on to clothing.

RETRIEVAL OF FILM FROM STORAGE

The user researches the material in the indexes and on the

shotlists. This may give sufficient information about the film and he will order prints. Another user may have to view the film before he can select the piece he needs. In either case the film has to be withdrawn from the vaults and prepared for viewing and/or the laboratories. This procedure takes time and needs to be systematised to achieve efficiency.

In many systems the library assistant responsible for withdrawing film is provided with information on production numbers and can numbers. A vault requisition form can be used to detail exactly what film is required and who requires it, how it is to be prepared and where it is to be delivered. The requisition form can be duplicated and the information passed on to the appropriate department for recording.

The assistant takes the list into the vaults, goes to the cans and withdraws the film using the information supplied to tell him which stock is required.

Film is brought out into the handling area and prepared. Where it has been wound on to wooden bobbins it can be run off and the bobbins retained as a record of film out. The film is wound ready for viewing or printing, i.e. head out and celluloid in the correct position for the viewing or printing machine to be used. Some small viewers project the image differently from larger projection machines, while in the laboratories the film needs to be put through the machines so that print through is the correct way round. Leaders and scribes should be checked at this stage and renewed if necessary. Once the film is prepared it can again be secured with white tape on which the number is written for quick reference. If a lot of film is being handled there should be no need to open each piece of film until the scribed number can be seen; there should be an external mark. The film is then sent to viewing cubicles or laboratories as required. Distribution libraries may wind film on to a new spool for sending out to users, but examination of film is normally carried out when the film is returned to the library and before it is put back in the vaults. Distribution libraries wind film on to spools for users, can it up, book it out to the user and despatch it.

FILM MOVEMENT RECORDS

It is essential in any library to know where the stock is at any given time, and for this a film movement catalogue is important. Such a record can be amalgamated with other records or it may be easier to handle if it is compiled specifically as a movement record but also used for other purposes. It can, for example, aid retrospective selection by showing which material is being used. Ordinary 5 x 3in catalogue cards filed numerically by the production number can be used. The information recorded on the card is taken from the requisition form and includes the date of issue, to whom the film is issued and subsequently the date of return. The assistant dealing with the film movement catalogue checks the film on return against the original requisition orders to ensure that all issued film has to be accounted for. These assistants can also examine the film on its return to the library and arrange for any repairs needed.

This system is adequate when dealing with a library which does not issue loans, but has film always either within library control or in the laboratories for printing. Requisition forms are kept until all the film on any form is returned and are then destroyed. Items not returned are investigated at intervals, once a week or once a month, or as and when the film is required. When film is loaned to other departments within the organisation, often scattered over a wide area, further measures are needed to ensure recall and return.

Visible index methods can be used when the recall of film from several departments or external borrowers becomes a necessary task. If the film movement record is kept by this method a signal can be put on to the card to show date or period of recall.

Other libraries have problems of loan and recall which are large enough to consider the use of computer or mechanised retrieval methods. The BBC have an Ultronic machine in which a punched paper tape is prepared from an original requisition list and all loans can be controlled together with the recall of overdues or film needed for other departments. It is to be emphasised that the BBC film library has one of the largest problems in the loan of library film within its own organisation. The production departments and laboratories are scattered over a wide area in London and the regions have to be considered in addition. Some 1250 cans of film are issued each week. Some large distribution libraries use computer banks to keep track of all film and issue recall notices when required.

The film movement record has, like most other records in a film library, to be tailored to the particular needs of the library and if a simple straightforward system can be employed efficiently it should be preferred to mechanical aids used for their own sake, rather than that of improving the service of the library.

VIEWING PROCEDURES

When extensive viewing facilities are available for customers the library has full control of the viewers used. Library staff should be present whenever film is viewed, in order to handle the film, run the viewing machines and take requests from the customers for printing. The customer should not be allowed to run the film himself whether it is a viewing print or master. The library has to protect its stock and if some damage does occur to the film or machines the customer is protected against claims for recovery of film or equipment.

The librarian runs the film through, sorts out the material the customer wants printed and separates it from unwanted material. This unwanted film is returned to the film movement department at once, booked back into the vaults and refiled. Refile should be done as soon as possible to prevent quantities of film accumulating at the refile stage and consequent hold-ups in searching for material. One member of staff at least has to be on this job full time.

A customer may not require the whole of a film, in which case, subject to library policy and laboratory practice, sections of the film can be marked for printing up. Laboratories as a rule do not print sections under a certain footage, say 20ft of 16mm, and many will not print sections of colour film. It may indeed be cheaper to have a print of the whole film of some 60ft than a section of 30ft from it, and the librarian will be able to advise the customer on these facts at the time of selection for printing. When sections are to be printed, a slip of tissue paper can be wrapped around the film at start and end of section, marked with arrows indicating direction of printing. In addition a note on the printing order of the length of the section should be sufficient indication to the laboratories.

VIEWING MACHINES

Viewing machines in a library may have to serve a dual purpose of use by customers and library staff engaged on shotlisting or selection. Also film handling staff need to use the machines for checking when a winding bench and light are not sufficient.

If a great deal of customer viewing occurs it is better to have separate machines for customers and library staff to prevent one activity getting in the way of the other.

The viewing machines must damage the film as little as possible as many film libraries run original material, for reasons of economy, rather than show copies. Machines have to be provided for both 16mm and 35mm in many large film libraries and in addition 8mm machines may become necessary in the future.

(Many short industrial or educational films are being mounted in 8mm cassette form). Some machines are available which are interchangeable on 16mm and 35mm but they usually perform better on one or the other and the additional expense of the machine could as well have been devoted to two machines.

Library machines also have to cater for sound or mute film and should provide facilities for optical and magnetic sound in the one machine. Silent machines should be used for silent film to prevent film running through the two gates on a sound machine and risking damage, but sound film should never be run on a silent projector. Silent viewing machines are designed with double sprocket holes and sound film has single perforations. If a sound film is run on a silent projector the sprockets run through the sound track on the film and render it useless.

Black and white and colour film can be run on the same viewing machines, but the light will probably need to be increased for the colour material. It may be better to acquire new machines built specifically to deal with colour rather than adjust existing ones, as an increase in light intensity may cause overheating.

Essential qualities for customer viewing machines are smooth forward and reverse running, ease of stopping and starting the film without damage by jerking, adequate light and a good sized screen, alternative magnetic/optical sound heads, an inching device for framing shots and a footage counter. Variable speed is not so essential for customer viewing unless long reels made up of several subjects are used, and the film need not be rewound on the customer viewer, as this will be done on a winding bench when the film is returned.

Viewing in feature or distribution libraries where the customer is looking at the film with a view to purchasing the whole print should, for reasons of quality, public relations and marketing, be done by projection. Most film libraries of this type have access to preview theatres in the parent organisation and should use these facilities, rather than viewing machines. Viewing machines are ideal for editors and production staff to select short clips of film for possible use, but where the complete film is bought for projection to large audiences the customer should see it under the same conditions.

SCRATCH PRINTS

Sometimes it is impossible for the customer to attend the library to view material for selection, but he does not want to have a large amount of film printed when he is only looking for particular sequences or types of shot. In addition the library may not wish to supply a customer with an amount of material over which it cannot exercise reasonable copyright control. In these and similar cases scratched prints can be supplied to the customer. They are supplied at a basic print cost, but all film is defaced by a bar or scratch through all frames to ensure the film is not transmitted without the knowledge of the supplier. The customer views the prints, selects the material required and returns it with an order for printing. The returned prints are matched up with the original film which is sent to the laboratories for printing.

PREPARATION. FOR LABORATORIES

Once the customer has decided on the film he requires printed the library staff take over preparation for the laboratories. It is essential at this juncture to ensure that the library knows the precise requirements of the customer, whether duplicate negative, black and white print, colour contact prints, internegative etc. and what form the sound track has to take. It is also necessary to appraise the customer of any additional stages in printing which are necessary to obtain the material he needs and for which of course he has to pay. Prints from library fine grain positives, for example, may have to pass through a duplicate negative stage before the print emerges and both stages are charged to the customer.

Once the library has precise instructions on the type of film required this information is transferred to laboratory order forms. These can be made out in duplicate or as many as required. One form should go to the laboratories with the film, and one at least retained by the library for checking against the film's return. Other forms could be used for accounting purposes or put with the customer's contracts for reference.

The film is sent to the laboratories together with the order. Short films can be joined in the library into appropriate rolls, but often even in a big order each film needs different treatment and it is simpler to send over individual pieces. Where viewing prints have been shown to the customer the corresponding original film has to be withdrawn from the vaults for printing. Printing is done from the best quality material, but if an intermediate stage already exists between the original and the customer's requirements it can be used to save customer expense.

LABORATORY PRINTING

Some detailed consideration of laboratory printing is necessary at this stage to indicate which printing processes are relevant to customer requirements, the number of stages used to obtain these requirements and how many are chargeable to the customer.

Printing involves transferring a photographic image from one piece of film to another. In duplication of film there are six main processes as follows:

1. Print original negative to master positive
2. Develop master positive
3. Print master positive to duplicating negative
4. Develop duplicating negative
5. Print duplicating negative to black and white print
6. Develop black and white print

The developing stages can be removed from this table and counted as part of the printing stages for easy reference. This reduces the processes to three main ones: Original negative to master positive, master positive to duplicating negative and duplicating negative to black and white print.

The master positive has special characteristics: it is normally a duplicating positive with very fine grain and copies of fine grain duplicating negatives can be made from it. These are useful for further printing because the quality is high.

If a customer needs a dupe negative and print and the library has an original negative this will have to go through the master positive stage in order to obtain a good quality dupe negative. The library can retain this master positive and use it to make other dupe negatives to cut down printing costs to customers and incidentally as an insurance against loss or damage to the original negative.

The further away from the original a film goes in printing the greater the accumulation of errors and distortion, and the first print from the original negative should be fine grain to ensure reasonable quality extension through more phases. An ordinary black and white print from the original negative is not of sufficient quality for further printing and making duplicate negatives.

A customer needing a duplicate negative and work print for re-editing uses a black and white print from the dupe negative rather than a master positive. This is edited and then the negative cut to match. A fine grain print is not necessary for this work print, but the customer has to pay for the master positive phase in any case.

There are four main types of printer resulting from combinations of the following techniques. In a *continuous* printer the film moves at a set speed as opposed to a *step* printer where film is moved intermittently one frame at a time. Printers may also be *contact* where film being printed and printed film are in contact with one another during printing, or *optical* where an optical system intervenes and transfers the image from the printing to the printed film.

Continuous types of printers are used for speed and economy and step printers are more useful for duping older film or making separation negatives for colour film. Continuous contact printers are used for most straightforward duplicating work. The two films travel in close contact, emulsion surfaces facing, past an aperture where a light shining through the printing film exposes the printed film. Additionally the machines can be provided with two printing heads, one for picture and the other for sound. This produces a combined or married print and involves the customer in no extra charge for sound. Continuous optical printers are used for reduction and blow-up between 16mm and 35mm.

Reversal printing gives an image of a very fine grain and has many uses in film library work when intermediate printing stages are not needed. Reversal printing occurs when a positive image is developed on the film exposed in the camera. The negative image is developed as normal and then destroyed or bleached out. The film is re-exposed and developed again. The resulting fine grain reversal can be used to make fine grain duplicating negatives and prints in the usual way. Reversal development adds three processes to normal negative development and is correspondingly more expensive but does not produce so many 'wasted' stages in between. Colour film is often on reversal stock and here the saving in the number of processes makes a considerable difference to the cost of colour prints.

Sound can be put on to the film as either a magnetic or optical track or it can be reproduced as a separate magnetic track. Magnetic recording makes no use of the photographic properties of film and separate processes are used to transfer magnetic sound from one film to another. The additional equipment required increases the cost. Many film libraries find it more convenient to put their sound optically on the film although magnetic stripes and separate magnetic tracks are provided if required. When sound is put on to an optical track the only problem to be overcome is synchronisation. Projectors have separate sound and picture heads, therefore the appropriate sound has to arrive at the sound head at the same time as the matching picture reaches the picture head. It has therefore to be printed a number of frames before the picture, that is some 20 frames in 35mm aand 26 frames in 16mm.

BREAKDOWN ON RETURN

Film returns from the laboratories in two batches, one of library originals and another large roll of customer prints or, for longer films, single reels. The rolls of shorter film have to be checked, broken down, numbered and prepared for sending out to the customer. The original film, if it is not required for cross checking or matching, goes back to film movement to be examined, booked in and sent for refile. The roll of customer prints should be checked to make sure all films have been printed and correct sections made. The prints are in a continuous sequence but differentiated by short sections of blank film where they can be separated and labelled. The production numbers should have been printed through, but where they have not they can be scribed on to the leader of the print. It is not usually necessary to run the shorter film on bobbins for sending out. Longer films and features can be spooled for customers. Hire and distribution libraries have to spool film ready for the loan department and if so these are wound head out for convenience. Other lending libraries wind the film end out and transfer to another spool before lending the film. However it is better for hire libraries to check film on return from a viewing and therefore film is usually wound head out, ready for the next customer. Most hire libraries request customers not to rewind film for this reason, the film is returned end out and only one rewinding is necessary to inspect the film and make it ready for the next customer.

Matching jobs are also done at breakdown stage for the customer by the library staff, that is matching the key numbers on negatives with prints to assist in the final editing of the material.

When the order is complete each print is wrapped in fine tissue for protection and enclosed in shipping cans or boxes carefully labelled with the contents, i.e. production number, quick title and any other relevant details. The containers are then passed on to the traffic department for dispatch or collection. Shipping to customers in hire libraries is a more detailed process. Hire libraries send film out ready for projection, usually on a spool so that the customer does not have to supply two spools for his projector. Details of the film hired, customer and borrowing or account number are noted, the copy number is taken together with the title and film number.

EXAMINATION BEFORE REFILING

Whenever a film is withdrawn from the vaults the condition

should be closely examined before its return. Any damage can be detected and dealt with immediately. Leaders to protect the film are replaced and missing scribes redone as a matter of course, but more serious damage should also be dealt with, such as perforations, scratches, missing sections, etc. This examination should be done immediately before the film is returned to the vaults. The cause of the damage should be investigated to see if any machines are malfunctioning and causing damage. In hire libraries if the customer has damaged a print he may be required to reimburse the library for the value of the film or that part of it which has been damaged.

In addition to examining returned film a constant examination of older film has to be carried out. The film preservation officer has responsibility for this, but all other members of staff should be aware of the signs of damage or deterioration and be able to bring it to notice. Some libraries do not have a film preservation officer as such, but leave it to the constant watchfulness of all members of staff. Even libraries with a large amount of old film work on the assumption that all film will be looked at by one member of staff or another over a period of some ten years, and any deterioration will be seen and dealt with. Other film libraries who suspect much of their early material is in danger of deterioration employ a film preservation officer to go through the film systematically searching for deterioration, mending, cleaning and organising back collections which may not yet be fully documented. A close watch has to be kept on the colour collections of the film and television news libraries. These collections are of recent origin and much has yet to be done on the quality of the colour. Stock and dyes are often in the experimental stages but the film is being housed in the libraries. Storage problems, particularly the question of temperature have not yet been solved, or understood in some cases, satisfactorily, and there may well be a sudden and rapid deterioration and loss of colour quality. If this occurs duping is necessary to preserve the collection.

If deterioration in the film is discovered it has to be sent to laboratories for duping or stretching or other remedial measures. These laboratory processes are charged to the library either at cost if the laboratory is internal, or at commercial rates if the film has to be sent out. Laboratory processes are highly specialised and the rescue operations on early film often require particular machines which are not available in all laboratories, e.g. for stretching shrunk film. In these cases the library has to pay full commercial rate. Duping of film which is in early stages of deterioration can often be done by non-specialist laboratories and here the library is charged only for stock used by its own laboratory. It is therefore in the library's interests to maintain a close watch on the stock so that deterioration can be detected early and drastic remedial measures can be forestalled.

REFILING

Original library film is returned via film movement and examination. Any missing scribes are replaced, leader attached and the film rewound on to its original wood bobbin. Examination and rewinding can be done at one and the same time. This film does not necessarily have to be stored end out or head out as it will always be rewound on coming out of the vaults to remove the bobbin. Feature films which are spooled are normally stored head out. Having been rewound on to its bobbin the film can be refiled in the vaults using the can number on the bobbin. This is one of the most crucial steps in the whole procedure for if the film is refiled wrongly it might as well be lost. Although the job of refiling is usually given to junior members of staff the importance of concentration and accuracy has to be stressed strongly and repeatedly to ensure that the system continues to operate efficiently.

Trolleys for moving film in the vault area are very useful. They give the assistant a working top for the requisition forms and quick checking and have other shelves for holding film extracted or for refile. These shelves can as easily be racks for taking larger cans of film if this is necessary.

When all the operations are completed the various pieces of information are assembled on each customer enquiry. The original enquiry, the film viewed, film selected, how much ordered and processed for use. The file is then handed to the administration staff who deal with contractual and royalty payments and the completed file is retained for reference purposes on a library schedule.

5

SHOTLISTING OR SEQUENCE LISTING

S OME WRITTEN or verbal description of the contents of a film is essential for reference and cataloguing. The aim of shotlisting is to produce a written or readable record of the contents of a film which reduces the necessity for viewing it to determine its contents. Repeated viewing causes considerable wear and tear on the film and is a waste of time.

PRINCIPLES OF SHOTLISTING

A shotlist is a descriptive list of shots in the order in which they appear in a film and includes camera positions and footages relating to these shots. It is useful to both the reference and cataloguing processes in film libraries where the location of sequences or shots within films is important. It has less relevance for feature or entertainment films where the whole film is normally reshown. Some listing of sequences is necessary, however, together with a precis of the action. The type of library involved determines the detail of the listing. Production libraries can use the shooting scripts for detail of shots or sequences. Archives need to make sequence lists with inclusive footages.

Short films are rarely used in their entirety, but particular sequences are recut into a new production. A written description helps to locate shots for reuse before direct recourse to the film. Unsuitable material is eliminated more quickly using written descriptions rather than the film. Working from these secondary sources the researcher is able to compile more accurate viewing lists for final selection. Shotlists act as a guide to people who are unable to see the film before selection. If the most complete version of a feature or documentary is required, or only a particular sequence, the search could extend over several libraries in many countries. It would not be feasible to have prints of all the films made for viewing, nor could the researcher travel around looking at the originals. An accurate shotlist solves such problems for him.

The shotlist may also be used for cataloguing purposes, for two main reasons: to save time and duplication of effort. Once the film has been viewed and shotlisted further reference can be made to the shotlist rather than the film. While many film libraries compile their own shotlists, some are supplied with them as part of the syndication service and if large amounts of film are dealt with the cataloguers may use these secondary sources in order to keep up with the intake.

It is clearly a waste of time and effort to have a film editor compile a shotlist for syndication, while a cataloguer compiles another for the same film for library purposes, especially when the syndication shotlist is detailed. Of course if the syndication shotlist is not adequate for library purposes it has to be redone. The better the verbal description the less need for constant viewing of the film, but it should be stressed that no verbal description can give a complete impression. If verbal description were enough there would be no need for the film.

Shotlisting is the precursor of cataloguing. The cataloguer should wherever possible see the film, because working from secondary sources may not be enough for indexing purposes. When shotlists are produced in a library the cataloguing staff should be responsible for compiling the shotlists as well as cataloguing the film. They will produce an index-orientated shotlist and the co-ordination between documents referring to the film should be strong as a result.

The cataloguers need access to the film they are working on, whether they produce the shotlists or not, and should be able to view the film before cataloguing either on library machines, or in film viewing sessions which may be designed for the information of several staff members. In many production libraries it is possible for cataloguers to see these general staff viewing sessions, but special cataloguing viewing sessions should also be provided for the specialist work involved.

Newsfilm agencies often have showings of the day's output, and these are attended by the cataloguers on duty. Other cataloguers attached to television news can watch final transmissions, although normally because television services use cue sheets rather than shotlists the library has in any case to make shotlists after transmission.

HOW TO SHOTLIST

Many of the features in shotlisting can be derived only from the film itself, but in information film, documentary and newsfilm the content of the shots relates to external events, and the film may illustrate current events, scientific processes, research work and so on. When possible therefore some information about the film should be obtained before viewing. The viewing session is easier if the shotlister knows in advance particular points to look out for: more information can be gained from the film if he is aware of the date of an event, the location, the story line or what is happening and who was there. For instance, if he does not know the personalities involved in a documentary or newsfilm, the shotlister may miss several important people who are not prominently featured but appear on the screen. This is especially true if the film is not a current story. Working from the title of the film in the accessions register the shotlister can do some preliminary research on the event featured.

Assuming that the library staff are to compile the precis or shotlist the next step is to view the film. This viewing session should pick out all the relevant features of the film and note all necessary information for the final shotlist. It should not be necessary to return to view the film over and over again for information which has not been noted in the main viewing session. The film may be run through more than once in this viewing session, but it should not be necessary to have more than one session. On the first run through of the film the viewer will gain a general impression of the content, subject and approach of the film maker, and notes can be taken on these features and any other special features to be looked for in compiling the shotlist. Then the film is rewound and put on to a special viewing machine for shotlisting purposes.

After the initial viewing for general impression the shotlister is ready to begin the final shotlist. All relevant features are noted as the film proceeds: titles, credits, footage, content of sequence or shot, type of shot in detailed shotlisting, sound — commentary, speech or natural sound effects. With all this information to be gathered shotlisting can become a laborious and time-consuming task if properly carried out. Nevertheless plenty of time should be allowed for this part of the operation because it makes the following tasks easier in direct relation to the thoroughness with which it is done.

VIEWING MACHINES FOR SHOTLISTING

Viewing machines for shotlisting purposes need some additional features to those used for customer viewing, but the same machines can be used for both purposes if necessary. If a great deal of shotlisting and cataloguing is carried out in the library and much time is also devoted to customer viewings, separate machines should be provided, but if one function takes precedence the timetable can be arranged to accommodate both jobs on the same machines.

Machines used for shotlisting and cataloguing should be equipped for running both silent and sound material. If sound is on a separate track it should be run on the same machine as the picture, with positive synchronisation of sound and picture, that is the sound and the picture should match when viewed. Optical and magnetic, separate or combined sound tracks can all be accommodated on the one machine, or one machine can be reserved for optical and one for magnetic, as long as the picture and track can be viewed simultaneously.

Library machines have to be provided for each gauge of film stored. Some machines are capable of running both 35mm and 16mm, while others are designed for only one gauge. Those which are designed for both often show a distinct preference for one, and it is often better to limit the use of the machine to one gauge, or to employ two less sophisticated machines dealing with one gauge each to prevent inadvertent damage and allow greater flexibility for the viewer.

An essential part of a shotlist is its location of shots by means of footage counts, therefore any shotlisting viewing machine should have an accurate footage or metrage counter and a time counter or clock. For very accurate location of shots two footage counters may be incorporated in the machine, one for total footage and one which can be reset for certain sequences to give inclusive footages. The viewing machine should allow the shotlister considerable freedom to operate the machine, to stop it at will, alter focus, alter racking of film (to make sure the whole frame is visible and the picture is not cut by frame lines), reverse film and replay, inch the film a frame at a time, and change the speed of running.

ESSENTIAL FEATURES OF SHOTLISTS

When the film is being shotlisted certain essential features must be recorded. These include:
1. Title
2. Credits
3. Footage
4. Type of shot
5. Description of shot
6. Sound

These are considered under separate headings in the following pages.

FILM TITLE AND NUMBER

The first feature to note is the title of the film and its production or location number. The title may be derived from the film itself in which case it should be used verbatim. With some films the title is usually a made up one indicative of the contents of the film, especially in the case of newsfilm. When the film is likely to be known by its title, for example a feature film, it is referred to and indexed by this title. But where the film subject is the likely reference, the title becomes indicative and other index headings are used for reference. In newsfilm the production number assumes greater importance in identifying the film. This production number may be assigned before shotlisting begins, or the film may be accessioned by the shotlister and given a number. If the film has no title, the shotlister devises one that is concise and informative on the contents of the film, and non-controversial. As well as being part of the objective aim of all film cataloguing, this is important for newsfilm which is being sent around the world. Care is taken not to upset various factions by implication or the use of a misnomer. The use of Biafra for secessionist Nigeria, for example, offended more people than it pleased, as many countries did not recognise it as a separate state. Occupied countries resent being named as part of the occupying power and it is often difficult to sort out complicated questions such as these.

Misleading titles can and should be changed in film work, where the title has been made up, but not where it appears on the film. If it appears on the film and is still misleading, then a brief explanation or correction should be given in references and catalogue entries, but the title should stand for identification. Misleading or inaccurate titles can occur when untitled film is booked in before being viewed, and in this case the title can be changed to conform with the contents of the film.

TREATMENT OF CREDITS

Production credits naming companies, artists and technicians involved in the making of particular films are of importance in most films and should all be recorded on full shotlists. Feature films can be indexed according to cameramen, directors, actors etc., in separate name indexes and all this information can be taken from the shotlist by the indexer. Copyright considerations make the production and distribution credits important. The position is different in many film libraries which own copyright on their material, and do not normally retain non-exclusive copyright material. Newsfilm credits seldom appear on film, the cameramen are not named and the company name may only be attached in a special leader which can easily come adrift from the film. On the other hand older newsreel companies which make up programmes or reels may title their stories and the company name appears on the title frames. Any collection of film which covers the work of several companies, whether they own copyright on the film or not should quote the original company on any shotlist to assist in identification of the film.

RECORDING FOOTAGE

Footage or metrage is recorded as the film runs through. It can be recorded as a total or running footage or inclusive according to the catalogue requirements. On the shotlist a running footage is usual. Each shot is listed with the total footage at the end or beginning of each shot. It is more common practice and easier to understand when the footage count is made at the end of a sequence rather than at the beginning. Footage counts are also useful for sequences in feature films.

e.g. NOT
      0′ PICCADILLY CIRCUS   but 12′ PICCADILLY CIRCUS
     12′ ADMIRALTY ARCH   18′ ADMIRALTY ARCH
     18′ THE MALL   22′ THE MALL

Running footage is shown in this way:
      6′ EIFFEL TOWER
    12′ ARC DE TRIOMPHE
    15′ ELYSEE PALACE

or

Eiffel Tower (6) Arc de Triomphe (12) Elysee Palace (15). This indicates that the film opens with a 6ft shot of the Eiffel Tower, followed by a 6ft shot of the Arc de Triomphe, followed by a 3ft shot of the Elysee Palace. The total length of the film is 15ft.

In indexing the film the total footage can be quoted on all cards, or only the footage which refers to the particular sequence, i.e. cards indexing the Arc de Triomphe can show the total 15ft or can break down the footage to 6ft and so on. If the system is designed to indicate inclusive footages the above shotlist could read:

    6' EIFFEL TOWER
    6' ARC DE TRIOMPHE
    3' ELYSEE PALACE

or

    Eiffel Tower (6') Arc de Triomphe (6') Elysee Palace (3').

This will be useful if the film is broken down into individual components, but as many film stories are normally left intact, it becomes important to know where the particular sequence occurs in the total footage, and the former shotlist is more useful.

Compilation films, magazine type film or newsreels are shotlisted in the same way, but may be broken down into individual stories, or left in the original reels. In the former case they can be treated as an individual item and the footage will refer only to the item being shotlisted with no reference to other sequences in the original reel. If the reel is left in its original form a running footage for the entire reel should be given and the whole film can be shotlisted at the one viewing. Inclusive footages for individual items can also be included if necessary. In considering stockshots both footage and location or key numbers have to be quoted to assist retrieval.

Finally the footage on a film starts with the first frame of the title or picture. Leader is not included in the footage because it is not an integral part of the film and its length varies in an arbitrary manner.

Duration of film is more useful to quote for feature and documentary material where the whole film is likely to be shown and timing is needed to assist programme planning of film shows. Footage can be included on these films as an added bonus. Footage alone is less helpful for feature material because the user has to do constant conversion to timing. Timing or duration is the most helpful method of indicating length where the film material is held in several different forms, e.g. 35mm, 16mm, 8mm, cassetted etc. The duration of the film should be the same for all gauges, but the length of film will be different in each.

INDICATING TYPES OF SHOT

This refers to the placement of the camera, its angle and movement, and the distance of the subject from the camera. It is cited in many different types of shotlist and can even appear in feature sequence lists to indicate a particularly noteworthy shot or sequence. However it is more commonly used for information films, newsfilm and some types of educational film. Where a description of the type of shot is required, the user of the film needs to know in advance if the shot is an interior or exterior, whether the camera is shooting straight ahead, or tilted up or on top of the subject, whether the camera pans across a scene, zooms in to it, moves around it, and if the subject is in close up to the camera or distant. Reuse of particular sequences in many cases will depend on the type of shot, whether it is close enough to give a clear view of the subject or far enough away to give the desired general impression.

In quoting type of shot on contents lists certain standardised definitions and abbreviations are used. This enables the user of the shotlist to understand its meaning and if he is using film from several different sources he will not have to readjust to each new shotlist, but can carry the definition over from one to another. Although shotlisting has its subjective side and opinions may differ on the closeness of a closeup, or what constitutes a medium view, sufficient uniformity has been achieved to allow for the drawing up of generally agreed definitions and abbreviations used in shotlisting.

The following have been in common usage and many are taken from the Film Cataloguing Rules of the Aslib Film Production Librarians Group.

Abbreviations in shotlisting to describe type of camera shot

GV – General View	Shot where camera is set well back to take in the whole scene.
LV – Long View	Shot where camera is far enough to show entire subject. Usually concentrates on one aspect of a General View.
MLV or SLV – Medium (semi) Long View	Camera apparently nearer to the subject than a long view, but not so near as for a Close up. In relation to the human subject, a shot of entire figure at short distance.
MV or SV Medium (semi) View	Closer shot than Medium Long View. In relation to the human figure a shot taken from about the knees up.
SCU – Semi Close Up	Shot taken in relation to a human subject from head and shoulders.
CU – Close Up	A shot taken with the camera close to the subject. In relation to the human figure, a shot of the face only.

TV or TS — Top View	Shot taken from above the level of the scene looking down on the subject. High Angle and Elevated also used for these shots.
EXT — Exterior	Outside view.
INT — Interior	Inside or indoor view.
EST — Establishing	Sequence used to introduce subject of story or film, location shot.
PAN	Panoramic shot, in which the camera is moved horizontally across a scene.
TRACK — Tracking Shots	Camera on moving carrier. Tracking shot can be forward, backward, left to right etc.
CRANE — Crane Shots	Tracking shots, lift up or down.
LAS — Low Angle	Camera below the level of the subject looking up.
HAS — High Angle	Camera above the level of the subject looking down.
ZOOM — Zoom Shot	A sharp apparent movement toward or away from the subject photographed by use of a zoom lens.
Inter-Elemental Shots	From one of the following elements to another, or to the same element : air, ground/land, space, water, e.g. AIR to AIR, AIR to GROUND.
Special Photography	Includes underwater, fast and slow motion, high speed, time lapse.

N.B. One point which has been noticed is the use of S in SV or SCU. This is often widely misread to be 'side' when in fact it should stand for 'semi'. The confusion is understandable and it may be better to disregard the S and use the less equivocal M for 'medium'.

The more these definitions are adhered to by the shotlister and the more widely they are used together with the abbreviations, the more useful will be the shotlist. Standardisation in the early stages is of great importance as in many other aspects of the film librarianship.

DESCRIPTION OF SHOT

Once again the type of film being shotlisted influences the shotlist content and wording. Scientific film has a different emphasis from feature, a newsfilm is different from both. In a feature, continuity and action are emphasised; scientific film is minutely described and newsfilm attempts to include the general scene as well as central theme. The description of a shot is an objective account of what is on the film. The opinions of the shotlister should never intrude and the language should be kept straightforward, concise and factual. There is not room in a shotlist to expand at length and an imprecise description is a poor reference tool.

Note is taken of the central subject in all types of film, but other points are described according to the purpose of the shotlist. In many films, information on locations, particular buildings and interesting features is noted in addition to the general subject because they may be of considerable interest later when the actual subject of the film is not. All personalities should be identified, and this can involve the cataloguer in considerable research. Today's face in the crowd could become tomorrow's personality. However it is obvious that even with the greatest care one can miss many who later become important. To aid this identification of personalities and locations a collection of stills and press cuttings should be readily available to the shotlister for comparison. If a shotlister has to work on several pieces of film from a certain period he should familiarise himself with the personalities of that period. Many personalities can be picked up by the alert shotlister, but the more remote the period, the more difficult it is to recognise people 'on sight'.

SHOTLIST FOR NEWSFILM

Seq.	16 mm	Secs.		Shotlist
1	3	5	GV PAN	Mass crowd gather for congress
2	5	9	SV PAN	Crowd seated on ground
3	7	12	CU	Man with headdress
4	12	20	SV & CU	Band playing
5	13	22	CU	People clapping
6	16	25	LV	Crowd waving
7	18	29	SV	Kaunda speaks
8	19	32	SV	Audience
9	22	35	CU	Kaunda speaks
10	25	41	SV	Kaunda speaking
11	28	45	CU	Zoom in Gore-Browne on platform
12	31	49	GV	Mass crowd

The shotlist may be confined to a list of actual shots, or it could be a list of sequences where an attempt is made to relate one shot to those surrounding it. This has to be objective, but it does help to maintain the continuity of the original film, and produces the more informative shotlist for newsfilm. Other lists of the contents of film which can be used for cataloguing and information include those produced for the longer films where a shotlist as just described would be too detailed and unnecessary.

PRECIS SHOTLIST

GV Pan mass crowd (3)   SV Pan crowd seated on ground (5)   CU Man with headdress (7)   SV & CU Band playing (12)   CU People clapping (13) LV Crowd waving (16)   SV Kaunda speaks (18)   SV Audience (19) CU & SV Kaunda speaking (25)   CU Zoom in to Sir Stewart Gore Browne on platform (28)   GV Mass crowd (31)

DEALING WITH SOUND CONTENT

In short films all sound effects, natural sound, speech and/or commentary should be transferred to the shotlist and inserted at the point at which they occur. Depending on the design of the shotlist it may be included at the correct place, or cue words or sounds may be shown where they occur and references made to another part of the shotlist for a full transcription. Transcripts of sound may be available for longer films or scripts. It is not necessary to transfer this information to a description of the action or story line. Normally with feature film it is enough to note that sound is available without giving other indication such as sound cues. Sound cues can however be inserted in documentary sequence lists as an added indication of the sequence reached by the viewer. In these cases separate transcripts may be available, but not necessarily.

Sound can be encountered in several forms, such as dialogue, music, natural sound, speech and commentary.

Dialogue if available is normally in the form of a transcript and is too detailed to be included in the shotlist. The script is held in separate form, but dialogue cues may be transferred to the shotlist if required although normally this is not helpful.

With music it is normally sufficient to note in the credits the music performed and by whom. These are included in the performance credits. However for copyright purposes it may be necessary to give inclusive timing to each piece of music used. These timings can also be included on the script, rather than the shotlist.

Natural Sound or NAT SOF indicates crowd noises or sounds

made by certain activities, such as tennis balls bouncing or being hit, cars racing on a circuit. These are often self explanatory and no more than the indication NAT SOF need be included in the shotlist.

SHOTLIST WITH SOUND CUES

Seq.	16 mm	Secs.	Shot List	Commentary
1	4	7	CU U.N. tapestry	The United Nations Security Council resumed its debate yesterday on Yemen's charges of British aggression. Sir Patrick Dean spoke for Britain.
				SOF UP AT 4 feet 7 seconds
2	91	2.25	CU Patrick Dean speaking	SOF Begins: "The representative of the Yemen . . . SOF Ends: " . . . activities in the Yemen".
				SOF DOWN AT 91 feet
				2 min. 25 secs.
3	92	2.27	SV Council	Then Dr. Pachachi replied for the Arab countries.
				SOF UP AT 92 feet
				2 min. 27 secs.
4	109	2.54	CU Dr. Pachachi speaking	SOF Begins: "It is not a matter . . ." SOF Ends: " . . . in Southern Arabia".
				SOF DOWN AT 109 feet
				2 min. 54 secs.
5	114	3.2	CU U.N tapestry	Dr. Pachachi is the delegate from Iraq. Additional speakers are being heard today.

Sound on Film or SOF is used for shorter information films such as newsfilm and indicates speech, interview or commentary. Here the speech should be transcribed verbatim wherever practicable. A phrase used in a particular speech can come to characterise that speech and a verbatim record of speeches helps the researcher to find the particular one he wants out of several which may have been made at about the same time. An example is the 'Wind of Change' speech by Macmillan. In some film libraries only extracts of longer speeches are recorded and a verbatim record of the part of the speech actually on film saves time in fruitless searching for a speech which was not recorded.

In compiling the shotlist for a film with SOF it is often easier to cue the sound and put the full speech on another card or sheet.

Commentary used on film is not always recorded on the shotlist, but may rather be used by the shotlister for information as to film content. The commentary on many newsreels in particular is no longer the copyright of the owning companies and cannot be used with the film. Sentiments expressed twenty years ago about an event may no longer apply and the user will want to interpret the events in his own way. Even with television news today there are too many references which are irrelevant to anything except the actual day the event is happening for reuse to be useful. Additionally the user may not want to reuse the whole sequence which goes under the commentary. Commentaries were often recorded elsewhere in background material at the time of making up the newsreel and many of these records survive to be referred to if necessary. Newsfilm agencies are not working on the same basis today as the newsreels and they supply film without a commentary to obtain maximum international use. A written commentary can be supplied instead for news readers to use over the film. Usually when shotlisting a film therefore the commentary is used for information by the shotlister, but not transcribed. Documentary commentaries are part of the film itself and as well as providing information for the cataloguer can also be used as the basis for sound cues. However as they are extensive they are better transcribed in a separate record to reduce the length of the sequence list.

ADDITIONAL INFORMATION

Finally, though not necessarily a part of the shotlisting procedure, certain information about the film itself can be noted at the time of shotlisting. Information on the original accessions record can be verified as to gauge (16mm or 35mm), negative or positive film, black and white or colour and type of colour, and whether the film is original or telerecording. The sound and type of sound can be checked, whether the film is mute or combined sound, or has separate track, and whether the track is optical or magnetic. This information can all be incorporated in the shotlist or reference cards to save looking in two or more places for information which is all relevant to the selection and ordering of the film.

STANDARD SHOTLISTING ABBREVIATIONS

Standard abbreviations are in use as follows:

mm	Gauge in millimetres, e.g. 8mm, Super 8mm, 16mm, 35mm, 70mm
NEG	Negative film
POS	Positive film
INTERNEG	Internegative
COL POS	Colour positive
MUTE	Picture only, no sound
st	Silent
sd	Sound
COMOPT	Combined picture and optical sound track
COMMAG	Combined picture and magnetic sound track
SEPOPT	Picture and separate optical sound track
SEPMAG	Picture and separate magnetic sound track

TYPES OF SHOTLIST

Shotlisting can be recorded in several ways, and the type of shotlist produced in any one library will depend on the other systems involved and the possible as well as actual usage of the shotlist. If the shotlists are sent out with the film as part of the service before the library acquires the film, they will probably be recorded in separate paper form. Rather than re-shotlist the film or retype the information on to the catalogue cards, the library retains the shotlists separate from the index and compiles separate shotlists for unused film to conform with the majority. If on the other hand the shotlists are compiled by the library staff the opportunity arises to keep indexing and shotlisting records in the one place, and the shotlist may be typed on to the catalogue cards. As long as certain information is included in the contents the main functions of shotlisting can be met. Many shotlists can be incorporated on the catalogue cards, either in abbreviated form on each card, or on a main index card in more detail. The essential features to include are footage (or timing), type of shot, content of shot and sound.

The system of shotlists and the information contained in them varies with the type of library involved. If the library deals with only one type of film a single system can be devised for shotlists and catalogue cards. If several types of film are kept there may have to be several systems running parallel. For example it may be possible to include all details on a catalogue card for short films included in the shotlist, sequence list or precis. For longer films the shotlist may have to be separated from the catalogue card. In these cases it is normally not necessary to have larger catalogue cards, and the longer shotlists will not fit on to even large cards. It is better to have only one place to look for information, and the catalogue should attempt to encompass all film in the one sequence where possible. Where film is similar in type and content and reuse only one filing system should be in force.

An additional consideration in deciding on the type of shotlist is the future use of the information, possibly in some mechanised system or in publication of lists of library material, either complete or in specific sections. Can the one record on a catalogue card be used for photographing to produce a published catalogue or index? If this usage is envisaged it will be useful to record all information to be used in final publication on the card at the outset to save laborious re-editing or additions in preparing copy for publication.

LAYOUT OF SHOTLISTS

Any future co-operative schemes, either on a national or international basis should be taken into consideration. But anticipation of format and requirements is even more difficult than trying to envisage future use within an organisation. Probably the closest one can come is to put all information of use on to the card as if the library itself were to publish the final version. Any bureau attempting to centralise information could collect it from several libraries and re-edit to fulfil its own requirements. Whichever way it is viewed there will be a great deal of tedious work involved. There is little uniformity in the ways used to record the contents of the film. Standards for shotlisting have been achieved to a considerable extent in the type of shot and abbreviations in use, but the actual layout of shotlists is by no means uniform.

The shotlist may be produced on its own record form separate from other records. When the list is produced outside the library, many additional facts not of immediate use to the library may be included, such as running times, background information to the film and a commentary to be read over the film if required. In the shotlist on page 88 only the section actually listing the shots as marked is really necessary to the library for future reference.

Such a shotlist or literally list of shots could be incorporated on other records, for example catalogue cards. A large card would be needed for this, and if the system were of any size catalogue drawers and space would rapidly be filled. Alternatively this shotlist could be put on the main index card, for instance an arrangement by production number, or date, and smaller cards could be used for subject and personality indexes referring back to the main card for a full shotlist.

MARKED SHOTLIST

Seq.	16 mm Feet	Metres	Secs.	Shot List	Commentary
1	2	0.6	3	LV Fire	Fifty thousand bales of
2	7	2.1	11	GV Firemen hosing PAN TO smouldering cotton bales	cotton were destroyed when fire swept through a textile mill in La Paz, Bolivia. The cotton was
3	9	2.7	14	GV Fire engine	valued at about four hundred and ten thousand pounds sterling.
4	13	4.0	21	LV Smoke	As the smoke cleared a
5	21	6.4	33	SV PAN Firemen hosing flames (2 shots)	police investigating team moved into action to check out the theory
6	25	7.6	40	SV Smoke rising	that the fire may have been started by economic saboteurs, intent on disrupting the country's production.
7	29	8.8	46	SV Fire Engine PAN TO Firemen	Three firemen were injured in the blaze
8	31	9.4	49	GV Building smouldering	which also seriously damaged the textile mill.
9	33	10.1	53	SV Damage next day	Fires are rare in La Paz
10	39	11.6	1.03	GV PAN Ditto	because of the high altitude and thin air.
11	41	12.5	1.06	GV Troops clearing	After the fire had died
12	45	13.7	1.12	GV PAN Troops clearing up	down troops moved in to clear up.

Use of unitised microfilm and mechanised retrieval is feasible here. The shotlist could be microfilmed and the aperture card used in a punched card retrieval system.

Another shotlist type is the precis which incorporates type of shot, content and footage in a continuous sequence. This is most used for publications and lists where contents are included. It looks neater, takes less space and can be adapted to normal published catalogues more easily. Less alteration and amendment is needed to such a shotlist before photographing for publication. On the other hand it is less easy to select sections rapidly from this type of precis than a list of shots. This point indicates why the list is more favoured by newsfilm companies than the precis where rapid selection of shots is needed for reuse and the whole film is seldom shown.

INSTANT CATALOGUING

Finally a word is needed about a stop-gap practice used for expediency only. The library may have to resort to this where there is a shortage of staff and time, to allow the film to be reused. It is not a complete answer, but is more useful than no index or shotlist at all. In such cases shotlisting is not done on the film, but it is viewed and all titles, main subject and any suitable sequences for indexing as guides to the film content are noted. This information will fit on to even a small catalogue card and can then be incorporated with other indexing. It is especially useful for silent film with titles. The titles on silent film usually give the subject of the film and any well known personalities shown. This information can be added to the catalogue cards as an annotation. If staff is not available for full scale cataloguing similar practices to this can often reveal much valuable film. This type of cataloguing is suitable for short films; if a feature film is viewed in this way it takes little more effort to produce a complete record for the catalogue.

6

DOCUMENTATION AND STORAGE
OF DOCUMENTS

THIS CHAPTER deals with material which describes what is on the film — such as shotlists, commentaries and related material which can be consulted instead of viewing the film. It also covers the physical records of the film and the reference materials needed to compile the shotlists.

PRODUCTION RECORDS

This is the physical record of the film handled by the library. In a film library the record may be the product of another department which first handles the film, such as the traffic department who book the film in. The traffic department makes up the accessions record and, in order to keep track of the film throughout its progress, prepares several copies and distributes them to the departments which require them. The production record has already been described in the section on film handling.

The library uses the production record to show film received, whether used in service or not, the stock and any spare material received in library and whether it was selected for retention or junking.

The record is of most use to the library when a large proportion of the total acquisitions of the organisation come into the department. Production records can be very detailed and take up space, so that their retention needs to be justified by constant reference to the majority of numbers.

In an organisation where the film enters the library direct, elaborate production records are not necessary, and the record of acquisition can be combined with other information, either on the main entry in the catalogue, or in a separate index. This separate index can also be used as a film movement or usage catalogue by the library.

The filing and control of production records depends on the type of record, but a numerical sequence of production or accessions numbers should prove the most useful, and the files used to hold the records should anchor them securely to prevent loss, but be sufficiently flexible to allow for easy addition or withdrawal. The records are constantly referred to over a long period and should be filed securely and not allowed to gather dust. Lever arch, loose-leaf files holding a set number of records each are fairly successful if care is taken in filing on shelves.

New developments in mechanised handling of information are also being used for this type of record, and computer storage of information has some advantages over other methods. Several pieces of information can be retrieved at once if the record is compiled and used properly. It is more certain than many paper records, which can go missing, become damaged or fall apart. The BBC are using an Ultronic machine for acquisition and film movement records. Other organisations with computer systems for accounting could adapt them to hold production record details. The larger hire libraries also use computers which hold accessions records as well as the distribution records.

SHOTLISTS

These are direct descriptions of the contents of the film, used instead of the film for research, and with the film when viewing. In addition to the shotlist, cameramen's information sheets and other related information are available. This information can be stored in several ways, but the method is determined in part by the type of film in the library, and the way it is filed. If the storage of film is itemised, the related material has to be itemised for quick reference. The main question is whether to collect all the material on one film in one place, or to combine material on several films together in some way and store in one place. In the former case a lot of space is used quickly and mechanical or micro-storage may have to be employed to conserve space. In the latter case the system of storing film may be according to the transmitted newsreel, i.e. all film transmitted on one day is kept in a can labelled with the day's date. All related material can then be stored in one box, or folder. For reuse of library film however this is not always the most convenient method of storage. For instance if one short sequence is required out of a half hour compilation, documentary or current affairs film, it will mean looking through several sheets of related material before the exact sequence is located.

Itemised storage system. The shotlist and related material in this system refer to the one piece of film. In a feature library, the catalogue is arranged by title. The film itself may be filed by title or more probably by a production or vault number, but the related material will be more easily filed by production title. This means that there will one sequence to look under for information about the production. If the related material were filed by production number the user would have to look up the production number in an index before locating the title, adding an extra unnecessary step to the retrieval process.

Where a user does not get sufficient information from the catalogue record or where related material is bulky it can be filed separately in a lateral file or in envelopes, or both. Envelopes are very useful for this type of filing. The material is often flimsy, small and difficult to handle, like press cuttings containing news of a film or reviews etc. Folders are also useful but for small items an envelope closed on three sides is more secure. Such containers arranged in title order are easy to consult.

In a newsfilm library where the film is filed in small reels, several to one can, the location or can number becomes of equal importance to the production number in withdrawing the film from the vaults. Therefore a system has to be devised to enable a research worker to use the catalogue to select film, pass on to the shotlist for further information and then to the film if need be. If the main catalogue card includes the shotlist, it is also advisable to include the location number on the card. If the shotlist is separate for some reason, and the time lag in permanent canning-up means that the location number is not available at the time of cataloguing the film, the location details have to be added to the shotlist or its container. One such system refers the user from the catalogue card to the shotlists which are filed in numerical order within the year, e.g. 6972/66, 7754/69. Each shotlist is contained in a separate folder which is made out for the film on final storage. The label on this folder gives the production number, the can number for locating the film in the vaults and the stock of the film in the can on that particular item. In researching or preparing viewing lists a list of production numbers is taken, the corresponding files are located and shotlists consulted. Using a lateral filing system any one number is easily located without having to disturb other material. If copies of film are located in several different cans, the additional can numbers and related stock can easily be put on to the folder label, e.g:

7754/69

Can No. 6723   16mm Neg & Pos
Can No. 6788   16mm Colour Pos & Interneg.
Can No. 6759   16mm Opt. Trk.

With a substantial intake of film, however, this method does grow fast, and locating several files may mean the researcher has to cover a considerable distance if several years of film are involved. Working on the same system as that already mentioned, microfilm has been used to reduce storage space. Itemised aperture cards are used and the information from the folder label is transferred to the aperture cards containing the microfilmed contents of the folder. This means a considerable saving in space, the researcher has less ground to cover, and the microfilm card cabinets and microfilm readers can be strategically placed closer to the catalogues than hanging files.

Daily storage system. Other newsfilm libraries, especially those connected with television stations find it more convenient to store all the film transmitted on a certain day in one can, the location number of the can being the day of the year involved, e.g. 60/69 is day 60 of 1969. This system means that all shotlists for the film of that day can be stored in one folder, again labelled 60/69. The location number can be put straight on to all records in this instance, because it is known at the time of cataloguing.

STORAGE EQUIPMENT

There are several possible ways to store the shotlists and background information. They can be stored in paper form or in some mechanised retrieval system such as microfilm. The two types of storage so far considered may influence the choice of storage equipment.

Storage of itemised material. Initial selection of film is through the index cards and shotlists. Therefore, where separate shotlists are supplied with the film, they need to be readily available for use and supply. They should be in close proximity to the catalogues and linked to both catalogue and film by some common quickly located factor, either production or location number.

If the shotlists are incorporated on the index card the equipment needed for storage will be card filing cabinets.

Some shotlists are too detailed or long for an index card and have to be stored either in their paper form or on microfilm.

Even if microfilm is used the shotlists may be retained in paper form for a short period. Several copies of a shotlist can be retained and used as required to save reprinting or photocopying each time a film is sent out.

The shotlists can be stored in file boxes, but each time a shotlist is needed the boxes have to be taken off the shelves, opened, closed and replaced. File boxes also take up a lot of room. Using foolscap file boxes and retaining about a dozen copies of each shotlist the shelf space needed for one month or 1000 films is about 30 or 40ft.

Other material is usually filed with the shotlists, such as cameraman's shotlists, exhibition pamphlets and explanatory matter, and finally some additional location mark may be needed for individual pieces of film. It then becomes practical to separate material relating to each film.

One of the quickest and neatest ways of dividing one set of paper from another is with the manila folder. These can be used over and over again if necessary by the use of sticky labels like address labels. When the material inside the folder changes, the label is retyped. These folders need not be heavy quality. If large numbers are filed in a lateral filing system they will not be disturbed much and if they are not too thick will take up less space. An ordinary quality manila of neutral colour so that it does not mark readily is adequate. The folders can then be stored in some form of lateral filing.

The pockets in lateral filing which hold the material are suspended from rails end on to the user with only the edge showing. They can be easily removed and the number held on any one shelf can be varied according to the amount of material to be stored. There is no need for empty pockets on one row and too much space or too few pockets on another. The pockets will hold several folders each, and the number is determined by the fullness and weight of the pocket when loaded, but it is wise to have a set number in each pocket as an aid to quick reference — unequal numbers slow the retrieval process.

An additional advantage of lateral filing with folders stored end on to the user is that the folder need not be withdrawn each time the contents are used. If only one copy of the shotlist is needed it can be extracted without moving the folder thus eliminating a problem of box filing, where the box has to be taken from the shelf before it can be opened. This method also decreases the risk of misfiling by removal and incorrect replacement. If lateral filing is used in conjunction with folders with a raised back edge, the production number is easily read without withdrawing the folder.

Guides are available for both the pockets of the filing system and the individual folders within these pockets. Each pocket has a protruding edge or guide holder where the contents of the pocket can be displayed. These guides can be angled so that they are visible above and below eye level. Guides are also built into the shelf rails of the filing system. The folder guides are of the stick-on label type, easily replaced and quick to process.

Lateral filing cabinets of any size take up a lot of space and mobile storage is often used for a more compact operation. Less access space is needed than for free standing files. Also power assisted movements of banks of files can be used, although where only a few banks (three or four) are in use hand operation is quite feasible.

On all equipment which covers a large area and is consulted frequently it is advisable to have some provision for working tops. These can be incorporated into the shelves of suspended lateral filing to be pulled out and retracted as required. The difficulties are obvious with mobile lateral storage, a shelf may jam in the out position and be damaged when one file is moved up against another, and protruding shelves are a danger to unsuspecting passers-by. Normally working tops are not provided with mobile storage.

Other filing equipment is needed for holding film lists, research work in progress, correspondence and other paperwork. Ordinary suspension filing cabinets can be used, but it should be remembered when space is at a premium that any cabinet with drawers needs access space. Small lateral filing units can be employed instead.

Daily Storage. When the film is stored by date of transmission the filing systems are simpler to guide but all systems so far mentioned can be used effectively with this type of storage. A day's scripts or shotlists can be stored in file boxes or in the pockets of a lateral filing system.

PHOTOCOPYING METHODS AND REQUIREMENTS

Material in the library needs to be copied for internal record systems, research and sending out to customers for information. The range of equipment available is wide and the type of original, size, number of copies and frequency of use all have to be considered in deciding on the equipment to use. The original may be card stock, book pages, pamphlets, single sheets of paper, hand or typewritten documents or illustrations. Some processes do not reproduce illustrations, others will not reproduce handwritten records, some machines have an external flat platen and reprint from books or cards without difficulty, while in others the original has to be fed into the machine for printing and these cannot cope with loose cards or bulky books. The number of copies from each original may also determine the machine to be used because some machines print single copies economically, while others are only viable for multiple copies. A machine which prints by feeding the original in with the paper to be printed is time consuming for several copies. Each copy has to go through the same process, whereas other machines print multiple copies from the one presentation of an original.

Photocopying covers a wide range of processes from the wet processes which need chemicals and sensitised paper to the dry processes. The wet processes give a clearer long lasting print, but require specialised handling and are in some cases only economic for long runs. The dry processes include thermal copying which can only reproduce from single sheets of copy and gives poor quality prints and xerography which can reprint from originals at speed giving one or several copies as required.

Xerography can provide a valuable alleviation to storage problems in many film libraries. Single copies of shotlists can be stored and reproduced for customer use when required. Using xerography in this way provides a considerable saving in space by eliminating the need to store a large number of copies of the same shotlist, or stencils of the original. Even when several copies are kept they will be used up in a short time and Xerox copies can then be made.

Xerography can print at speed using a variety of different papers and it will copy all colours, types, prints and handwritten documents whereas some copiers will not take handwritten documents or print from some colours, e.g. Thermofax processes involving a heat transfer of impression, will not reprint handwritten pieces. The Xerox will not reproduce illustrations and half tones adequately, but this is rarely needed in a film library.

Xerography can also be used successfully for copying catalogue cards to produce lists of material for a rapid enquiry service.

Xerography has of course much wider applications than those mentioned. It can be used to duplicate many records, but its main usage in a newsfilm library is to duplicate information about the stock, i.e. shotlists of the film and subject lists from the catalogue cards. The Xerox machine will probably be used by several departments in an organisation, but the nature of commercial film library copying, which needs immediate availability for only one or two items at a time, usually means that the machine should be sited in the library itself.

APPLICATIONS OF MICROFILM

Microfilm in a film library can be used for reducing film

shotlists to manageable proportions, or integrating the shotlist into a mechanised retrieval system for other records in a library to keep them in a permanent form or for filing of older records to help to preserve them and reduce the space problem.

Shotlists are microphotographed according to the filing system already in use. They are usually microfilmed after the filing system has been operating for some time and this dictates the microform used. For day-to-day filing a fiche might be advisable or for itemised filing an aperture card could be used. Roll film is not successful for filing this type of record, which is better suited to a continuing record like a newspaper, book or periodical. Aperture cards have the additional advantage that they could be integrated into a punched card retrieval system either immediately or at a later date if the need and opportunity arise.

Other records, such as accessions, can also be microfilmed to reduce the space needed. A factor that may limit the use is the quality of the original, which has to be clear, and sometimes only a carbon copy is available as a library accessions record.

There has been some investigation into the possibilities of microfilming older records, either for publication as a reference tool to external researchers, or as a preservation measure within an organisation. The accessions or issue records of early film companies are of considerable interest to archives and research workers, but are often found to be deteriorating badly. They were not usually regarded as important records and were not initially recorded in a lasting form, and the more these records are consulted the more they deteriorate. Copying this material on to microfilm often makes it easier to consult and preserves the record. Roll film can be used successfully for this type of recording. In some cases however a company can only claim copyright in the material by producing the original record, and the originals may have to be kept for this reason.

TYPES OF MICROFILM

The three microfilms which are applicable to film libraries are microfiche, roll film and aperture cards.

Microfiches are made up from transparent photographs set on a thick film base. Several pages are contained on the same fiche. The application of this microfilm is best adapted to the daily type of storage, providing that enough of the fiche is used for any one day's shotlists to make it economically sound. Space should not be wasted on the card. The microfilm can be filed according to the date in a simple filing system. One drawback with fiche is that it is more difficult and expensive to convert into hard copy, and if a great deal of printing has to be done from the fiche another less expensive microform should be found.

Roll film micro images are photographed on to 16mm or 35mm film, of which 35mm is the most commonly used, because there is less reduction and print out is easier as a result. But roll film is not always suitable for the straightforward numerical filing of news-film. The user is referred to one item and it wastes time to have to scan through rolls of microfilm which have no relevance to the item searched for. Roll film is also difficult for records which have to be withdrawn or amended. Roll film is more useful for microfilming newspapers or book records where continuity is more relevant.

Aperture cards are useful for itemised filing where the shotlist consists of from one to four pages. One card represents one film and the cards are filed numerically in production number order. The cards have a microcopy of the shotlist inserted in them and the same information that appears on the folder label in a lateral filing system, i.e. production number of the film, location or can number and the stock held in each can. The rest of the card could also be used for the film movement record or the card could be used in a punched card retrieval system.

MICROFILM EQUIPMENT

For a full microfilm operation based on the aperture system the following machines are needed: a microfilm camera, a copier for duplicating microcards, microfilm viewers and a printer or reader printer for printing the microcards back to readable size. Storage cabinets are also necessary for the microcards.

Material can be sent out for microfilming but in most film libraries the records have to be constantly available and cannot be allowed off the premises for even a few days. The microfilm camera can be operated by normal library staff. It is a repetitive job, but requires attention to detail, a reasonable mechanical and photographic aptitude and the ability to sort out the material which needs to be copied from other material which can be discarded. The camera should process the aperture card, and it should not be necessary to cut roll microfilm and insert into the aperture cards by hand.

A duplicating machine is also advisable for making additional copies of the microfilm. The card produced in the camera is used as the master card for security and further duplication, and the duplicate cards are used for viewing and printing. The duplicates can be produced in separate process much more cheaply than the photographic process by contact printing. The duplicates can also be used for a mechanical retrieval indexing system.

The library will probably need several viewers for reading the microfilm. These should be available in viewing cubicles, research areas, and the microfilm unit itself for quality checking.

Because of the high cost of microfilm readers and the incompatibility of microfilm systems as a whole, many customers of a film library have no facilities for reading microfilm. Therefore a printer or reader printer is necessary to reproduce the microfilm copy in readable form for external users. A microfilm printer has to produce a clear, lasting print (though not necessarily a permanent print) of readable size which is easy, cheap and quick to produce.

Custom built storage cabinets are available for microcards fitted with drawers which are easily withdrawn for easier filing high up in the cabinet. These should be fire resistant, or better still of fireproof construction, and lockable for additional safety of records. Data processing equipment firms have an extensive range of equipment as well as the manufacturing firms.

Microfilm cabinets should be stored as near to the catalogues as possible for quick reference purposes. Being more compact than lateral filing units they are at an advantage when quick retrieval is needed and can usually be placed more conveniently for the user.

COMBINING RECORDS

As space is usually valuable in any film library, records should be combined wherever possible. Only where considerable additional work and duplication of effort would be caused in combining records should they be left separate, e.g. retyping long shotlists on to equally large catalogue cards is unnecessary. Shotlists and index cards can be combined, but this is usually done when the cataloguer has to compile the shotlist. The shotlist can be put on to all index cards, or on to a main card if the shotlists are lengthy.

Production and accessions records should be combined wherever possible. Cinema newsreel collections often have an accessions record of all film received and a 'production record' or contents list of film included in the issue maintained as two separate records. Unless the accessions record includes a note of usage of the film it is necessary to search two records where one would be enough.

Other records which can be combined are production and

accessions with film movement. A film library has to know where
all its film is at any given time and film movement records are
designed to show this. Film movement cards are filed under the
production number and indicate if the film is out for any purpose,
viewing, processing, awaiting refile. As the record is filed in
numerical order in the same way as the production record, it is an
easy matter to combine the two. All production details are
included on the card, with space left for future usage.

It is also often convenient to combine the shotlist and the
production record and this is easier when the library accessions the
film and makes the production record. It is assumed that all film
will acquire a shotlist in this system. The location number or
record can be combined on this record as well. The aim should be
for the most comprehensive and compact record for ease of
location and handling of all forms used, i.e. the indexing system,
the shotlist and the film.

TYPES OF REFERENCE MATERIAL FOR SHOTLISTING

If the library shotlists film, reference material has to be
organised and retained to assist in these compilations. The type of
material required includes reference books, periodicals, reviews,
pamphlets and handout material. For newsfilm, press cuttings or
press tapes should also be filed. Some film libraries use shotlists
compiled by other departments for current material, but have a
large collection of older film to be shotlisted and identified. For
this type of work other reference material will have to be kept.

REFERENCE BOOKS

The reference material provided in a film library should reflect
the nature of the collection. Libraries concerned with feature film,
for example, need a backup collection of books on film history.
Biographies of particular directors or actors are useful to date film
in the collection as well as having intrinsic interest. Books on film
production are needed where this is an important feature of the
collection. Archives, for instance, need material on film history
and production as well as critical works on the art of the film and
biographies. Film libraries with modern collections need reference
material to cover recent productions only.

Apart from the compilation of shotlists for current material a
film library with a large collection of earlier material needs
reference works on film art and production and twentieth century

events. These books should be comprehensive for any film or period covered by the collection, both to inform the shotlister as fully as possible and to aid the researcher trying to find specific films or filmed material on events and personalities.

Reference works particularly relevant to current events and documentary subjects include good encyclopaedias. These are essential for the variety of articles and summaries of events, e.g. the World War I article in the *Encyclopaedia Britannica* is a compact source of information for the researcher. International reference books on current affairs with back numbers are useful. For early material access to a complete run of a daily newspaper, such as *The Times,* is often of great assistance in tracing dates, and gives personalities involved and background information. This is not to suggest that the film library should obtain its own microcopy of *The Times,* but *The Times Index* plus access to a large public reference library which already holds such a run is invaluable. In addition back numbers of *Whitaker's, Who Was Who* and *Who's Who* as well as early maps can be of considerable use.

For reference and as an aid to research in the catalogues some noted reference books provide information from which the researcher can start to find all the relevant material on a particular topic, e.g. up to date encyclopaedia articles about particular events or period in the twentieth century. Gazetteers and current atlases assist in locating areas of interest. *Who's Who* is of use and *Whitaker's* gives the main events in a year, lists government members in all countries and contains the latest peerage lists etc.

Other general reference books will apply to the type of coverage, for instance *Jane's Fighting Ships* and *Jane's All the World's Aircraft* annuals are of considerable assistance in identifying vessels or aircraft.

Keesing's Contemporary Archives is a compilation of news articles on current affairs that can assist in a news library for back checking. The enquirer may want to find a particular event or may want to know when a certain speech was delivered. For this kind of enquiry Keesing's is often the quickest route to take.

In general, reference material in a film library which deals with news material is of the quick reference type — encyclopaedias, directories, yearbooks and annuals, or abstracts of the more learned type. Information has to be available quickly and in a concise form. The researcher does not want to be referred from one book to another for his facts; he wants to be referred to the film. Reference tools are used to sort out the relevant headings to be investigated in the index to film, either a date, a personality, a useful subject heading or a location.

REFERENCE PERIODICALS

Periodical literature also reflects the purpose of the library and includes journals on film art and production. Libraries with up to date film on general release use the periodicals for lists of latest productions available and reviews of current productions. Educational libraries use periodicals for this type of current awareness.

REFERENCE CATALOGUES

Published catalogues of film, both national and local, are also useful for any library which has to hire film for users or purchase film material. The British National Film Catalogue deals with all non-fiction material released in the UK, while fiction material can be monitored through the *Monthly Film Bulletin* of the British Film Institute. Other catalogues are published for particular subject areas, from large hire libraries and for particular audiences or users. Subject catalogues include those put out by the Royal Institute of Chemistry, Educational Foundation for Visual Aids, and the British Industrial and Scientific Film Association. Large hire libraries issue their own catalogues, whether for general hiring or, as in the case of the Inner London Education Authority (ILEA), to their own circuit of users. Other hire libraries include Guild Sound and Vision, Contemporary Films, Central Film Library. Catalogues aimed at particular audiences include the British Universities Film Council Catalogue.

REFERENCE PAMPHLETS

Exhibition catalogues, programmes, handouts and publicity material are useful reference material. They often refer to a particular piece of film, e.g. the programme and full credits of a feature film, programmes and detailed contents of information or educational films, the catalogue of an art exhibition or the handout on the first flight of a new aircraft. In cases where the material is essential to that film it can be retained in the same file as the shotlist. Otherwise, if the material is of more general interest than one particular film it could be kept in the separate subject file. With catalogues of exhibitions however the position may be different. A film of an exhibition will concentrate on certain exhibits. The shotlist should list these, but the catalogue will list all other exhibits. The catalogue can be retained for its intrinsic value as a reference to the subject or artist. As catalogues are usually bulky they will be best among the general reference collection rather than in boxes or files. The catalogues may have no value beyond reference to the film and once used to compile the shotlist can be discarded according to the library's general policy.

PRESS CUTTINGS

Press cuttings can be used for compiling current affairs shotlists and are especially useful when dealing with news material. Newspapers and press cuttings are often the only source of information available for reference of this particular type of film.

Newspapers can be kept on files for use in shotlisting. The articles are used to explain the event, what happened and who was involved. With this knowledge the shotlister knows what he is looking for and can identify more useful material. Press cuttings can also be used but this is not as prominent a part of the work as in other news organisations. Many press cuttings have little value to the film library once the relevant facts are transferred to the shotlist, although review articles can be kept in this form. A press cutting can be used to assist in compiling the shotlist, but the cutting does not refer to the film, and cannot substitute for a shotlist. It serves rather to inform the shotlister. Press cuttings are therefore only retained for a short period before being discarded. Some cuttings have longer use, especially major summary articles which can be retained for later reference, e.g. those which illustrate the diary of events in a military operation such as the Six Day War in 1967 or progress in political or economic negotiations. Press cuttings need not be kept separate from other flimsy reference material in these circumstances, but could be retained in cabinet files or pamphlet boxes in sections covering broad subject headings. Other material included in these files and boxes are pamphlets, handout or publicity material.

PRESS TAPES

These are of even less permanent value to a newsfilm library than cuttings. They are retained for current information only, but are so often overtaken by events and do not refer directly to any piece of film that their retention for other than a short period is unnecessary. They can be retained in a file separate from other reference material, probably in a drawer file under parallel subject headings to the press and pamphlet boxes. They must be discarded regularly and ruthlessly if the library is not to be overrun by them.

The treatment of pamphlets, press cuttings and tapes is connected with the object of combining records discussed earlier. Wherever possible the relevant information should be transferred from the flimsier reference material to the shotlist and then the reference material discarded. The discarding procedure will have to be part of the general library routine and carried out according to set rules.

OTHER REFERENCE MATERIAL

Additional reference material may be in a different department serving its own customers or a small adjunct to the film library used primarily for reference by the library. This material includes stills and slides.

Some film libraries are now finding a demand for stills as part of their general service. Stills can be used as an integral part of the reference system, to assist in identifying places, buildings and people, or they can be kept in a separate section dealing in stills as part of the service. Other film libraries offer stills for other purposes, advertising film in film societies, book illustration etc. These are not often used for library reference purposes, however, for other material serves for identification purposes. Stills can take the form of photographs or slides.

Photographs will probably only be used by the reference staff for comparison purposes. They can be filed in subject or name order within protective envelopes. If the collection is of any size an additional index record can be made out with entries for subject and personalities. Additional information is not so important when the collection is being used for staff information in this way.

Slides are probably of more general use in a television or newsfilm service because they can be used for compiling back projection in programmes.

The collection of slides will probably grow fast when once it is used outside the library. Slides will need greater care and protection as they will have to be viewed and reprinted constantly. Two copies should be kept, one for viewing and one kept only for reprinting. Indexes to slides will be as detailed as those for film. If necessary indexing can be included in the main catalogue on similar cards (most economic with 5 x 3 system) with some index symbol to indicate that the card refers to a still — either a different colour card, or symbol incorporated in the number of the still. The slides can then be filed in a numerical sequence referred to through the indexes. In a more elaborate system, slides are kept in sets of personalities, subjects, locations etc. This is useful for large collections of slides alone, but probably not necessary as part of the reference collection of a film library where they can be filed in the main reference system.

7

CATALOGUING

ONCE THE film has been stored in the film library and shotlisted, the physical nature of film makes it necessary to limit access to it. Some written catalogue entries have to be designed to contain sufficient information to help reduce the number of times the film has to be handled. The shotlist provides a list of the contents of the film which can be consulted to preselect film for viewing, but film shotlists are sometimes lengthy and not designed to provide all the necessary information. They may instead form the basis of a catalogue card which can be filed under the several index headings necessary to trace a filmed subject. Separate catalogue entries also have to be designed for all film to aid retrieval of both shotlist and film and provide the main source of information about film available in any particular library. The catalogue entries form the initial approach to a film and should also assist the user to preselect and to avoid wasted research time and damage to the film caused by unnecessary viewing.

There are two main sections into which cataloguing theory and practice can be divided: the choice of main heading and the descriptive part of the entry itself. In discussing these it will be possible to indicate the problems which arise in cataloguing film, and how cataloguing of films differs from that of books.

CHOICE OF MAIN HEADING

The main entry heading for a book should be the author or 'person or corporate body chiefly responsible for the creation of the intellectual or artistic content of the work' (AACR Rules). Film has no such easily identifiable 'author'. The film 'author' is usually found to be a combination of production company, producer and director, each contributing his own mixture of commercial and artistic expertise to the final product. Directors and producers, however large their contribution, could not be used as the main author entry for the film. The nature of the collaborative authorship of films makes an author entry inappropriate. How then are films commonly identified? Feature and documentary films are most widely known and recognised by title and this is used as the main entry in most film libraries. Added entries can be made for other aspects of film-making, e.g. under production companies, directors, actors, cameramen where appropriate, but the main heading will be under title.

Other films do not fit into even this pattern, notably stockshots and newsfilms, because there are no titles as such, only written indications of the subject content which cannot conveniently be used as filing titles. This indicative 'title' does not identify one film sequence from another in its wording and cannot be used to file the entries in any logical sequence or under which the film will be searched for because these films are not remembered by title or exactly worded description. Stockshots are generally entered under a descriptive heading with or without a notation. The heading is normally followed by a synopsis (or shotlist) of the content of the film. Newsfilm can be entered and identified in one of two ways according to the type of library it is being held in. It can be filed by date or an arbitrary main heading can be used. Stockshots and newsfilm do not mix well with other types of film and the choice of main entry serves to underline this factor. Where this type of film is contained in a large collection such as newsfilm in the National Film Archive or stockshots in a production library, it is separated from feature and documentary film and treated differently. In the National Film Archive features are indexed directly under title, while newsfilms are indexed directly under the date of the event with added entries for personalities, locations and subjects. Other libraries which contain newsfilm and stockshots may file them together, if the stock material is held in sequences, but if the stock material is considerable, different criteria apply and they may have to be filed and handled in separate operations. Most feature libraries with stock material keep two sequences for ease of handling and access.

An arbitrary main heading may have to be decided on in order to begin the cataloguing process with these special types of film. After all, if the film is to be filed for retrieval it must have a heading or headings by which the reference or catalogue cards can be filed. The film may need a country or location heading plus one or more subject and personality headings. Newsfilm generally requires several of each type of heading. One of these can be selected as the main heading for convenience, not because it is a standard rule for cataloguing film. The heading chosen as the main one depends on the indexes used and how they are used. For example a newsfilm agency could have an index filed by date of event but further divided into country of origin. Information about newsfilm has to be available as soon as possible after the film is received and, because the country and date of event are known or can be quickly arrived at (any serviced material will have this information on all shotlists), and anyone searching for a current news story is likely to have this information also, the country and date card can be made up immediately and filed in the catalogue. In this instance the country and date card has become the 'main entry'. The arbitrary nature of this assignment of main headings soon becomes obvious. The researcher cannot remember the exact date or even place of an event and the film is searched for by subject or one of the personalities involved. This is not the case with film filed by title; the title is remembered and its use as a main heading is justified, as is the use of an author as the main heading for a book. Stock material may have an arbitrary main subject heading although in true stock libraries there may be only one subject per piece of film. Unusual types of shots may be selected as main heading, e.g. zoom, stop-action, time lapse. However this use of shot as a heading is not really practicable. The heading soon becomes overburdened with material, and the user tends to want stop-action or time lapse film of specific subjects.

Some film therefore cannot be referred to by title, either because there is no title or the provided title is too indefinite. A descriptive sentence about the actual subject content is used instead of a title and such a sentence is not distinguished from others describing films about the same event or the other 10,000 stories which may be issued by only one organisation in a year.

Date may be used as a filing device for news material in some film collections. Date is not particularly relevant in filing stockshots — the date of shooting may be very relevant, but not as a filing device. Date is not used for features and documentaries, partly because they already have an adequate heading in the title and also date is not a useful heading. Archival newsfilm is often filed by date of event, or if this cannot be established, the date of issue. However too much film is shot on any one day for this to be a useful filing device any longer. Even with early newsreel material there are difficulties, as when all the film in an issue was not shot on the same day, and in some cases there may have been a delay of several months between shooting the film and screening it in a newsreel.

Because these solutions are not all entirely successful as a means of retrieving a piece of film other methods have to be employed. Most stock and newsfilm is referred to by a number, either an accessions number or a location number or both. This number cannot be used as the 'main heading', but in stockshot and newsfilm work it is the main key for retrieval of a particular piece of film and therefore assumes an importance which the accessions number of a book does not have.

The allocation of accessions numbers to film and the form of these numbers is an important first step in the whole cataloguing process and will have to be considered in more detail when cataloguing procedure is discussed.

FORM OF HEADING

Once the main heading has been decided, the form of heading also requires standardisation. This standardisation of citation is as important a consideration for film as it is for books. Film is normally referred to by title, except for the film which does not have an identifiable title, for example stockshots and newsfilm. In these cases the title is supplied by the cataloguer but not necessarily used as a main heading because it is unknown to the searcher and therefore an unsought title.

Where film title is used as the main heading it is transcribed in full from the copy held, and any alternative title is added to the main heading. If the original is known to be different from the copy title this is given in square brackets following the copy title. If however the title is missing from the film copy but known or can be ascertained the fullest available title is given as the main heading followed by the explanation (title missing). If a film lacks a title an appropriate one may have to be supplied by the cataloguer and enclosed in square brackets. This ruling can be used for feature and documentary materials, not stockshots and newsfilm which are discussed elsewhere. Some libraries may have an alternative rule for citing the title. Archival film is usually entered under the original release title in the language or origin of the film but this is less helpful for other libraries and may involve considerable research to determine the original title. Reference should be made from the original title if this is ascertainable.

Existing rules for standardising the form of the main heading, especially where this is an author, are more applicable to film than the rules for choice of main heading. The rules governing the choice and form of name of authors are particularly useful in film libraries which have extensive indexes of personalities and are faced with all the usual problems of the correct form of entry of personal names. A newsfilm library for instance will probably find these rules of greater use than many conventional book libraries or even other types of film library because of the numerous personalities shown on newsfilm, many of them with foreign and 'difficult' names. Other rules for the form of heading which can be adopted from a standard code such as the AACR include those for citing geographic names, particularly those dealing with the preferred language version of geographic name, and problems of transliteration.

DESCRIPTIVE CATALOGUING

The aim of any descriptive cataloguing is to describe each item, whether it is a book, film, slide, gramophone record, etc., in a consistent way, and to distinguish one item from other items and allow for accurate retrieval. The descriptive part of an entry is cited after the heading and includes the title of the work, an author statement, edition, imprint, collation and series. This is in a normal descriptive entry, but several of these parts of the entry have to be reconsidered when dealing with non-book materials. In feature film, for example, the title is used as the main heading whereas in other types of film the 'title' is normally a synopsis or summary of the content. The film is not known by this synopsis and it is not used in asking for the item. Newsfilm does not have a title, but does need a synopsis or shotlist of the contents in order to indicate what is on the film and prevent constant viewing.

The choice of main heading is of less importance or relevance in some types of film than in others, or books. Stockshots and newsfilm cannot be distinguished successfully by the use of the main heading. The main heading (author) chosen in cataloguing books reduces the number of entries under any one heading to manageable proportions, and so does the main heading (title) chosen for feature films, but the arbitrary heading chosen for newsfilm (country and date of event) or stockshots (subject) results in a large number of entries under the single heading. Descriptive cataloguing is therefore even more essential in distinguishing one piece of newsfilm from another than in distinguishing one book or feature film from another. In newsfilm cataloguing the descriptive part of the entry assumes more importance in locating an item than the main heading, and rules for descriptive cataloguing are of more concern in the cataloguing codes.

The 'author' has already been discussed, and it is seen that production credits including actors, cameramen, directors and production companies may all have been mentioned in the 'author' statement of a feature film. Newsfilm usually ignores the author statement; it is simply implied in the source of the material if this is quoted. The imprint is treated similarly, the production company and place of production are mentioned in feature film, but in some film cataloguing the production company is implied. (For instance with newsfilm it is usually the newsfilm company concerned and need not be repeated on each entry). The date and place of production are included in the entry, but may not necessarily occur in the normal imprint. The place of production is less relevant in feature films than the place where the production company's main offices are, i.e. the nationality of film production is important, not the location of filming. A British production filmed in Spain is a British film, not Spanish. The situation is different for other films such as news items, where the place of event is probably cited at the beginning of the synopsis and the date is part of the heading or part of the location number. The date of a feature film is normally taken as the date of first release (similar to the date of publication of a book), but the date of a newsfilm is the date of the event. This date is a more useful way of citing newsfilm than the date on which the film was issued. On the other hand the date of a television film is taken to be that of the first transmission.

The collation statement of a film is one of the most important parts of the entry. It indicates the type of film involved at once and can eliminate fruitless searches through quantities of film by indicating the length, gauge and physical properties of the film. If a colour film with detailed or long sequences and sound is required, all the silent, black and white, short film can be eliminated by using the collation statement of the entry. The collation of a film should include the length, duration, gauge, sound tracks and type, and a note on colour system used. Feature and longer documentary film collations should also note the number of reels in the film.

Descriptive cataloguing for film should include a detailed statement of the physical properties of the particular item and its contents in order to avoid handling the actual film wherever possible during the search for particular items. This means that the entry has to include a lot of information in as succinct a form as possible and also the layout of the entries should be consistent to allow for fast identification and retrieval.

USE OF SECONDARY SOURCES

Information included in the cataloguing entries for books comes from the book itself. That is the primary source and cataloguing rules designed for books include sections on how to cope with any information which is derived from secondary sources.

In film cataloguing secondary sources are so frequently necessary that the rules do not provide for entries to distinguish between primary and secondary data. In feature films a certain amount of information is available with the film itself as a rule although this information may often be erroneous or misleading. The date of release, for example, may not be the date of the original release but of release in a particular country. Details of distributor may change and have to be taken from secondary sources. The original distributor mentioned on the film copy may have sold his rights in the film. With short film clips, stockshots and newsfilm the position is even more marked. There is rarely any sort of 'label' or 'title' frame on the film. The print may lead straight from the name of the distributing or producing agency to the first frame of the picture, with no title, no date and no location.

For reasons of flexibility in editing and handling, stock film and newsfilm is usually issued without a sound commentary, so information about the event is not available from such a commentary. This means that a shotlist or synopsis containing further information about the film has to be compiled and issued with the film. This is a secondary source but it provides the cataloguer with most of the information he uses to compile the entries.

PERFECT COPIES

Book cataloguing is based on perfect copies wherever possible. If the library contains an imperfect copy this fact is noted in the entry. This is not relevant to film cataloguing where the entry has to be based on the film available for the user to consult. With many films it can be argued that 'perfect' copies are never produced, there are frequently several versions of a film of differing lengths and containing different scenes but all valid records of an event. Other libraries hold incomplete films or sequences, some may hold copies edited for special purposes, or censored copies. In the case of much archive film the material has been acquired when the film was damaged and sequences or clips may have been impossible to replace. The negative may be destroyed and only imperfect prints available with no definitive reference to the original material. The user has to be referred to the version which exists in the library and catalogue entries are compiled from the scenes and sequences contained in that version.

Catalogues listing material released in a country, e.g. national catalogues where the material is not being held by the organisation issuing the catalogue are in a different position here, but there is still difficulty in acquiring information about the final exhibited version. Again the censor may remove sequences or the exhibitor may remove sections to bring the film to manageable length.

CATALOGUING PROCEDURES

There is no real substitute for viewing film and whenever possible cataloguers and others responsible for information about films should view the material they attempt to catalogue and classify. No verbal description can give a complete impression of a film sequence, or substitute for viewing that film. Much of the information which exists about a film may be misleading. This applies particularly to the title, which is generally concise and leaves out both detail and description and may be designed to catch the imagination or amuse rather than convey information. With a short title many personalities who appear in an information film are unmentioned as well as several incidents. All the personalities and incidents should be indexed in some way and a film cataloguer should never go by the title alone.

The ideal in film cataloguing, therefore, is to view all the film, shotlist, catalogue and classify it. One person should in fact be responsible for carrying out all these processes for any one film. In television and newsfilm libraries, however, time is an important factor and to work only from the film would prove impossible. Users of the library have to rely on the catalogue entries and shotlists when choosing their material for usage or viewing sessions. In the same way the cataloguers may have to work from secondary sources in order to keep up with the intake. If it is necessary to work from secondary sources, there should be an attempt to make these as objective as possible and without personal bias or colouring. A shotlister is trained to observe what is actually shown on the film and not to interpret the events or allow his own opinions to be expressed in the shotlist.

Cataloguers in some organisations can use the shotlists for indexing purposes when time will not allow a viewing of the film. Such shotlists should be made in detail rather than a précis type. Précis shotlists, like a film title, leave out a great deal of information and shorter scenes which appear to have little relevance to the event may be omitted. Much of the detail a cataloguer requires does not appear. A full shotlist with each shot, type of shot, length and content is necessary.

The catalogue entry is then prepared from the shotlist or viewing. Any details which may not be apparent from the shotlist should be researched and added, i.e. date of event, physical format etc.

In the preceding discussion on the choice of the main heading for stockshots and newsfilm it was stated that the main heading was decided on a fairly arbitrary basis and before continuing to discuss the form of entry compiled from a shotlist the importance of the accessions or production number should be noted.

ACCESSIONS NUMBERS

This number (it may well be the same number serving both functions) is essential for the retrieval of the many shorter or incomplete films, especially newsfilm and stockshots. The main entry, subject heading or classification number cannot be used to find film in the same way as it can with books. Even the title of feature film is not a satisfactory means of filing film on the shelves. Accessioning in book libraries is often used as a stock control. Books are not filed by accessions number, as this would mean that several copies of the same book were located in different places on the shelves and no subject arrangement could be achieved on the open access shelves. Films cannot be treated in this way, they should not be on open access and without the intervention of a viewing machine do not constitute the type of material which can be 'browsed'. There is no advantage in attempting to file film by subject even if this were feasible. Also with information film there are several subjects often of equal importance in any short piece of film and decisions as to which subject the film should be filed under would be difficult to make and of no value. Films are therefore normally filed by a location or production number which may derive directly from an accessions number. There are several points to consider about such numbers including uniqueness and the form it should take.

The number allocated to each piece of film should be unique to the particular filmed story or event. It is the means of retrieving the film either alone, or in conjunction with a location number or date of transmission.

The number also has to apply consistently to the one piece of film, and should not be reallocated if the original film is destroyed. It is safer to allocate a new number for every story than to risk the confusion that could arise from duplicated numbering. But how unique should this number be to a film? Should every piece of film be accessioned separately, despite the fact that they are often only different physical versions of the same film, such as negative, positive, or colour versions. Normally instead of using different production numbers and records referring to the same sequence of events, all negatives, positives and colour versions plus related soundtracks of the same film are gathered under the one production or accessions number. A code may be added to indicate the stock, but this system normally relies on further instructions being given to the person retrieving the film to pull out the negative or positive as required. All the stock held on a particular number is noted on the record cards and location records. This method reveals all the stock held on a particular story quickly rather than having to search several numbers to locate stock which has come in at intervals after the story has been released.

This system does not prevent the separation of stock in storage if necessary. As long as the separate locations are clearly marked on the record cards, negatives, positives and colour material can be housed in different stores. Cuts can also be accessioned under the same number as the related cut story.

Uncut stories and film of the same event as the cut or issued version on the other hand are given different accessions numbers. All film of the same event is not the same, the cameramen are different, have different angles, and shoot scenes of different length. Uncut film is treated as new film and accessioned separately. This assists cataloguing, indexing and reference to particular sequences and assists more specific retrieval.

NUMBERING METHODS

The accessions number can be either a running number, an issue number, a location number or a date code. If any of the last three are used there is usually a parallel sequence of running numbers used for the unissued material.

Once again the purpose of the library and the way it issues film helps to determine the most useful numbering system for the film. Distribution libraries normally use a location number for retrieving film. Feature film libraries use a production number similar to a location number as do film archives. Television libraries use a date code, i.e. date of transmission for current affairs or a production number for series and longer programmes. Stockshot libraries need location or a combination of location and key numbers. A newsfilm library which issues separate news items each day but does not attempt to package these items or present them in any order, needs a running sequence of numbers to label the film. A newsreel company which issues complete newsreels at regular intervals needs two sets of numbers, one issue number for the complete newsreel and a parallel set of numbers for unused items retained in the library. A television company presenting daily news programmes uses the date of transmission instead of an issue number, and also files the film within the date of transmission by individual accessions numbers.

Running number. This is the most widely used numbering system for accessioning and there are two main ways of using a running number. If the number of items issued each year is not great, the accessions number can be allowed to run on indefinitely. i.e. 1 — 100,000 etc. If there is a large number of items issued each year, as in newsfilm agencies, then the numbering system can be restarted at 1 each year providing that the year is quoted with the number, e.g. 1001/67 and 1001/69 or 67/4593 and 69/4593. The running number can be combined with another number code to indicate the content or subject matter of the film. This happens often in distribution or hire libraries where a number code is attached to the accessions number to indicate level or general subject area, e.g. 400-9124 Language film, 500-6235 Science film.

Issue number. The issue number is used for news or current affairs material and can also be either a running number or numbered within a year. Issue numbers are used for those films which actually appear in the final newsreel, and unused film is numbered separately. For example, a parallel system of undated numbers which distinguishes unused from used film might consist of the issue number 127/35 or 35/127, representing issue number 127 in 1935, and parallel library numbers running from 10523 to 10540. Newsreel accessions registers list all used and unused film in running number order and record the film used in issues. In addition there is an issue register which gives the number, date, descriptive title and length of each item together with the total footage of the newsreel issue.

Location number. This number is used to retrieve the film from the library vaults, often in conjunction with one of the other numbers mentioned. In stockshot libraries location numbers are used together with key numbers to retrieve film accurately. The location number may be a can number or a sequence of cans and when once the appropriate reel is found the key numbers are used to locate the exact shots required. In a newsreel library where several films are stored in one can, the retrieval system uses a running number for the film and a location number for the can.

Location numbers are less necessary in newsreel libraries where each issue is stored in a separate can and the issue number is the can number. Location numbers are usually indicative of the sequence in which a film may be found, rather than actual vault numbers which become altered as the collection expands and film is moved from one vault or area to another.

Date of transmission. This is the television equivalent of the newsreel issue number. It is also a location number. One newscast is selected as the main issue of the day and stored in its entirety. All the film used in the news programme is stored in a can labelled with the day and the year, e.g. 60/69 represents Day 60 in 1969. Each individual film or story is also numbered separately with an accessions or running number. All untransmitted film is given a number in the same numerical sequence and filed separately. Date of transmission and/or running number are marked on all records to assist retrieval.

OTHER FORMS OF NOTATION

Other forms of notation may be used in addition to the numbering system to indicate types of film, sections of longer films or parts of issues in newsreels.

The film number may be used, for example, to indicate the physical form of the film; negative, positive, black and white or colour. N usually stands for negative and P for positive and they can be used as prefix or suffix. It quickly becomes important to indicate which films are issued in colour or black and white only. If the information is available on acquisition it can be built in to the film number. Some companies use C as a mnemonic for colour, but this is easily confused with the part or section C. The BBC elected to use K for colour, while other organisations use the prefix X.

Sections of longer films as opposed to separate items are often indicated by a letter A, B, C, etc., interposed between the number of the items and the year showing that more than one film has been made from the same roll, e.g., 1001/A/70, 1001/B/70. The letter is interposed between the numbers to avoid confusing it with other prefixes or suffixes which may be used. Letters are best used for this interposition rather than numbers which may be confused with the film number.

Where a newsreel issue is retained in a complete reel there should be an indication of the placing of individual items in the reel, e.g. Issue 101/41 (1), Issue 101/41 (4). If the issue has been broken down into individual stories it will still be necessary to denote each story in this way and numerals are less clumsy for this than letters.

COMBINING RECORDS IN THE MAIN CATALOGUE

Combined records may be feasible for the collection which covers one type of film. In feature film libraries all material can be accessioned and retrieved by the use of running numbers and it is easy to pull out all the records in one catalogue filed by title. But the position is complicated in libraries which either cover several different types of film or which have acquired several collections of the same type of film already numbered in similar sequences of accessions number, such as newsfilm.

Archive collections usually maintain separate catalogues for material which has to be considered separately and catalogued in different ways. For example an archive may maintain one catalogue for feature, documentary, cartoon film, filed by title and another catalogue for newsfilm filed by date.

Newsfilm libraries have a different type of problem when information about more than one collection has to be combined in the one catalogue. To save time, and reduce the risk of missing material indexed in several sequences, it is desirable from the user's point of view that all available film is recorded in the one place. The material could be split up into indexes according to date span, e.g. all collections covering silent material before 1930 in one index, all collections covering 35mm newsreel material up to 1954 or the end of the newsreel material in a second, and all television newsfilm collections in a third index. But this does not assist a research worker looking for material on a particular subject or personality, which could be filed in at least two of the catalogues. It is desirable therefore to have only one main catalogue, but there must be strict control of the filing order of the various collections.

When several collections in the one library have similar numbering sequences, letters are used to distinguish one collection from the others, e.g. Paramount newsreel is P 15269, Gaumont British becomes GB 15269 and Gaumont Graphic GR 15269.

FILING ORDER

If it is necessary to file material in a sequence using the accessions, production or running numbers, a straight numerical sequence applies for all feature and documentary material. The numerical sequence is most used in distribution libraries where film is coded for quick reference and computer retrieval by using the film number rather than the title.

As one of the main ways of approaching newsfilm is by date, the filing order for production numbers and collections can usefully follow date order. When the date is taken into account the collections themselves will be filed in a set order, e.g. Gaumont Graphic, Gaumont British, Paramount, current newsfilm. Within each collection the logical filing order is the issue number first and then the uncut number.

One final anomaly may be encountered with a newsfilm numbering system made up of an acquisitions number, and the year. This is the year of acquisition, not event. With most film this is a reasonable system, but there is the odd exchange of film with other libraries and a film may come in to the library which was shot in 1896. Because it was only acquired in 1965 the acquisitions number is dated 1965. In this case the date of event has to be used to file the material and it will be filed at the end of the sequence for other collections.

FORM OF ENTRY

Consistency of treatment and in the form of entries is important in any form of information exchange and the accuracy of the content is essential. Cataloguing codes can be used to determine the form of entry, but the following features of the film should be noted on the catalogue card; title, subject and/or classification number, production details (i.e., production company, place and date), production and performance credits, physical format including length, production or location number, summary or synopsis and notes including such details as restrictions on future use. The order of these elements varies according to the type of film catalogued. In some entries elements have to be omitted because there is no element in the film, in others they are cited differently because one aspect is more relevant to the type of film than another.

Title. The main purpose of descriptive cataloguing is to describe each item as an item and distinguish it from other items. With a book the main entry is a combination of author and title, but principally author. However film has no author as such and the most common main entry is title. The title is taken as that of the copy in hand and in the language that appears on the copy. If the original title is known to be different it may be appended in brackets. If the title is missing, but known, it is transcribed on to the card and the explanation 'title missing' is appended in brackets. In many instances with feature and documentary films the title may be both missing and unknown. In these cases a title is supplied by the cataloguer and put in square brackets to indicate this is a supplied title. This is a cataloguing convention, but if there is any likelihood of the convention being unknown or misunderstood, 'title supplied' should be appended in brackets.

Stock material and newsfilm require different treatment. Titles have to be supplied and they should include all elements present in the picture; place, date, personalities, subjects. The entry is usually a short sentence indicating the contents of the film, but it may be spread to a shotlist if independent shotlists do not exist. An entry in the form of a shotlist can be shown in either the normal shotlist layout or as a précis of the action, such as:

Sequence	Footage	Time	Shot	Descriptive Detail
1	7	12	GV PAN	Exterior of Building
2	10	16	CU	Entrance to Building

or as a running précis with type of shot, descriptive detail and a running footage:

GV Exterior of Building (7) CU Entrance (10)

The aim is to summarise the contents of the film and, if independent shotlists exist, to refer the user to them for additional information. However, as concise and informative a summary as possible should be included on the index card to prevent the user looking in several places for information, and the entry should be specific enough to serve as the basis for subject classification.

Newsfilm today is not given a title but one of the content summaries described. A title is not transferred to the film at all, but it goes directly to the action. Newsreels are in a different position. Whereas television uses a newsreader to link and introduce the filmed items, newsreels used captions, or titles, to let the audience know what was coming next. Unfortunately these titles were meant to catch the eye rather than be informative and may even be misleading. Where a newsreel title is quoted on the catalogue cards, a short additional summary is often desirable to explain the title.

Silent newsreel titles were designed to be less misleading as there was no commentator to explain the situation to the viewer, but they also need some additional explanation. The silent newsreels also had internal titles in addition to the main title of the story, and all these should be quoted either on the catalogue card or the shotlist.

As a rule the amount of information given on the catalogue card depends on the amount of other information available about the film. If a separate shotlist is available, for example, a shorter entry can be used on the card. If there is no separate shotlist, a lot of information is needed on the card.

Subject. This is the classification heading by which the film is filed in the indexes. There will be more than one subject heading for each film, but each card has one heading to file by. This takes the form of subject key words or classification numbers according to the system used.

Production statement. This is equivalent to the imprint statement for a book and contains details of production company, sponsor, distributor, place and date. The production company and sponsor may well be available on the film but the distributor may be harder to discover. Normally, accompanying data has to be consulted, but the distributor is the part of this statement most likely to change and, in such cases, it may even be wise to omit this information from the catalogue card and record it elsewhere.

In newsfilm libraries the main credit goes to the production company, but this is taken for granted unless otherwise stated in the entry. If the film has come from an outside source this should be noted. The BBC and Visnews, for example, have reciprocal agreements concerning foreign and home news. If film from either company is retained in the other film library acknowledgement is made. Other newsfilm libraries that have bought up additional collections also name the source as part of the production number or elsewhere on the card. Other production credits, e.g. cameramen, may be included on the contents sheets or other records, but are not necessarily on the catalogue cards.

The place (of origin) is normally cited as a country for film, rather than the city or town quoted for books. The country of origin for most feature film is taken to be the nationality of the production company. No attempt is made to indicate the location of shooting of a film, at least not in this section of the entry. Films are shot on location all over the world, but these locations have nothing to do with the origin of the production company or its nationality.

Stockshot and newsfilm again do not comply with this rule. Imprint place is normally irrelevant to these films, but location becomes of paramount importance. It is necessary to indicate the location of particular shots and these locations are given greater prominence than in the imprint, being included usually at the beginning of the main entry. In newsfilm libraries in particular, where date is also very important, it may often be useful to combine country or location with date in the catalogue. This reduces the amount of film to be searched for under any one date.

The date is normally taken as the year of first release or issue of the material, but there are several variations to the rules according to the type of film and also the information available. Complete films are given the year of first release if this information is available, but if not the date of completion of production may be used. Copyright date is another possibility, but many films do not receive copyright dates and those which do may be given copyright date after the first release. This date should also be used with caution.

Archives may have to do considerable research to ascertain the date and may resort to a stock date as an approximation. However stock dates can be misleading and should be treated with care and some scepticism. Film companies did not necessarily use recent stock, film may have been transferred from one stock to a later stock with different markings and several other practices can produce inaccurate dating of film.

Another difficulty arises when a film suffers long delays in release. Where there is a considerable lapse between the date of production and the date of release the production date should be mentioned in a note.

An increasing number of films are never released publicly, for example government research material and educational material produced by particular institutions or departments for internal teaching use. The date of production is cited for these films. Stockshot, television films, newsreels and newsfilm are all exceptions to the ruling quoted. Stockshots use the year of production or filming.

Television material is given the date of first transmission. This may be cited as either a year in the case of complete programmes, or a date in the case of news broadcasts.

Newsreel and newsfilm should both use the exact date of the event shown, to the day, wherever possible. If the date of event is unobtainable, especially in older material, the date of release of the newsreels is used instead. An exact date assists retrieval, especially if an event goes on for several days or weeks and only one particular occurrence is required. As will have been seen most film entries cite only the year of release or copyright but newsfilm should give the date of the event to assist retrieval and recognition.

Production and performance credits. These are more necessary for complete feature and documentary film than for other types, where such details may not exist or be relevant. Performance credits include production credits, such as director, producer, cameraman, editor as well as contributors, narrators, actors etc. They are normally cited in a set order with an abbreviation of the function appearing before the name.

e.g. p. (producer)
d. (director)
ed. (editor)

Physical format. This is equivalent to a book collection and is a statement of the physical properties of a film. It should include gauge, projection speed, length, sound, form of material.

The gauge or width of the film is given in millimetres, e.g. 35mm, 16mm are most commonly found for newsfilm. Details of film package can also be included here, that is if the film is in an 8mm loop or cassette.

With the increasing admixture of television and cinema film in the same collection it may be necessary to indicate the projection speed. This is quoted in frames per second (fps).

The length of a film is quoted in feet. The measurement is taken from the first frame of the picture to the last frame and it includes any titles. Blank film, whether it is attached leader or an actual part of the print, is not included in the footage. More recently in newsfilm the metrage has been added for the benefit of foreign subscribers, but there is difficulty in quoting metrage for film for exact lengths. The number of frames per foot is not directly convertible to frames per metre. However metrage can be used for longer sequences if required. Some film libraries include running time of the film as well as or instead of the footage. Running time is recorded in seconds.

Details such as whether the film is sound, silent or mute and the type of sound can be entered here, i.e. combined or separate, magnetic or optical.

The form of material includes negative, positive or colour and type of colour. Additional factors are the type of film recording, especially if it is a telerecording or satellite recording, because this is an important indication of quality. It should also be stated whether the film is an answer print or a show copy.

The detail included in the physical format depends on the purpose of the library or catalogue. If it is intended to print from the film held, fuller details are needed on the catalogue card, or some equally accessible record, than if the film is simply for showing or distribution. However it is important to include any details which indicate the quality of the film held and for this reason telerecordings should always be shown as such.

Production/location number. This is an important key to retrieval and should appear on the catalogue cards. The main entry of many films is in the form of contents sheets or shotlists or cards prepared from this material and is filed, like the film, chronologically according to the 'serial number'. This number is the production number of the film which has been variously described as the acquisitions, accessions or production number. The production number retrieves any separate shotlists and perhaps the film, but it may also be necessary to have a location number to find the film, especially newsfilm libraries where, because of the delay in final selection the location number of the film is not put on to the catalogue cards, but is lodged with the contents sheets. The catalogue cards are filed several weeks before the location number of the film is known and it is an unnecessary waste of time to have a member of staff continually searching for all catalogue entries in order to put the location number on the cards. In stockshot libraries this number is usually the key number and is an essential tool to retrieval. The key number is usually incorporated in a longer code which indicates the can or reel on which the number can be found as well as the location of the particular shot on that reel.

Summary or synopsis. The summary should describe the content of the film accurately and objectively and should be specific enough to serve as a basis for classification. It is not necessary to repeat this information in some types of film where either the summary is in the form of a shotlist which is too long to be included on the catalogue card, or the summary is in fact the main entry, e.g. stockshots and newsfilm.

Notes. These include notes to clarify the main entry, such as details of other versions, language of version held, any related material, physical condition, peculiarities of production and any restrictions on usage, such as restrictions of supply or special copyright conditions which have to be observed. These should appear on the catalogue card for quick reference purposes, especially if they are long standing. Information that is liable to change could be recorded separately, but if there is a risk that supply of the material may be made without reference to the other records the restriction will be best recorded on the main index record.

The main index cards should also have a note of all the subjects, personalities and locations the film has been filed under. This assists retrieval of the cards for amendment or destruction and may incidentally provide additional clues to the content of the film to an astute user. These tracings could be on the reverse side of the card. Tracings are also used for reproducing the required number of entries in the main cataloguing processes.

Evaluations. One final section which may be included in the entry is an evaluation of the film. This is most commonly used in published catalogues to indicate the level of the film being considered and the audience to which it will be most appropriate. Educational film catalogues usually include an evaluation because it is necessary to know in advance the level of the audience the film is intended for, especially at school level. But the argument will continue to rage for some time as to how many evaluations are valid. Each evaluation should only be taken in the context of the catalogue for which it was made and not transferred to other records for which it may be less relevant. With newsfilm an evaluation is seldom relevant or useful. Each user will want to judge the content of the film himself and use it in his own particular way. A stockshot or newsfilm should be of general interest to the public and an age or educational level judgement is therefore inappropriate. Also an evaluation of any film does destroy some of the objectivity of the item. The cataloguing is done by a 'committee' whose opinions differ widely so that the final outcome is uninformative.

ENTRY FOR FEATURE IN ARCHIVE CATALOGUE

1926 THE LODGER; a story of the London fog [F.1020]
Credits: *p.c.* Gainsborough Pictures; *p.* Michael Balcon; *d.* Alfred Hitchcock; *asst.d.* Alma Reville; *sc.* Eliot Stannard, Alfred Hitchcock; *ph.* Baron Ventimiglia; *ed.* Ivor Montagu: *a.d.* C. Wilfred Arnold, Bertram Evans; *t.* Ivor Montagu; *a.t.* E. McKnight Kauffer
L.p: Marie Ault, Arthur Chesney, Malcolm Keen, Ivor Novello
Drama: A notorious murderer is at work in London. In Bloomsbury a young man appears and takes lodgings with the Bunting family. The daughter, Daisy, is attracted to him, to the annoyance of her sweetheart, a policeman. The policeman obtains a search warrant and finds cuttings in the lodger's room relating to the murders. The young man is arrested, but escapes with Daisy's help. The real murderer is caught by the police. The young man explains that his sister was one of the murderer's first victims, and he had vowed to track him down. (5,664 ft)

TYPE OF ENTRY

The type of card used in the catalogue is also connected with the type of entry decided upon. Two main types are the unit entry or main unit entry with analyticals and the multiple entry.

ENTRY FOR FEATURE IN FILMOGRAPHY

TROJAN WOMEN, THE

U.S.A. 1971   **Director: Michael Cacoyannis**

Cert—U. *dist*—Cinerama. *p.c*—Josef Shaftel Productions. *exec. p*—Josef Shaftel. *p*— Michael Cacoyannis, Anis Nohra. *p. sup*—Carlo Lastricati. *p. manager*—Paco Lara. *asst. d*—Stavros Konstantarakos, José Maria Ochoa, Roberto Cirla. *sc*—Michael Cacoyannis. Based on the translation by Edith Hamilton of the play by Euripides. *ph*—Alfio Contini. *col*—Eastman Colour. *ed*—Michael Cacoyannis. *a.d*—Nicholas Georgiadis. *sp. effects*—Basilio Cortijo. *m/m.d*—Mikis Theodorakis. *cost*—Annalisa Rocca. *sd. ed*—Alfred Cox. *sd. rec*—Mikes Damalas. *sd. re-rec*—Gordon McCallum. *l.p*—Katherine Hepburn *(Hecuba),* Vanessa Redgrave *(Andromache),* Geneviève Bujold *(Cassandra),* Irene Papas *(Helen),* Patrick Magee *(Menelaus),* Brian Blessed *(Talthybius),* Alberto Sanz *(Astyanax),* Pauline Letts, Rosaline Shanks, Pat Becket, Anna Bentinck, Esmeralda Adam, María García Alonso, Nilda Alvarez, Victoria Ayllon, Elizabeth Billencourt, Margarita Calahora, Elena Castillo, Anna María Espojo, Maria Jesús Hoyos, Conchita Leza, Margarita Matta, Mirta Miller, Conchita Morales, Virginia Quintana, Yvette Rees, Carmen Segarra, Esperanza Alonso, Consolation Alvarez, Adela Armengol, Gloria Berrogal, Maria Borge, Carmen Cano, Renee Eber, Katie Ellyson, Gwendoline Kocsis, Maureen Mallall, Ivi Mavridi, Livia Mitchell, Ersie Pittas, Catherine Rabone, Clara Sanchiz and Laura Zarrabeitia *(Women),* Maria Farantouri *(Singer).* 9,969 ft. 111 mins.

Troy has fallen to the Greeks after ten years of war. The Trojan men have been decimated in the fighting, and now the order comes from Menelaus, King of Sparta, for the captive Trojan women to be taken to the Greek ships; among them, separated from the others, is Menelaus' adulterous wife Helen, pretext for the war and long despised by the women of Troy. Talthybius, a messenger from the Greek camp, arrives with the news that Cassandra, the prophetess daughter of Hecuba, King Priam's widow, has been chosen by Agamemnon as his personal slave. Deranged by the war, Cassandra prophesies that the Greeks will pay dearly for the fall of Troy. Andromache, widow of Hector, the bravest of the Trojans, learns that she is to be the slave of Hector's conqueror Achilles. She takes comfort in her young son Astyanax, only to find that the Greeks have resolved to have him killed. Horrified, Andromache resists, but Talthybius puts his orders before his sympathies, Andromache is led away, and the boy is hurled from a cliff. The Trojan women now turn their bitter anger against Helen, who proudly and cunningly puts her case before Menelaus. Confused by Helen's guile, Menelaus rejects Hecuba's plea that Helen should die in Troy; her fate, he decrees, will await her in Greece. After supervising the burial of Astyanax, Hecuba is led away with the Trojan women from the city which now burns with Greek fire.

ENTRY FOR DOCUMENTARY IN FILMOGRAPHY

711—TOWN & COUNTRY PLANNING
711.4(421) — Environs of London. Urbanisation. Control
  LONDON—THE UNIQUE CITY.—dist.: Concord Films
    Council, Hire: 1971.—30 mins.: sd.: B & W. 16mm.
    Credits: p. Nancy Thomas. ph. Charles Parnal. ed. Peter Pierce.
    Where other cities have grown upwards, London has ever increasingly
    edged her boundaries outwards into the Home Counties. This has been
    partly due to the denizens' desire to combine housing with areas of
    greenery. What methods can be used to solve the problem of London's
    sprawl?

ENTRY FOR STOCKSHOT

629;23.4 : 626.1   N.P. 13/1
Cargo boat in Manchester ship canal

                                            198ZG 19572—592
                                                   594—624

ENTRY FOR NEWSFILM IN ARCHIVE PUBLISHED CATALOGUE

1929 Issued April 11   [N.2110]
    ITALY'S WAR HEROES PAY HOMAGE TO POPE, KING AND
    MUSSOLINI. A square crowded with people waving and displaying
    banners (36). PIUS RETURNS THE GREETING AND BLESSES THE
    VETERANS. Shots of the Pope standing at a window and of the crowd
    waving to him (60). SURGING BEFORE THE ROYAL PALACE THE
    CHEERING SOLDIERS HAIL KING EMMANUEL. The King on the
    balcony of his palace and a shot of the crowd (87). AT THE ANCIENT
    COLISEUM — A TREMENDOUS OVATION FOR MUSSOLINI. An aerial
    view of the crowded Coliseum (117) and a close shot of Mussolini
    making a speech (127). LONG LIVE IL DUCE! A further shot of the
    crowd (135) and Mussolini. (142)
    PATHE

    cApril 12   [N.2111]
    LONDON'S WELCOME TO THE SPEED KING: MAJOR H. O. D.
    SEGRAVE, WINNER OF THE WORLD'S LAND SPEED RECORD
    AND INTERNATIONAL MOTOR-BOAT CHAMPIONSHIP, COMES
    HOME. Close-up of Segrave (18). IT IS ANNOUNCED THAT H.M. THE
    KING HAS BEEN PLEASED TO APPROVE THAT THE HONOUR OF
    KNIGHTHOOD BE CONFERRED UPON MAJOR SEGRAVE. Further
    close-up. (25)
    EMPIRE NEWS BULLETIN

ENTRY FOR CURRENT NEWSFILM

U.S.A.	MAY 1967
U.S.A.: Bankers from 40	4420/67
countries meeting in New	38' 16 mm
York to see 'electronic	X 4420/67
banking'	38' 16 mm
PRINT MASTER	

If the shotlist is to be included on the card (and this happens most frequently where no shotlist exists with the film, but is made by the indexing staff and typed direct on to the cards rather than typing on to a separate record) then one card should represent one film. If the shotlist is long it may only appear on the main card and the other indexes contain either a unit entry or multiple entries referring to the main cards.

Multiple entries occur when the films are listed several to a card usually in accessions or production number order. The cards are given a title, subject, location or name heading and filed accordingly. This reduces the number of cards to be stored considerably, but can become untidy when films are withdrawn or come into the library out of sequence. It may not be possible to retype the cards each time an alteration is made and the cards have entries crossed out or added out of sequence. The result is unattractive and confusing. For a static collection which is intact at the time of cataloguing and will not require foreseeable alteration, the system is useful, but not for a current, changing collection.

Unit entry takes more space but can be manipulated more easily, and it can also be reproduced easily by mechanical means. When there are several cross references for each piece of film the mechanised reproduction of cards is a useful tool, but unit entry is a prerequisite for the reproduction of multiple copies in this way. If the entry has to be adjusted and sections inserted or removed the system defeats itself. Unit entry is normally used with separate shotlists unless the shotlist is short or in précis form and can be put on a 6 x 4in card. This increases the amount of space needed for the catalogue, but saves the space needed for storing the shotlists.

In a library which produces analytical entries the situation is further complicated. Analytical entries are usually single entries indicating a particular subject or sequence within a film. The advantages of unit entry are lost, but there may be a greater advantage in having the specific subject entries in the catalogue.

This point has to be weighed up by the cataloguer before analytical entries are embarked on. They are normally of most use for longer films, feature, documentary or educational. Unit entry may still be employed for many of the entries but the analyticals will have to be done separately.

TYPES OF CATALOGUE

The form the catalogue takes should be determined by the type of information it is required to carry and the use which will be made of it. There are four main types of catalogue: sheaf or loose leaf, visible types of index, computer or mechanical retrieval, and card catalogues.

Sheaf catalogues. These are useful for a static collection, that is one which is not being added to continually or altered. If much alteration is required it means breaking open the sheaf file to extract or insert sheets and the physical wear and tear on the flimsy paper which is used in sheaf catalogues eventually leads to a destruction of the records. These characteristics make sheaf catalogues impractical for many film records.

Visible indexes. This includes indexes where several main entries are visible at one time and the full record cards overlap one another to reveal only this main entry. e.g. Kalamazoo type binders, where the 'cards' containing full details are laid over one another to show only the main title of the film on the bottom of the card. Apart from being a very bulky record, these suffer from the same drawbacks as the sheaf catalogue if alteration, interfiling or replacement of records are continuing operations. However the National Film Archive are using them successfully with their feature collection.

Another type of visible index is the one line entry, but this is not used for main entry as insufficient detail can be put on to the one line. Visible indexes of the one line type are better employed as guides to the main catalogue where the subject and its location or notation are displayed on the strips and show the layout and relationships of the subjects; something which is often not appreciated in a card index to the subject file.

Computers or mechanised storage methods. A need has been felt in many film libraries for some mechanised form of storage and retrieval because of the amount of data, the lack of space, and the labour involved to produce and retrieve data and list the contents of the library.

In any large film library, the amount of data quickly becomes a problem. Data builds up in all the recording systems including the catalogue. Putting it into a mechanised system does not reduce the amount, but it can improve handling efficiency. Some libraries keep accessions in computer form and link this record with film movement and recall systems. The BBC film library, for example, use an Ultronic machine for a loan system which deals with 2000 cans of film a week. Distribution libraries keep records of borrowing and film movement in computers where there is a large volume of traffic.

Lack of space becomes a problem when a catalogue that has been built to answer immediate enquiries for a few items at a time grows rapidly and the physical problem of storing it appears. Computer storage sometimes solves the problem, but punched card systems seldom do. There is still the problem of storing the punched cards for use in the sorter and in addition punched card handling equipment is bulky.

In an established library the labour of transferring the data into a machine readable form may preclude the use of this form until economic and staff resources are built up. In many film libraries continuity of service is essential and while transferring systems the data has to be made available for current consultation. This complicates the issue further.

If microfilm is used in the library it may be converted into a punched card system with less expenditure and labour than other systems. The microfilm will have to be punched or put on to an optical coincidence system.

The retrieval of the data and the usefulness of the data processing system may depend on the type of question asked in particular libraries. The sort of question asked in a newsfilm library for example is not always well adapted to mechanised systems of retrieval. The questions are usually specific, require a rapid answer rather than an intensive search and may refer to only one item being sought. To run a computer for this sort of rapid enquiry service is wasteful of economic resources and a punched card system takes too long.

Mechanised retrieval methods are more useful and less laborious, for quantities of information such as subject lists, catalogues of holdings and union lists either national or international. It is not usually worth the expense to one library to list its holdings in this way as the lists may be required infrequently. But for a wider range of libraries, inclusive of several types, use of these methods by a central information bureau for film holdings becomes practicable.

Card catalogues. Most film libraries use card catalogues. Cards can be inserted in filing or removed easily for alteration without disturbance to the rest of the catalogue. Card catalogues are easy to consult and are flexible enough to contain as much or as little information as required. The size of the card depends on the information to be incorporated on it. The 5 x 3in size is widely used for unit or unitary entry, but 6 x 4in or 8 x 5in are also often used, depending on the type of film, amount of information or type of cataloguing carried out.

If the shotlist is to be included a 6 x 4in card may be adequate, although if a feature or perhaps a newsreel is shotlisted intact the larger 8 x 5in card is needed to contain the full shotlist. Full shotlists may be put on to the main card only and all subject and locality references may contain only the relevant part of the shotlist, or a unit entry with the title or subject of the film and reference to the main card for the shotlist. In this case the main entry is on a larger 8 x 5in card and the references on smaller 5 x 3in cards.

A subject catalogue in a film library often has changes of headings and additions of new subheadings to keep up with trends in film history or current affairs and the guides should be easy to alter. For example guides which have a stiff plastic extension on top of a stiff board can serve this purpose well. Individual strips of tough board or card are typed and inserted into the plastic. They are easily removed when the heading no longer applies and a new guide inserted. Damage to the guides rarely occurs because they do not bend, dogear or chip and are easy to keep clean and clear.

In order to comply with fire regulations in film libraries the catalogue card cabinets are of metal. Some film libraries are still able to use wood cabinets, but only where they are well away from the film handling areas. As even metal cabinets will melt in the fierce heat of a fire additional fireproofing is wise, especially if the catalogue contains the only record of the film library contents. Fireproofed cabinets take one or more catalogue drawers or ranks of drawers in one cabinet. This means that a double drawer has to be opened in order to get at the catalogue and consulting the catalogue is a little more awkward. This is a small price to pay for securing some 50 years of work.

STANDARDISATION

In spite of differences in the functions of libraries all need to maintain catalogues and indexes to show the material available. These catalogues would be of most use if some uniformity could be achieved between libraries in their systems of cataloguing and classification. Different practices in each library do not lead to efficiency and make co-operation and the exchange of information more difficult. Unfortunately many film libraries were already well established before principles of standardisation were drawn up. As a result, by the time codes of practice were agreed on and introduced, the libraries were faced with a large task to remedy the faults which made co-operation less effective than it could have been.

The purpose of catalogue codes is to prevent the idiosyncrasies and inconsistencies which result when verbal instruction is interpreted by several people over a period of time. A codified set of rules once accepted can be used to guide both the cataloguers and the user. The cataloguers can be uniform in their approach by using the code and because of this the user is helped in finding his way through the indexes as easily and quickly as possible.

The codes being discussed at this point refer to descriptive cataloguing and not to subject cataloguing or indexing which are more closely related to the question of classification.

Codes of practice. Many of the cataloguing codes have been based on the experience of librarians working in a particular medium, or committees of librarians working in the same medium who co-operate to try and agree about general rules or practice. Where the work is done by a committee or group of librarians the resulting codes have a broader reference and can be used in a wider context. Because of the small number of film libraries any one group will probably be representative of several different types, i.e. distribution, production, stockshot, newsfilm, archive etc. Narrowing the field of interest when compiling rules works against the very compatibility they are designed to achieve. There is now a further broadening of rules for film libraries to include the many developing 'multi media' libraries, that is libraries which store and index many sources of information such as books, films, slides, audio and videotapes, gramophone records, etc. Any attempts to establish rules for only one media should also be related to the national and international codes being drawn up by book librarians. Certain fundamental differences do of course exist between the cataloguing of books and films. The film, for example, is usually referred to by title, whereas a book is better referred to by its author. Other rules can be of use to both disciplines, such as rules of alphabetisation, many of the rules for descriptive cataloguing, filing order, and the citing of personal names. Film librarians can therefore use the longer established codes of book librarians as a basis from which to work, but should not attempt to follow these rules too rigidly and become enmeshed in details which serve no useful purpose and do not apply to the film medium.

The particular problems which the rules should account for include the choice of main entry, location number, production statement, country of production or origin, date, collation, summary, notes and added entries. All these factors have been discussed in the form of entry and many of the problems noted. According to the main codes which have been designed for use in film libraries the main entry of the film is under the title, but it has already been noted that some films, notably stockshots and newsfilms, do not have 'titles', only descriptive statements or summaries of the subject content. Alternatives are therefore necessary for the first rule in a film cataloguing code to deal with stockshots and newsfilm. Entry of stockshots can only be made under subjects, because that is the most important element for stock material. Titles are usually descriptive titles supplied by the cataloguer and non-retrievable. Entry of newsfilm can be made under the date of event, but this is not satisfactory in most newsfilm libraries, although it is feasible in archive collections. Later rulings suggest the main entry for newsfilm is filed in serial (or production) number order. Newsfilm and stockshot librarians may both argue that their films will be searched for under subject and that the subject entry should be the main one, but newsfilms usually consist of more than one subject and each is equally important for re-use purposes. In such cases a further choice has to be made to select one main subject, and as this is a somewhat unnecessary exercise the citing of newsfilms by production number has been selected as the most convenient way.

The added entries for film will be concerned with alternative titles, additional subject headings, locations and name entries for production and performance credits, or personalities on film, and a code of practice should be laid down with reference to the citing of personal names especially. Many of these rules can be adapted from book librarianship codes, e.g. the entries for compound surnames, surnames with prefixes, use of forenames, titles, pseudonyms, and Oriental, Arabic and Indic names. These last present many problems, especially in newsfilm libraries where usage in the country of origin, English usage and the cameraman's idea of English usage combine to cloud the name with confusion. Extreme care is needed to avoid several sequences arising in the personalities index which relate to the same individual. Newsfilm libraries probably have a larger proportion of Oriental and Arabic names to contend with than many other film libraries and therefore the problem is magnified. The rules concerned with personal names should be carefully constructed and standardised and available with the general code of practice for each film library. It may be necessary to have a set of rules separate from the main code because of the detail and number of alternatives to be accounted for, but the rules should be available to the cataloguers together with the main codes of practice. A useful reference work is A. H. Chaplin, *Names of Person, National usages for entry in catalogues,* IFLA 1967.

Other appendices should be included in the codes to assist in the production of standardisation and uniform entries. These include problems of capitalisation and punctuation of the entries themselves.

It is also necessary to have clear definitions of the many unusual and often synonymous terms in use in the film industry. The terms should all be defined and where possible one synonym decided on for use in the code and therefore in the library catalogues. This can be done by a system of 'see references' in the list of definitions, referring the user from the terms not preferred to the selected one, e.g. SPROCKET HOLES *see* PERFORATIONS.

A list of standard abbreviations should also be added for reference.

Filing order. After the catalogue entries have been decided upon and drawn up the filing order becomes important. Most codes do not make any recommendations on the alphabetical arrangement and it is left to the devices of the cataloguing staff to draw up their own rulings. However some reference should be made to the British Standard 1749 : 1969. *Specification for alphabetical arrangements and the filing order of numerals and symbols.*

Cutter's Rules for a Dictionary Catalogue were formulated a long time ago, but are still sound and, used in conjunction with the American Library Association Rules for filing, provide a valuable tool. The problem of filing order is not specific to film libraries and codes used by all librarians are equally applicable and should be used. It is not so necessary to include rules for filing order in the film cataloguing rules, although mention should be made of the problems and the standard rules and codes available to solve these problems.

CODES OF PRACTICE

There are several codes available for use in film libraries, both specialised and general:

1. *Rules for use in the Cataloguing Department of the National Film Archive.* 5th ed. revised. 1960.

2. *Rules for Descriptive Cataloguing in the Library of Congress:* Motion Pictures and Filmstrips. 2nd prelim. ed. 1958.

3. Unesco. *International Rules for the Cataloguing of Educational, Scientific and Cultural films and filmstrips.* Prelim. ed. 1956.

4. Aslib Film Production Librarians Group. *Film Cataloguing Rules,* 1963.

5. Joint Code. *Anglo-American Cataloguing Rules,* 1967. Part III. Non book materials.

National Film Archive Rules. These were designed specifically for use in the archive's cataloguing department. They cover all types of film, feature, documentary, experimental and newsreel and go into considerable detail. They were published partly for the benefit of the archives and partly as an incentive to other film librarians in the UK to realise the problems involved and the need for a codified set of rules.

The rules are divided into four main sections dealing with the Title catalogue, Newsfilm catalogue, Indexes and Style. The NFA established the entry of film under title. Detailed rules are included for quoting the title of a film as a substitute for the normal detailed rules for quoting the author entry of a book. The National Film Archive enters the film under the original language title of the film, for example, to allow for international recognition of the item. This would involve the small film library in considerable research and the rule can be waived for the small 'non-archive' type of library. The familiar title of a film helps to find it more quickly in a small collection and a system of references serves to help the user who has only an original title reference. Rules for dealing with missing titles are included, an occurrence far more frequent in film than in books and a fact reflected by the importance of the rule.

Credits are mentioned and the order and ways of citing participants in a film are codified. The 'imprint' includes the country of origin of the film and the date of the film is taken as the date of first release in the country of origin. The collation entry for a film consists of the physical properties of the film, namely the gauge, the form of the film, whether silent, sound, colour etc. and the length. A table appended to the rules indicates the most commonly used abbreviations and designations for film.

The distributor of the film has also to be included in the main entry, especially in archive copies. However this information is liable to change and amendment as distribution companies and contracts change. Although the information should be recorded with other information on the film it should really be recorded in a part of the entry which can be easily altered or amended to save retyping an entire entry for one part.

A summary of the film sequences is included in the archive catalogue entry in the absence of a separate shotlist. This should indicate the content of the film, and footage counts for the more important sequences (especially any which will be given added or analytical entries), together with the beginning and end of each reel of the film and a note of any missing sequences.

Review references are included for archive film to give the user additional information about the film, especially from contemporary sources. Notes on other versions and related material are also helpful in this connection. Tracings are recorded to allow for future control of the catalogue.

Rules are quoted which are specifically designed for archive record keeping: the donor of the film is mentioned in the main entry,together with the date the film was received by the archive, and the selection committee decision is recorded to indicate the reason for acquisition of the film.

Newsfilm is treated in a separate section of the rules and each item of news is treated as a separate item and filed by date of event. The archive holds newsfilm as a chronological record of events, but in other collections newsfilms are held for their subject matter and the archive rules for the cataloguing of newsfilm have therefore only a limited application.

In addition to the main catalogues detailing all the film held in the archive there are several indexes and a section of the Archive rules is devoted to these. Users of the collection will want to approach it from several different angles and indexes are provided for production credits (i.e. directors, production companies, cameramen), subjects (i.e. an alphabetical index to the classification scheme in use), biography (i.e. personalities, actors etc.), form (fiction and non-fiction), and treatment (i.e. cartoon, television, compilation, experimental).

The rules for style include alphabetical arrangement and capitalisation and attempt to follow standard cataloguing procedure in order to make the indexes easy to follow and use.

The rules, therefore, while they form a valuable starting point for film libraries were not designed for anything more than the National Film Archive's own cataloguing department and include several rules which are either irrelevant to many other film libraries or too detailed to be usefully adopted in their entirety.

The rules for newsfilm especially have to be extensively altered before they can be used in a commercial newsfilm library. Nevertheless the rules did establish standards of film cataloguing which have continued to develop since.

Library of Congress, 1958. These rules were designed for general collections of film, and to meet the needs of the national collection of film in the United States. In the introduction to the Rules the compilers state that for the cataloguing of special types of film and collections of film assembled for special purposes the rules will require adaptation. Because the rules are general they can be applied widely to the less specialised film libraries, but the provision of rules for dealing with newsfilm is inadequate and any other specialised types of film library will have to devise their own rules to cope with individual problems.

The first section of the rules deals with the choice of entry, the second with the imprint and the third with the physical description. Like the National Film Archive and the Unesco rules the principle of title main entry is formulated. The difference between the rules lies in the choice of language of the title. Whereas the National Film Archive chose the original language title for reasons of international identification and co-operation the Library of Congress prefer the title in the language of the copy held. This is more topical for a non-archive collection where prints or copies of the film are normally held in the language of the country concerned. These may be dubbed or original sound tracks, but for quick reference the familiar language title is more useful. Rules for supplied titles and subtitles are also included, both similar to the rules for the Archive, i.e. supplied titles are enclosed in brackets and subtitles or alternative titles are quoted after the main titles with added entries where necessary.

The imprint includes details of production company, country of origin and date of release. The information for the imprint may be taken from secondary sources, but the difference between information taken from the film and other sources is not drawn. The distribution or releasing company is included in the imprint in addition to the production company and the date of the film is given as the date or year of release.

The rules covering the physical description of the film include the length of the film quoted in running time rather than footage in this particular set of rules. Many commercial film agencies quote both the running time and footage in the shotlists but use a footage count on the index cards. This is an economy of space and forms a quicker reference than quoting minutes and seconds for short pieces of film. Running time is more helpful for longer feature or documentary films where it is quoted in minutes, but footage is more useful for short pieces of film especially where charges are to be levied. Laboratory printing charges are based on footage and constant conversion to duration would increase work in commercial libraries unnecessarily. It is better to quote both running time and footage whenever possible, especially in a catalogue which contains several types of film.

The physical description includes details of the sound track or notes that the film is silent. In film cataloguing it is frequently helpful to differentiate between the types of sound on a soundtrack. For example, the sound may be only natural sound effects, background music, or there may be sound on film, of dialogue, interview or speech, e.g. NAT SOF for natural sound and SOF for sound on film for speeches etc. The Library of Congress Rules include rules to cover the physically different types of soundtrack or film which has to be run on special equipment in the rules for Notes as an extension of the physical description. Optical sound, for example, is treated in the rules for sound, but magnetic sound is mentioned in the extension notes, and kinescope film, Technicolor, tinted stock are all mentioned in the extension notes, not in the physical description. The rules should really allow for different types of soundtrack as well as different types of sound to be mentioned in the main section on physical description. Different types of soundtrack include OPT (optical sound track which may be separate from SEPOPT or combined with COMOPT the picture track) and MAG (magnetic sound which may also be separate SEPMAG or combined COMMAG). The physical description also includes a note to indicate if the film is monochrome, sepia or colour and finally the width of the film is given in millimetres. It may be necessary to extend the colour description for film today to indicate the particular colour system used to assist the film editor in deciding which pieces of film can be edited together and reused. A note on whether the particular film is a colour original or a print from colour or in separation negative or internegative form is needed.

Further rules deal with series and notes including extensions of the physical description, changes of title and related or source material which can be consulted. Production and performance (cast) credits for motion pictures are dealt with although no abbreviations are cited for the various functions, i.e. producer, director, etc. Rules for compiling summaries are suggested which provide much useful guidance concerning the need for accuracy and objectivity in compiling this section of the card. Summaries should not be confused with evaluations. They describe the contents of the film as objectively and concisely as possible while evaluations give an indication of the type of audience and the relative usefulness of the film.

Rules for continuities include collected series, serials and newsreels. The Library of Congress Rules do not consider stockshots or newsfilms as such and give only one specific rule for newsreels. They recommend the use of an open entry using the latest title, e.g. Industry on Parade. No. 1. This rule cannot be applied to newsfilm with its subject interest and is designed rather for a general film library which contains only a small proportion of newsreels. The rules are primarily applicable to libraries which hold complete film where most of the film can be entered by title.

Unesco Rules, 1956. These rules were drawn up for international usage and they endeavour to cover several aspects of the cataloguing of film. The rules are divided into three main sections, and each of them attempts to standardise one aspect: The *descriptive* catalogue, *appraisal* entries, and *availability* of entries.

Of these rules, the standardisation of descriptive catalogue entries is the most important in the present context. The appraisal or evaluation of entries is best left to the user with the aid of a shotlist or summary of the contents to indicate further detail. The standardisation of the availability of film is also less important today because of the considerable difficulties in itemising short films or stock material for example. An international index or union catalogue of film can give only a general idea of the extent of short film collections by indicating the subject areas covered, and leave detailed research to the individual enquirer.

The Unesco rules were intended to be applicable to both individual film collections and in a wider context to national catalogues of film produced in each country. In order to give these catalogues wide acceptance and make them useful internationally the Unesco rules consider the format and layout of cards in greater detail than most of the other rules considered. Several examples are given of different layout for different purposes and types of film. Four types of card are envisaged for each film, a descriptive catalogue card, an evaluation card, an international availability card and a national availability card. The different format and layout required are coded and rules devised to cover each type. The cards for national and international availability are ambitious in coverage and it is doubtful if for even a small proportion of the films such full details can be supplied on demand. So much film distribution is dependent on individual agreement and negotiation

which cannot easily be documented. The exchange and availability
of newsfilm for example depends on several agreements based in
some instances on the number of television receivers in a country
or area and in others on whether the prospective customer for
library film is already a 'serviced' customer of the newsfilm
agency. Such factors make a considerable difference to the terms
of availability and are difficult to chronicle in card form. The rules
for different types of cards are ambitious and in the event of
subsequent experience somewhat impractical.

Part II covers the actual rules for descriptive cataloguing. These
have been adapted for international use from the Library of
Congress Rules in the 1953 edition. They also take into account
the modifications suggested in the Rules for use in the cataloguing
department of the National Film Library in the 1952 edition.
Rules are quoted for entry under title or a supplied title in
brackets. The imprint includes the production company and date
of release. The physical description includes the length given in
running time, whether the film is sound or silent, in colour or
black and white, and the width of the film in millimetres as well as
an extension of the physical description for different copies, i.e.
varieties in the physical characteristics of the film, different gauges
or colour and black and white versions of the same film have to be
noted. Explanatory notes are also included in the rules, that is if
the film belongs to a series, changes of title, other language
versions and related material. Credits and cast should be listed and
a non-evaluative summary included in the entry. Tracings for
added entries should also be on the main entry. Again there are no
specific rules which apply to stockshot or newsfilm although
several can be adapted for use. Even the Unesco rule for
continuations does not specifically mention newsfilm as the
Library of Congress Rules do. Otherwise the two codes for
descriptive rules are very similar and the comments made in
discussing Library of Congress Rules apply equally here.

The Unesco rules are more extended than the others to include
sections of rules for recording evaluation and availability data.
Despite the shortcomings of evaluation and also the enforced
selection and restriction of items to be included in the national
and international catalogues the Unesco rules for availability and
evaluation cards form a useful guide for future compilers of
international catalogues.

One section of the rules is set aside to consider the assignment
of card reference numbers for each film catalogued. This is based
on a country code, the date of cataloguing and a sequential
reference number for the film. e.g. USA—67—1249 indicates a film

catalogued in the USA in 1967 number 1249. This is an attempt to do for film on an international scale what BNB does for books on a national scale. The plan is very ambitious and has several pitfalls, but is worth some consideration. The main difficulties lie with the date and the number. The date is that of cataloguing rather than release or event and may cause confusion, and the number will be independent of the finding number for the film used by the library storing that film. The number would have to be allocated after cataloguing by the central bureau while the originating library would need its own numbering system to locate the film for its own purposes The library will have to include the international number on its own catalogue cards or provide a key to match international and library numbers to deal with enquiries which come from the users of the larger catalogue.

Envisaging the larger catalogue being run by a central bureau the Unesco rules also provide a section of rules for the completion of the data sheet this bureau will use to compile the catalogue. The data sheet will be completed by the originating library.

Regrettably the Unesco rules, because of their general nature and ambitious coverage, have not been widely adopted, certainly not in the international sense aimed at. Libraries have tended to use rules drawn up nationally rather than for international usage.

Aslib Film Production Librarians Rules, 1963. These are the most recent rules, aimed at specialist film libraries, drawn up and published in the UK. They were designed by the Aslib Film Production Librarians committee which consisted of members from several different types of film libraries and as a result the rules take account of more types of film libraries than others have done in the past. For example the first section deals with complete films and these rules can be applied to feature production, archive and documentary film libraries. A useful section is included on newsfilm which emphasises the essential difference in treatment required for newsfilm. A third section entitled 'picture material other than complete films' is aimed to assist the library which specialises in extracts or stockshots. A further section is devoted to sound material associated with film and its special problems. Additional sections include rules or suggestions for added entries, especially the form of name selected and lists of definitions and abbreviations used in working with film.

The section devoted to complete films considers the main entry for a film to be the title as in the other rules mentioned, but suggests that the title cited is the original release title in the language of origin. This follows the National Film Archive rule, but it is not always the most familiar title of a film and may present difficulties for the small film libraries. Additionally the original release title may have changed subsequently and the film becomes better known by the later title. Although these two sections of the rule allow for reference from other titles, the main rule itself needs further consideration and amendment in the light of experience in small general film libraries. Useful rules are included at this point for transcription of the title and dealing with alternative titles.

In the production statement for feature films the sponsor is mentioned, as well as the production company and the credits and cast. The imprint as it is normally understood is here divided between three rules, production statement, country of origin and date. All the elements exist the Aslib Film Production Librarians rules, but the arrangement is often different from other codes. The country of origin is taken to be that of the original producing company and the date is the year of first release in the country of origin.

The collation includes the usual elements of gauge, material or form, and length. In the Aslib Rules the length is given in feet rather than running time as suggested by many of the other rules. This makes it easier to include other types of film in the same catalogue when the length can be cited uniformly. Rules for summaries and notes to expand the main entry are also included. A separate rule for compilation films expands the rules for summaries and analytical entries to suit the particular case. Other rules deal with continuations, that is serials, series and magazine type film, and rules are attached for some specialised types of short film including trailers and commercials. These are the only rules to deal with commercials, a developing phenomena on television as well as in the cinema. Commercials are entered under the name of the advertiser, not the title, because many commercials have no specific title.

Section two of the rules deals with newsfilms and this makes these rules of more relevance to newsfilm libraries than any of the others cited. The Aslib Rules are the only ones which attempt to cope with newsfilm as such. Others may deal with newsreels but the two types of film require different treatment and a separate set of basic rules is needed. Even so the Aslib rules do not solve all the problems. The choice of entry is taken to be that of a continuation with an alternative rule for archive purposes. The rule for continuations indicates that the main entry for newsfilm could be a shotlist, commentary or contents sheet and cards prepared from this material should be filed serially in chronological order. The alternative rule for archive purposes indicates that each event is to be regarded as a separate item and filed chronologically under the exact date of the event. In newsfilm libraries these two rules are in effect combined: the entry is made under the date of event and filed by one of the principal features, such as the country of origin or event and the serial number, as in the country and date file. Other rules for newsfilms indicate that mention has to be made of the location number, production statement, collation, summary and added entries. Most of the information in these sections can be taken from the production statement or shotlist but if these are not compiled viewing the film will provide the necessary information.

A useful section of the rules deals with picture material other than complete films. This is especially helpful for stockshot libraries and refers to such items as key numbers and their organisation. This, together with the sections on sound material, is one more indication of the wide application of the Aslib rules to specialist film libraries. Section III itemises the special considerations needed for this type of picture material, for example the main entry is made under subject, not title, the description of the action is given in camera treatment or type of shot and a précis of the content. Key numbers are used to locate the material in the original negative and these key numbers are different from any of the other numbers so far discussed and need separate consideration and treatment. Other rules are similar to these for other types of film and cover the source of material and the date of production.

Rules are also devoted to the cataloguing of sound material, both for sound effects and dubbing tracks. These are designed for special libraries concerned primarily with sound or those in which sound effects assume an importance equal to or greater than the film material.

The next section of the rules is concerned with added entries and is largely based on the normal cataloguing codes, such as the Anglo-American code, for different forms of name entry including how to enter names with prefixes and compound surnames as well as considering entry under forenames, pseudonyms, etc. The rules for entry of foreign names are useful for newsfilm work especially Oriental, Arabic and Indic names.

A further section deals with the standardisation of capitalisation, punctuation and the use of figures. Most of these rules are based on conventional cataloguing codes, but it is useful to publish them in the specialised codes for materials other than books.

A large section is devoted to definitions of terms used in the film industry and by film libraries, and a further section deals with standard abbreviations. Again it is useful to have all this information drawn together in the one source code.

The Aslib Film Production Librarians code is the one most used by film libraries in the UK for reference and it is hoped that it has achieved some standardisation in the field by its adoption. The code should be considered by anyone starting a film library today and many established film libraries have tried to re-organise parts of their catalogues in accordance with the rules suggested by the code.

It is the most specific code devised for film libraries in the UK and has more relevance to the current situation than most of the other codes devised.

In recent years film librarians and indeed conventional book librarians have been broadening their interests to take in all the carriers of information, not specifically books or films, but a combination of the two together with gramophone records, audio and videotape as well as other sources. The trend today is therefore away from codes designed for one medium alone to those designed to accommodate as many as exist. This change in interest and emphasis is to be encouraged, but there are still libraries which specialise in one medium and therefore require cataloguing rules for this speciality.

The 'ideal' set of rules has not been achieved for specialist film libraries and the film librarians interest should not be over-shadowed by the newer audio-visual interests. Rules for multimedia will be more effective if based on a consideration of rules for the several separate media rather than on more general unspecific cataloguing rules. In this way the requirements for each medium should be realised rather than extending the book cataloguing rules to take in other media without proper fore-thought.

This last method will result in some woolly rules which are so general as to make practical application impossible.

The Anglo-American Code. These rules are closely related to the Library of Congress rules, and the rules for motion pictures and filmstrips are included in the section relating to non-book materials. The AA code is a general cataloguing code intended to be applicable to all media, but based firmly on book cataloguing principles at present. Parts I and II of the code cover the choice of main heading and descriptive cataloguing of an item and a statement at the beginning of Part III implies that these rules are applicable to non-book materials unless specifically contravened by the stated rules in Part III. The media covered in Part III are widely different in type and appearance as well as their usage and control and need separate consideration. The section on motion pictures and filmstrips opens with notes taken directly from the Library of Congress rules noting the special attributes of film, the need to limit access to the material and rely on more detailed cataloguing, the difficulties of determining an 'author' for film and the consequent entry under title and the uses of secondary sources.

The rules are divided into Entry and Description following the layout of the main body of the code. Under Entry, rules for title entry are given together with rules for added entries. These added entries include the director, distributor, production company, alternative titles etc. While it is common to include alternative titles in added entries, distributors and production companies may well be found unhelpful as additional headings because so many titles will appear under the heading. It is less helpful to know which titles a distributor deals with, than to know which distributor deals with a particular title. The main entry of the film, under title, will give the information required and the entry under distributor will probably never be used.

Under the descriptive part of the entry, rules are given for including the production company, the distributor and the date of release. The physical description includes the length in running time as in the Library of Congress, not footage as in the Aslib rules, the type of sound and form of film material and the width. A series statement is inserted where necessary and provision is made for notes or expansions of the information given in other parts of the entry. The credits and cast are listed, and rules for summaries are included, again based directly on the Library of Congress rules. The rule for continuations is designed to include collected series and newsreels, but once again no mention is made of the more specialised types of film including newsfilm, as opposed to newsreels, stockshots and commercials.

These rules are disappointingly unenterprising in that they have been transferred with very few alterations and no major amendments from the Library of Congress rules of 1958. The criticisms levelled at the Library of Congress rules apply equally to the AA code and the compilers do not begin to formulate adequate rules for the cataloguing of newsfilm. Cataloguing any film is highly specialised and before attempting to formulate a set of rules covering all media, the rules for each medium should be advanced and standardised. Only when adequate rules exist for the control and retrieval of material in each medium should an overall code of rules be contemplated. The problems of cataloguing which face film librarians are sufficiently different from those of book librarians to warrant separate consideration. A new set of cataloguing rules is required for the film librarian based on the Aslib FPL model rather than the AA model, that is a code which covers the sort of material to be found in a film library and which recognises the essential difference between films and books. The main sections of the codes will remain similar, including a section to consider the main entry or choice of heading and a section to cover descriptive cataloguing but, to save confusion, the codes for books and films should be kept separate at this stage until the rules for film are more highly developed. A correlation can be attempted later when greater standardisation is achieved in the film libraries, but until then separate codes are required. There are areas in which it is sensible for film cataloguing rules to follow those already worked out for books, e.g. the citing of names in a heading, but it is simpler to include such rules in both codes rather than try to refer the film cataloguer back to the book catalogue codes for many of the necessary rules. Film and book codes should both aim to be independent and self-sufficient.

A co-operative venture is currently in final process of drawing up a set of rules for multi media which it is hoped to present to the Anglo-American cataloguing committee for ratification in place of the current Part III. At the time of writing the Library Association Media Cataloguing Rules committee in the UK had arrived at a set of draft rules for presentation to other bodies such as the main Library Association Cataloguing Rules committee and the Canadian Library Association, the American Library Association and the Library of Congress. If after consideration agreement on the new set of rules is reached it is hoped to replace the present Part III of AACR with this more relevant set of rules. However this will not solve the film librarian's problems in entirety. The rules are specifically being formulated in response to the needs of 'multi media collections in general libraries and resource centres'. It is hoped that they can be adapted to the needs of specialised institutions and single medium collections, but it may prove difficult for film libraries to extract the necessary information from the other detail. Of necessity certain compromises have to be made in designing a set of rules for multi media collections; the media are not similar and cannot all be treated in exactly the same way. The case still remains for a set of rules specific to film collections for film librarians.

AUTHORITY FILE

Even when he works from an existing code of rules, the

cataloguer has to take further decisions independently. It may be necessary to adapt or modify the code in certain areas to deal with a particular problem arising in one library. These decisions, together with decisions on indexing and classification, should be entered in a central file for use by the cataloguing staff, and this file should be kept separate from the staff manual which applies to the working procedures of all staff. To include the more specialised decisions of cataloguing and classification in this file would make it a bulky and unwieldy document. General cataloguing procedures and the method of working go into the staff manual but the more detailed decisions are reserved for the authority file.

All headings and references in the indexes are entered and a note is made of the ways in which the headings are used, that is what is included and which details are omitted. The file can be kept on ordinary 5 x 3in cards or in a loose leaf binder, although the card file is the more successful method and can be expanded more easily. Cataloguing rules can be amended in the printed publication, but one copy should be kept for this purpose and all decisions recorded in this central copy. Confusion will result if several copies with conflicting decisions are allowed to exist.

USER'S GUIDE

The authority file is reserved for the use of cataloguing staff, but the user also requires a guide to the catalogues — usually a shortened or simplified version of the code of practice to enable the user to approach the catalogue intelligently. The user's guide should be kept as simple and straightforward as possible. It should include notes on the layout of the catalogue, which indexes exist, how to approach a subject or location by the quickest route and how to use the subject indexes and the system of references. There should also be a key to the subject catalogue if it is a classified catalogue or a list of major subject headings. The latter is sometimes unnecessary when the user is at the catalogue and can as easily look at the heading in the catalogue as on a list of subject headings.

The key to a classified catalogue or one based on a notational system is necessary because of the unfamiliar nature of the notation. The user needs a key before he can approach the subject he requires. Again the classified key for the user should be part of the subject index and not confused with the authority file for the staff. Classified keys can be entered on catalogue cards and filed as part of the subject index or they could be entered on a visible index placed near the subject catalogue. A list of major subject headings could also be displayed on a visible index.

STAFF MANUAL

The staff manual is a record of the working procedures in force throughout the library. It includes notes on how each job is done in the library, that is the practical routines, and the order in which the jobs are done to achieve maximum efficiency.

The staff manual is designed for the guidance of the people in particular posts, and it also serves to inform all members of the library staff should they change jobs either through promotion or on a rota system. It will also serve to illustrate the sequence of jobs to be done in the library and why particular tasks are essential to the smooth running of other departments. The manual should be sufficiently detailed to enable a new member of staff to understand the principles of the work and be able to carry them out effectively. The manual becomes a code of practice and while additional training should not be dispensed with the instructions given should be explicit enough to allow any job to continue when staff members change or are away for some reason.

A staff manual in a film library has to take account of the intake and accessioning of film and related material, the shotlisting of film, the principles of selection and the practical routines, cataloguing and indexing, storage of film, research procedures, withdrawal of film for reuse, preparation of film for the laboratories and also of the attendant paperwork for accounting and contractual departments. The manual changes continually as newer, more efficient methods of work are found or as new problems have to be solved. It is therefore useful to maintain the code in loose leaf typewritten form.

8

INFORMATION RETRIEVAL

HAVING CATALOGUED the description of an item or film the next step is to design a system whereby the material required can be found or retrieved from the store. An entry in a catalogue consists of two parts, the description and the heading. The description informs the user of the relevance of an item, but the heading denoting subject or other necessary finding device becomes the most important part of the entry for retrieving relevant descriptions.

Information retrieval includes varied forms of cataloguing, indexing, classification and non-conventional forms of data retrieval. Items are labelled with some device which when turned up in a catalogue reveals the items required. The labelling presents difficulties because a label has to be understood by both searcher and indexer. A searcher has to be aware of the label an indexer has used for a particular item and the relative success or failure of a system can be judged by the ease with which it can be used.

Classification schemes do not solve all information retrieval problems in many film libraries. Classification plays only a small part if the definition is restricted to an arrangement of subjects according to a predetermined classification scheme. While classification assists with the retrieval of subjects, additional indexes are required to deal with other information which does not lend itself to classification. For example, specific credit indexes, e.g. actors, directors etc., geographical locations, especially where these are used for subheadings rather than the main heading, personalities, dates of events.

Indexing might be a better word for information retrieval in film libraries. Unfortunately, apart from classification, definitions of other types of information retrieval do not distinguish them clearly from each other. Indexing and cataloguing can be used synonymously in some circumstances and yet mean totally different things to different people. Cataloguing has sometimes been used to refer to the description of complete units and indexing to refer to parts of larger entities. This is not a

149

particularly clear distinction when one considers stockshots or short newsfilm sequences. With a short sequence a description of the whole is still required as if it was a complete unit — it will probably be reused as if it was complete — and yet it may be referred to as a part of a more complete film. For the purposes of the present discussion however it may be helpful to consider cataloguing as the description of the item and the formulation of the entry, and indexing as the labelling of the entries for retrieval purposes. A catalogue and an index can be used synonymously in film work as they both refer to the headings and descriptions used in finding the items, although catalogue does indicate the more complete unit and index may simply refer to a shortened entry or key to a more detailed catalogue.

WHAT TO INDEX

Film is often complex in content. Even feature films may contain a series of separate sequences only loosely linked together by one or more themes. In addition the film may have been shot in several locations, on different dates and may contain shots of several personalities involved in the main story. The film can be indexed in its entirety or can be broken down into specific sequences which have an interest of their own. The cataloguer can index the whole film, separate sequences, individual shots.

Whole film. This means indexing the central theme or subject content of the entire film. It is useful to have such an entry in the subject index for many films, but it gives an inadequate idea of the individual parts of a film which may be required on their own. Even when the whole of an information film is indexed, added entries are required for locations, personalities and any other notable features. If indexing is restricted to the whole film it creates very general subject headings which may not assist the user in finding the short sequences he requires as illustration.

Separate sequences. Film is often reused for purposes other than those for which it was shot. Short sequences featuring a location, personality or particular process or occurrence may be needed to illustrate a new film which is being compiled. Each sequence in the original film could be reused in different ways. In order to allow for flexibility in reuse the potential user has to be informed about each separate sequence in the original film.

Therefore each sequence is indexed separately under appropriate subject headings. Additionally all locations and personalities are indexed.

In practice it is usual in information film libraries to index under both the whole film and the individual sequences. Some films are short but designed to illustrate a particular event. The user may need to use the whole of this event to illustrate his point, but equally he may be interested not in the event itself but in one of its constituents. The film index should be designed to satisfy both these approaches.

Individual shots. Film is made up of many individual shots welded into sequences or moving pictures. When the indexer has to decide whether to catalogue these individual shots the reuse of the film has to be taken into account. Short sequences can be reused, but very short shots cannot usually be used effectively. They become a meaningless flash on the screen. Occasionally a short shot can be reduced to a still frame held for a period of time, but the quality of a still frame, especially of 16mm film, is not particularly good and if a still is required it is usually better to use a photograph. This argument does not apply to stockshot libraries where the quality is necessarily higher than other 16mm film and individual shots are retained. Additionally in stockshot libraries the length of a shot is one of the useful determining factors in its selection. A longer shot of an item will be selected against a short shot of equal quality.

A shot in film is not usually indexed if it is shorter than 5ft of 16mm. This allows for a slight loss of length in re-editing and still allows the editor time to make his point. Decisions on length of shot to index are particularly relevant to locations or buildings. Subjects are usually of sufficient length not to bring the question up, and personalities may be treated differently as a matter of policy. Individual shots as a general rule are not indexed minutely except where they are of exceptional interest or rarity. This does mean relying on the observation and opinions of the indexer, but certain basic principles can be laid down in the department for guidance.

INDEX ACCORDING TO NEEDS OF USER

Film can be indexed in several different ways according to the needs of the user. If a particular actor or personality is required, all available pieces of film containing that personality should be retrieved from the same point in the catalogues. Similarly for a particular location, street or town, all shots should be indexed in the one place. If subjects are required they should be available in as minute detail or general description as the user requires. A good indexing system for film takes account of the sort of material it is storing information about, the types of questions the user has asked or can be expected to put to the indexes, and the most efficient and quickest way such questions can be answered.

As many entries as are required to cover all aspects of a film should be provided although some limitations may be placed on the systems by economics and space.

Some systems require more entries than others and considerations such as the conservation of time and space have to be taken into account when deciding the particular system to be used. It may be thought better to use more space for the catalogues, have more added entries and make the subject references more specific in order to save search time if fast retrieval of one or two items is required rather than providing browsing facilities under more general headings. Past experiences of the systems offered and working with similar collections of material are important guides to selecting suitable indexing systems.

ATTRIBUTES OF EFFICIENT INDEXING SYSTEMS

Indexing systems for film should:
1. Be accessible and easy to use.
2. Provide fast retrieval.
3. Expand to take new subjects or other index headings within the present framework of the index.
4. Be flexible.
5. Include an adequate system of references.
6. Use specific entries over a wide subject area rather than deep analysis of subjects over a narrow field of interest. This is especially relevant to information and documentary material. Research film on the other hand requires a deep analysis in a narrow field and stockshots require deep analysis over a wide subject field.

In order to achieve these ends it is generally necessary to have several indexes to the film rather than one very large dictionary catalogue. It is, of course, only feasible to have a dictionary catalogue when all headings are alphabetical. Therefore a system which includes a classified catalogue for subjects would have at least two indexes; one dictionary for alphabetical arrangement of headings and one classified for the subject index. In film libraries where production credits prove useful for finding material all personal names can be combined in one catalogue with a designation attached to indicate the work of the person concerned.

  e.g. CARSON, Jack, *cameraman*

    CARSON, Jack, *actor*

Production credits are necessary in all feature and documentary libraries, but are not usually necessary for newsfilm agencies where all rights in production and camera work are vested in the parent company. Newsfilm libraries separate indexes on a different basis and this is done in order to answer certain types of enquiry. Aspects of a newsfilm which assume an importance include the country the film was shot in as well as the more specific geographical location such as the town or street or building, the date of the film, the main subject of the film and any subsidiary subjects and the personalities involved. It may be convenient to combine some of these factors into the same index, such as the country and geographical location, or the country and date of the film if this can be done without difficulty, but it may be as convenient to separate the indexes to allow ease of access and straightforward filing.

INDEXES FOR FEATURE AND DOCUMENTARY FILM LIBRARIES

The prime function of feature and documentary film indexes is to answer questions such as the title of the film, credits for directors, actors, cameramen, music composition, arrangement and performance, date indexes for archival newsfilm, as well as subject indexes for all documentary film. Entertainment feature films are less likely to require subject indexing than other types and the title index may suffice to retrieve the film. However if a subject index is already established in the library for other types of film there may be occasion to include any notable sequences from feature film in the subject index.

It will be noted from the list of indexes needed that all except the subject index are *name* indexes. The actual organisation of these indexes is often a matter of convenience rather than set rulings. If the library is a specialist one in which the user comes in to find out which films were directed or shot by certain people, it may be easier to have separate indexes for directors or cameramen. There is one small difficulty here in that many cameramen become directors and more usually many actors become directors and may work in both capacities on one film. This would mean the duplication of entries in separate indexes for the same person, but it will be up to the indexer to decide whether separation of the indexes is more convenient than trying to include all names in a single index.

If all film is referred to by title in the library, it is best to keep the title index separate rather than try to include it in the name index and so produce a cumbersome tool which would be difficult to use.

INDEXES FOR DISTRIBUTION FILM LIBRARIES

Distribution film libraries need indexes for title, name indexes for production and performance credits, an index for the production company, a numerical index for film numbers and a subject index for documentary material.

The title index is straightforward. The name index for credits need not be as detailed as other film libraries. The index for production company is important to distribution libraries mainly as an internal finding device and also to indicate the volume of material being handled for each of the production companies being serviced by the distribution library. Production company index is seldom relevant to other types of film library where the index would be less informative than the title index and more difficult to retrieve from because the user would have to be aware of the production company in order to find the film.

The film number or numerical index is essential for distribution and accounting purposes where each title is given a number indicative of the type of film and the location within the library. Any large distribution library finds it easier to manipulate film numbers than titles, especially in machine retrieval systems. The subject index in distribution libraries is of a general broad subject type.

The film is handled and viewed in its entirety, cannot be cut or reused for purposes other than viewing and therefore it is the general, overall subject which is important, not the individual sequences.

INDEXES FOR EDUCATIONAL FILM LIBRARIES, NATIONAL AND OTHER CATALOGUES

Educational film libraries are similar to distribution libraries in the type of index required except for the production company, which is unnecessary. If the library is of a hire type the indexing follows much the same pattern, although subject indexing may well become more detailed to suit the needs of the user.

National and other catalogues of film have to index other

aspects of the film, although the subject index for non-feature material is the most important entry in the catalogue. The films are indexed complete, both general and specific subject headings being used where appropriate. Where there is more than one subject to a film the film may be included under one or more subject headings, but economy in the number of entries is an important factor and the indexer has to make decisions constantly on how many subjects to include for each film. Name indexes are used for title of film, directors and other contributors and distributors are normally appended in a separate list giving details of addresses, etc. The distributor or availability of the film should always be included in the main entries of a national catalogue and a list of addresses is essential for convenience of use.

INDEXES FOR NEWSFILM LIBRARIES

Newsfilm libraries may resort to different types of index to answer basic user questions. For example the four most basic questions asked result in these four indexes.

When did it happen? . . .	Country and Date
Where did it happen? . . .	Location
What happened? . . .	Subject
Who was there? . . .	Personality

Country and Date Index. This gives the actual date of the event or when the film was shot. A listing of film according to date is not however particularly informative on its own and as the searcher will usually know where an event occurred as well as the date on which it occurred the date has been combined with the country of origin. The country also serves as an additional aid because a searcher may know only an approximate date for an event. If he then had to look through all the newsfilm for two or three weeks without any further breakdown of the entries he would be consulting a large number of entries which would take considerable time. If on the other hand there is an initial breakdown into country and then the entries are filed by date there are fewer to look through.

The date referred to in this index is the date on which the film was taken, and must not be confused with the date of transmission, which might be several days after the date of event.

Date of transmission is used to file the film in television libraries, but it does not assist the independent researcher who is looking for a particular event and not the date when it was televised.

If several films are taken on the same day in any one country the entries for that date can be filed in accession number order.

If the film is a compilation shot in several countries, an entry can be filed in each country with the inclusive dates of release of the original items. This is more useful to the researcher looking for a general coverage than trying to break down the shotlist into separate countries and trying to determine all the dates necessary to refer the user to the country in which the city or town occurs, although a gazetteer kept close to the index for reference purposes should solve most of the problems. 'See also' references are rare in the locations index although they may be of the type quoted previously, referring the user from an old term to the new or vice versa. e.g. Eire, Dublin before 1922. See Ireland, Dublin.

Filing is alphabetical by country, then within a country by state or county if used and next by town or village. All the lines in the headings are used and when there are several cards under the last heading the card can be filed by production number.

e.g. USA
      TEXAS
      HOUSTON
      ASTRODOME

File by USA then all the Texas cards together, all the Houston cards and finally all the Texas, Houston, Astrodome cards filed by production number.

Locations. All locations are indexed and there may well be more than one location card for any one story. Locations are sometimes not very helpful for the researcher especially when they are unspecific, e.g. England, London becomes a large file of uninformative entries within a short time. But one cannot omit entries for all large cities, as Lebanon, Beirut, for example, will have few entries and it will be important to know that the film was shot in the city rather than in the mountain region of Lebanon. It is difficult to know where to draw the line in making a decision such as this and probably the only way to resolve the problem is to be as specific as possible in quoting locations in large cities, e.g. England, London, Regent Street rather than England, London.

Personalities. All identifiable personalities who appear on the film are entered in the index. This ignores the length of shot and the usual reuseability criteria of subject and location. No matter how long or short the sequence which shows a personality is, it should be indexed under that person. It is important for future biographies and compilation films to have all records of a personality available.

NAME INDEXES

In any indexing system for film the name indexes assume importance and before going on to discuss subject indexing one or two further points about name indexes generally should be considered. The names indexed include production and performance credits as well as the newsfilm personalities previously mentioned. As many production and performance credits as are necessary or likely to be searched for are included in the name indexes, either in separate indexes according to function or all together in one larger index. Many libraries index only the director, perhaps cameraman and the main actors or contributors. Others, for example the film archives, include as many names as feasible, especially if the user is likely to want to trace the career of a particular person. Much of the information for these indexes is obtained from the film itself or accompanying data, such as the synopsis and catalogue entry prepared by the cataloguer.

In newsfilm libraries the situation is slightly different in that all personalities who appear on the film should be indexed. To do this, the shotlists have to be searched thoroughly for all mention of people involved. The shotlister also has to be aware of all likely personalities at a particular event and do a detailed matching of the expected and filmed personalities.

This applies to all film in a collection and while recent personalities and events may be easier to recognise and match, the older the film the more difficult the task becomes. A shotlister or indexer working from the film has to do considerable research before approaching the indexing in order to recognise the personalities who appear on film, both expected and unexpected. This recognition probably comes from familiarity with the period and subject involved and is an imprecise quality to look for in a good shotlister. It comes from experience and training rather than any innate ability.

In any film library once the main principle of entering each name involved has been accepted the problems of how to enter these names in the index are encountered. The problems are in large part the same as those for citing personal (author) names in a more conventional catalogue. Personalities are usually entered under the family name in capitals followed by the Christian or forenames in lower case. If the forenames cannot be found the surname is used and a note is made in brackets of what the person does or what office he holds and the country he comes from.

Sometimes a film may be about a particular person but he does not appear on the film. In these cases the personality is noted in brackets to indicate that he does not appear.

In selecting the part of the name to use as a heading, standard codes are used to achieve some uniformity of reference and help the cataloguer to decide on a heading in the case of difficult names. If standardisation is not aimed for, the same personality may be filed under two or more places in the index, with no connection between the two different names. In these cases information will be lost.

The standard codes include the Anglo American Cataloguing Rules, and the Aslib Film Production Librarians Cataloguing Rules for Use in Film Libraries. The latter code is based on the wider standard AA code which covers other media as well as film. The citing of authors according to the AA code and personalities is not sufficiently different to warrant any new codes being formulated, but the AA code will help in deciding on the form of name and the choice of main heading in the case of difficult names.

New indexes in film libraries are likely to have a greater proportion of foreign names than author indexes in many book libraries. This is especially the case in newsfilm libraries where world coverage is given and personalities for Oriental and Arabic areas are frequently in the news. The main difficulties are encountered in dealing with these Oriental, Arabic and Indic names with several additional problems of transliteration among the Cyrillic languages. For example Russian personal names are not necessarily transliterated in the same way by different countries and a close watch has to be kept on these names to ensure that the name transliterated into a foreign language is recognised as the same name transliterated into English. If a code is followed closely and references are carefully prepared and inserted many problems can be solved even though it does mean the researcher looking in two places in the index. At least the second place he refers to will have all the entries he requires. Certain names, particularly the Arabic, have become so well known by the last part of their name that reference to any other part is seldom made and it is better to use the well known name to file under. e.g. NASSER, Gamal Abdel, not GAMAL ABDEL NASSER.

Other normal difficulties in citing personal names include the use of soubriquets or pseudonyms. Most actors do not appear under their own name, but it is of little relevance to enter the actor under his real name even if this is known. The form of name used in the performance credit should be the one used in the index as this is normally the best known name. In film work, nicknames are commonplace and the cataloguer has to decide when it is better to enter this nickname, or when a reference from the nickname will suffice. e.g. 'Che' Guevara, El Greco, Cassius Clay or Muhammad Ali. Many personalities in the recent television age are known only by their 'adopted' names and in these cases it is probably most useful to use these adopted names for the entries on the grounds of speed of reference.

FILING AND REFERENCE IN ALPHABETICAL INDEXES

Before going on to discuss subject indexing one or two further points about the name, location and other alphabetically arranged indexes should be made. It will be found in most film libraries that both alphabetical (name) and subject indexes are essential. Each type of index brings its own problem of citing and cross reference for assistance to retrieval.

Filing by date order. Except in the case of archive newsfilm, which can be filed in order of date of event, it is more usual to combine the date with some other aspect of the film, for example, country of origin. In practice it is found that in filing by date of event and country of origin the entries are filed in accessions number order. But if the exact date of the event is quoted this should be used to file the entry within the country of origin. Where several events occurred on the same date, the production or accessions number is the next element used to file the entry. Filing alphabetically by 'title' within a date has no relevance and should not be attempted for newsfilm.

The country of origin or event is filed alphabetically but one or two points are worth noting.

The use of initials for countries can be time saving at the input stage, it will save considerable typing of headings if USA and USSR are used instead of United States of America etc. Also in order to bring certain neighbouring or divided countries together the country is quoted first and then the qualifying term in brackets afterwards. e.g. GERMANY (East), GERMANY (West), KOREA (North), KOREA (South).

Country cross references. In any index a certain amount of cross referencing is necessary to refer the user from the term he may use to the term under which the entry has been filed. With countries this is usually a matter of referring the user from an old name, or an anglicised name, or a reversed name to the one used in the index. e.g. Siam *see* Thailand; South Korea *see* Korea (South);

Persia *see* Iran. If the index spans a period of years reference will have to be made from names by which a country was formerly known to those under which it is filed today. In these cases some *See also* type references will be necessary. Thus entries made under the former name are filed as such and those made under the later name are filed under this name with a reference after the last entry of one and before the first entry of the other.

e.g. IRELAND

After 1922 *See*	EIRE
	NORTHERN IRELAND
EIRE before 1922 *See*	IRELAND
GERMANY after 1946 *See*	GERMANY (East)
	GERMANY (West)

GERMANY (West) before 1946 *See*   GERMANY

The two types of reference in common use for library indexes, are the *see* reference which refers the reader from a term not used to the preferred term, and a *see also* reference which refers the user from one term under which entries are filed to other connected or related terms under which entries which may be of further interest are filed.

Filing by location. In stockshot and newsfilm libraries particularly filing by location is important. This may be done in the subject index by means of a classification number, but it can also be done alphabetically.

The locations file can be broken down into countries and then towns or cities and then buildings or streets. This results in a three line heading for ease of reference. It could be quoted on one line, but this is not an easy finding device. The eye of the user can pick up a reference if it is in the same place each time more quickly than if he has to scan across a page searching for the reference. Larger countries can be further broken down by county or state, but again this should not require too detailed a knowledge of the areas in other countries. Many users can cope with English location by county and American locations by states but beyond these two knowledge is hazy. In order to make the England and American files easier and quicker to consult, the county or state is mentioned.

e.g. ENGLAND   USA
      DURHAM   ILLINOIS
      SUNDERLAND   CHICAGO

This also means that towns of the same name are separated in their correct location and are less likely to be confused in retrieval.

More than one entry may be advisable for any one town, for

instance if the film was shot in both the town and a specific location within that town two entries should be made out. This is especially relevant if there are good exterior and interior shots of the building concerned which may be needed later as illustration. The main criteria in deciding whether to use a location entry is the further use envisaged for such an item. If the location is an important feature of the event it will be mentioned; if the shots of the location are long and detailed enough to serve for reuse as location shots then they should be entered in the index.

The location index can be combined with the country and date, but this is a further breakdown and it may be beyond the memory of the searcher to know exactly where an event occurred, especially if it is a very specific location. A combination of the two indexes would present additional filing problems, and would probably be less helpful and certainly slower to consult than the two separate indices.

Location cross-references. Again simple cross references will be required from the unused name of a country to the used name and from the reversed names like East Germany etc. In addition reference will be needed from a town in USA or England to the state or county heading in case the user is unaware of these. It may even be necessary to refer the user to the country in which the city or town occurs, although a gazetteer kept close to the index for reference purposes should solve most of the problems. *See also* references are rare in the locations index although they may be of the type quoted previously referring the user from an old term to the new or vice versa. e.g. Eire, Dublin before 1922 *see* Ireland, Dublin.

Filing by name. This index can present complex filing problems. The different ways of citing names have to be allowed for. Considerations such as the Western usage or surnames as last names, Spanish use of the names of both parents as surnames, Oriental use of the main name first and the use of titles and designations of rank as the first part of the name all have to be taken into account.

Once the form of name is decided, the filing principle of letter by letter arrangement will be found the most useful in this index. Letter by letter arrangement will assist in solving awkward problems in the filing of personal names, it is more straightforward and easier for the user and filer to understand when all the different forms of personal names are taken into account. For

example names with prefixes are filed as if they were one word:
   DE FREITAS
   DELACROIX
   D'OLIVIERA
   DE VALERA
Names which have been cited straight through like Chou en Lai
and Ahmadu Ahidjo are also filed as if they were one word.

Other standards are used in filing procedures. When the
forename alone has been used as the heading with Popes, Kings,
Princes of the blood, these are arranged before surname entries of
the same name.

Surnames alone or followed by a description are filed before the
same surname with initials or forenames, and the initials are filed
before forenames beginning with the same letter. Titles are
disregarded unless they are needed to distinguish otherwise
identical names. These are normal filing rules for any alphabetical
index.

Within a personal name the entries can be filed by title,
chronologically or by production number.

Name cross-references. The *see* reference is a very important tool
in this particular index. All names cited are entered under the
same part of the name, but it is essential that no matter which part
of the name or which name the user looks for, there is some
reference to the name which has been used in the index. These
references are all of the *see* reference type, referring from a
heading not used to the one preferred. References should be made
for names when they are first added to the index and any
subsequent references discovered later should also be included. *See
also* references should not be used extensively in this index,
although occasionally they may be necessary for groups or other
corporate 'personalities' whose members may later merit entries as
individuals, e.g.:

   the BEATLES *see also*   HARRISON, George
                            LENNON, John
                            McCARTNEY, Paul
                            STARR, Ringo

TYPES AND AIMS OF SUBJECT INDEXING

There are four main ways of dealing with a subject index: 1.
Classified. 2 Dictionary. 3. Alphabetico classed. 4 Mechanised.

The construction of subject indexes depends on whether the
arrangement is to be alphabetical or based on a scheme of
classification.

Both schemes have been used successfully in libraries of all kinds and an alphabetico classed scheme attempts to gain benefits from both types by using natural language in the choice of headings and arranging these headings into classes and divisions with subdivision when necessary.

Subject indexing aims to enable the searcher to locate information about something. Relevant material may well be found in films related to, but not the same as, the subject of the search itself. The index should be a network of terms which, by the use of indexing tools such as cross references, enables the user to enter the catalogue by one term and automatically have all other terms recalled or presented.

The classifier uses all information available to select subject headings or classifications and construct the index based on a study of the films themselves, synopses, shotlists, accompanying data and other reference material. Film titles alone are insufficient and misleading to try and index. Key Word in Context KWIC or KWOC indexes for example could never be based on film titles, only on an abstract written after viewing the whole film.

CLASSIFIED SUBJECT INDEXES

Classification is a division into groups which are then arranged in a definite sequence. Classification of information is the use of a predetermined scheme which sets out the logical pattern of subjects to reveal the general and specific in relation to one another. Classification schemes are usually based on a notation, either numerical or alphabetical or a combination of the two. Widely accepted schemes are normally devised by some central authority which is expert in classificatory method and has consulted subject specialists to assist in drawing up the scheme. Building a new system of classification is a formidable task, and it is difficult for any individual scheme to achieve wider application. Many librarians with special collections in need of classification face the problem that none of the general schemes can be recommended without considerable reserve and yet the compilation of a new scheme is difficult. A proliferation of small schemes is not necessarily useful because there is no standardisation across a wide enough field. Film covers the full range of most classification schemes if only in general terms. Some areas may be more heavily weighted than others, e.g. newsfilm needs a very detailed scheme for political activities, sports, riots, disasters etc. Research film may need only one section of a classification scheme for in-depth indexing.

A system in general use should be adapted whenever practicable. There is considerable need for national or international acceptance of standards in this area for any future amalgamation of records. There is a difficulty even here, because nationally we prefer Dewey for many schemes especially if it is hoped to associate with book classification through the British National Bibliography, while many specialised film libraries prefer UDC, including the National Film Archive, Film Centre, Royal Aircraft Establishment, BBC, Granada Television, BNFC etc. European and other international organisations based on Europe, such as Unesco, prefer UDC even if they only use UDC basic numbers and ignore all but the most elementary relationships. The United States on the other hand prefer the Library of Congress notations. One attempt to bring the two schemes together might be approached through the new Marc project which it is anticipated will be compatible with both LoC and BNB Dewey.

The purpose of the film library influences the system adopted and determines many modifications. For example the libraries may deal with similar subjects but have a different emphasis. The Imperial War Museum and the Royal Aircraft Establishment have an interest in aviation but IWM emphasises aerial warfare and RAE the technical aspects. The detail in sections of any accepted classification schemes would be different in the two libraries as a result. A film library with a general coverage which is not catering for one specialist type of user will classify the material in more uniform detail or generality because requests come for all facets of a subject. The choice between broad and close classification also depends on the purpose of the library, i.e. whether the subjects are arranged in classes and divisions (broad) or minute divisions under a class or division.

Some libraries have to build form classification into the system adopted. General film libraries may have to allow for different types of film, e.g. the British Film Institute expands the UDC number for film (791.4) by the use of auxiliaries to cover non fiction, newsfilms, documentary, propaganda, compilation, cartoon, experimental, television, etc. The basic numbers in the classification schemes are not altered by these means but the scheme can be adapted to suit the subject or medium being classified.

The main properties of a classification scheme are that it is:

1. Systematic, proceeding from the general to the particular.
2. As complete as possible and covers the whole field of its given subject.

3. Indicative of the relationships between subjects and permits classification from different points of view.
4. Explicit.
5. Practical in its notation. This should:
    (a) Show recognisable order
    (b) Be easily transferable in the mind to another record
    (c) Allow for intercalation of new subjects without disturbing the existing order.
6. Expansive and flexible in plan and use.
7. Supplied with an alphabetical index to the notation.
8. Published in a form which surveys the field covered by the system.

All of these points and aims are easier to accomplish in known and tested schemes rather than in one drawn up by a single organisation for use with one collection.

Alphabetical index to classifications. Additionally a classified index requires an alphabetical index or key to the classified order. This index has to be as carefully organised as the classification scheme itself and must be kept up to date and amended in conjunction with the classification. Some libraries have tried to combine this index with the published index to the classification scheme used, but this is not particularly successful. Headings in the published index may not be required and the user wastes time going from the index to classified order only to find no heading exists. Also the published index does not cover all the terms specific to the library or the cross reference terms which are needed. This is the serious lack in a published index when it is used in this way. The published scheme is not designed to be used as a subject index and will not cater for synonyms and other necessary references.

The alphabetical index includes the subject or reference and the relevant classification number. References need not be included in this index except to inform the user on the structure of the classification, but there should be a direct reference to the classification number on each card.

Another index which has recently been given prominence is the thesaurus of terms — usually a printed index produced by a computer. But this is more commonly used with computer retrieval techniques than the ordinary classified index.

Filing order for classified indexes. The correct filing order for entries in a classified index is generally indicated in the scheme itself and follows either the numerical decimal order involved or the alphabetic notation order. In a numerical classification the first sequence of numbers should be easy enough to file in order, but difficulties may be encountered with the filing of subheadings and punctuation marks. The classified scheme which is most commonly used in film libraries (UDC) has a set order for the filing of punctuation marks which may be followed. For example, the colon is the most important of the UDC connecting symbols and numbers divided by the colon are filed directly after numbers standing on their own without the colon. Apart from the filing order given in the UDC schedules, BS 1000A also gives a standard for the order of notation incorporating auxiliary symbols. Within a number when all auxiliaries and subheadings have been accounted for the cards can be filed in date or production number order as in the alphabetico classed system.

The filing of subheadings and the reversals or cross references may present more difficulties. The main objection to the use of UDC has often been the length of the notation needed to denote a specific subject, and the number of reversals which are implicit in these long subheadings. Some of the reversals may have no value, but it requires a decision by a cataloguer if any are to be eliminated, and these decisions may have to be reversed later thus leading to confusion. This problem is also met in alphabetico classed systems after a period of time. A subject heading, either because it is never used in a search or because the number of entries under the heading have grown so numerous, may become so uninformative and slow to search that it has to be withdrawn.

Many film library catalogues have to use geographical locations extensively. These can be included in the classified sequence or could be indexed in a separate alphabetical index as shown previously.

As a further aid to the user many notation systems can be guided by translations of the notation or featurings added to the guide cards below the notation.

Guiding can either be a simple matter of using cards to show when a notation changes or with featuring the changes of notation are shown together with the translations. This will mean the use of a deep index tab so that the translation on the tab is raised above the level of the entry cards and notation and feature are visible to the user.

Advantages of classified indexes. The main advantages of classified indexes are that they avoid many of the cross classification problems in alphabetical systems and can adapt to unexpected increases in certain subjects.

Classified indexes have achieved wider acceptance than the

alphabetical schemes where no two schemes are alike in their organisation or choice of subject headings. This wider acceptance means that uniformity and compatibility can be achieved between organisations and internationally. This factor assists co-operation, and classified schemes can be used as the basis of widely used indexes. Material can be drawn from many sources into central information offices and published for wider use if an acceptable classification scheme is available. In these cases much additional classification by the central body is avoided and misunderstandings from the use of subject headings to mean different things in different organisations. Numbers are easier to manipulate and understand than subject heading words in international co-operation where additional problems of translation have to be met.

Disadvantages of classified indexes. The disadvantages concern the speed of access and the unfamiliarity of the notation to the user. The speed of access is reduced slightly by the user having to consult a subject index before he can go to the main entries. Because the notation is unfamiliar to the user who is used to dealing with words, he will have to consult the index each time before going to the catalogue. Notation schemes are slightly more difficult for untrained staff to cope with and many of the staff in a film library who could deal with quick enquiries in a subject catalogue find it more difficult to use a classified index. Senior staff will have to do much enquiry work which could reasonably be done by juniors and will not have time to do more detailed research for users.

The notation in classified indexes for film can become too complex when all the relationships between subjects are taken into account plus detailed geographical locations.

Stockshot and newsfilm libraries among others may classify by the type or angle of shot, e.g., the UDC schedules may be adapted to allow for camera motion. These adaptations include:

1. Inter-elemental shots such as air to air, ground to air, water to air.

2. Tracking shots: forward, backward, up or down.

3. Pan shots: right, left, up, down, whip or zoom.

4. Angle and distance shots: high, low, top, close up, medium or long shots.

5. Special photography including underwater, fast and slow motion and time lapse.

DICTIONARY-STYLE SUBJECT INDEX

In a dictionary catalogue the subject entries are included with all other entries in a straightforward alphabetical arrangement. The subject entries are specific and this leads to the inevitable problem 'How specific is specific?' For example, the heading Ships is not specific enough to start a search for a shot of a submarine and yet to enter it under Submarine would demand a vast number of references to other types of ships and their applications. A major disadvantage of a dictionary catalogue is its bulk. This makes it unwieldy and difficult to consult. It also presents numerous filing problems to the cataloguer.

ALPHABETICO CLASSED SUBJECT INDEX

This is an arrangement of subjects in classes and divisions with further subdivisions. In an alphabetico classed index subjects are arranged alphabetically in certain broad classes. Animals are arranged alphabetically by type and the whole section is filed in A. Disasters can be subdivided by type and filed alphabetically in D. In this arrangement the classes are ANIMALS and DISASTERS and the divisions could be LIONS, MONKEYS, RABBITS; FIRES, FLOODS, LANDSLIDES. Decisions have to be taken as to the level of the main headings and the subordinate headings and how these subordinate headings are to be related to the main headings. For example, is the subject catalogue going to contain headings for TRANSPORT or is the main heading going to be more specific referring to only one form of transport, e.g. AIR TRANSPORT, RAIL TRANSPORT, etc.? Each group can be subdivided as minutely as necessary although a series of subheadings can result in losing the specific subject required. Further decisions have to be taken on the order of items within each subordinate heading. A chronological arrangement might be preferred or a further subdivision of the item using the country of origin and then a chronological arrangement can be used as it is in the system under discussion. Subdividing the headings by country of origin breaks down the number of entries under any one heading and makes it easier and quicker to research in that heading.

Advantages of alphabetico classed index. The alphabetical system has one or two advantages in special types of library work. For example, in newsfilm libraries it is particularly helpful.

A classified system is useful in small specialised libraries where the user can become familiar with the system from intensive work with it. A newsfilm library has a large number of users, but many of these do not research often or very intensively in the library. A classified type of catalogue does present an initial barrier to the casual user and may well impede the speed of access to the information.

The system is filed by words, that is the key used in researching is the one which newspeople are most familiar with — language. In newsfilm libraries the users are journalists and producers with literate rather than numerate abilities. It is easier for them to use a word scheme than a numerical scheme where they cannot remember the numbers easily and have constantly to refer to an intermediate index to the classified catalogue before finding the material they need. Anyone can come and research for the film he needs without having to learn a notational filing system before he can begin.

Allied to the last factor it is useful to have a straightforward system for researchers, editors and producers to do their own research. Unless the library employs research assistants of its own the editorial staff or producers will make constant use of the indexes and they should be encouraged to do this on the assumption that they know best what it is they are looking for and how the material they find could be used to the best advantage.

An alphabetical system may be better designed to answer the sort of questions asked in some film libraries. The catalogue can be designed for specific reference or generic survey. The generic survey is more of a browsing reference to the indexes to locate all material relevant to a broad subject and closely related subjects. A classified catalogue meets these requirements well. Alternatively specific reference applies to searching for material on a well defined subject. Those film libraries which have more use for the specific reference enquiry will benefit and their catalogues can be designed to answer such questions. Specific reference requests are more easily met by the alphabetical types of catalogue.

Construction of alphabetico classed index. Subject headings will evolve as the indexing proceeds, new subjects appear and others change their nature or emphasis. The cataloguer has to decide when a new heading is justified and how it will fit into the present system, i.e. whether it can be used as an additional subheading for one of the existing main headings or whether it is important enough to warrant a new heading. An initial decision has to be taken for the whole of the cataloguing system on whether to use general or specific entry. In information film work specific entry has been found more useful than general. If a general heading is chosen the material under that heading grows quickly and out of proportion and researching within the heading becomes a slow and laborious task. Specific headings mean more references have to be made but the speed of access is increased.

A list of subject headings is a useful tool for the cataloguer, but any established list should be used with caution as the headings chosen for the list are not always relevant to film subjects. *Sears List of Subject Headings,* by B. M. Frick is useful, and classification systems such as the Universal Decimal Classification schedules will provide subheadings and guidance on the breakdown of large general subjects.

The cataloguer, using both the lists of subject headings and the authority file for the library concerned, selects suitable headings for the subjects covered by each film. The number of subject headings which can be used for any one film need not be limited, but the usual considerations of relevance, length of sequence and reuseability apply to this index as much as the others. The film is usually concerned with a main subject, but several other subjects may be covered by short sequences in the film. Entries are made for both the main subject and all sequences of interest, although individual shots are not necessarily entered. Individual shots are indexed only when the library has poor or inadequate coverage of the topic or it is particularly unusual.

Added entries can all be cited in the unit entry form for speed of processing. Some libraries when making added subject entries enter the inclusive footage of a subject item and ignore the rest of the film for that entry. This is a useful guide to the importance of the topic in the film and the type of treatment it receives, whether it is only a 'passing comment' or dealt with more fully, but in much film work these analytical entries would take up too much staff time and would not allow for the fast processing of the catalogue entries. In a unit entry system the user has to read the content list or shotlist in order to find out the extent of the coverage.

Use of catchwords. In deciding on subject headings for a long-standing index one of the maxims has been to avoid the catchword or the sort of terms which change rapidly and become obsolete. But in documentary film the catchword is frequently used and this may be the only term one can use to refer to a subject, as in certain stunt sports like Dragster, Go-Karting. The indexer has to try and work with both the present and the future in mind. How is the subject referred to now and how is it likely to be found in the future? If the term is widely used and it cannot be cited as a subheading of one of the large classes it is best to use the catchword on the basis of specific entry but refer from a more general established subject heading. This means that a researcher in the future who is unaware of the catchword type of subject will be referred back to it when looking under a general heading.

Layout of headings. In order to achieve uniformity and quick identification of the parts of a subject heading some consideration should be given to the layout of headings.

Main classes should be cited in a prominent position on the top line of a heading. Main subheadings are more clearly located if they appear directly under the class heading. A location used as a subdivision should also be quoted directly under the other headings rather than on the same line. The eye can pick out the main subheadings much more easily if they are prominent in display. This layout will result in one to four line headings according to the number of subdivisions. With some main headings no subdivision is relevant, e.g:

UNITED NATIONS or
NORTH ATLANTIC TREATY ORGANISATION

Others require one or more divisions, e.g:

ELECTIONS   DISASTERS
ENGLAND   EARTHQUAKES
              TURKEY

These references are easier to read than:

ELECTIONS, ENGLAND
DISASTERS, EARTHQUAKES, TURKEY

This is especially the case when qualifying terms are added to one or other of the headings.

Reversal or qualifying terms can be cited after the heading to which they refer, separated by a comma, e.g:

SATELLITES, Artificial or
DEMONSTRATIONS, Anti Nuclear.

Other headings may have main subdivisions in brackets after the heading, e.g:

AIRCRAFT (Civil) RESCUES (Air Sea) WAR (Civil)

The colon can also be used for subdividing a main heading if preferred, e.g:

CRIME : MURDER or
POLITICAL SCIENCE : GOVERNMENT.

Several subjects may require a further breakdown than any so far mentioned. These are usually additional descriptions of the particular item involved and are put in for quick identification but ignored for example in filing, e.g:

SHIPS (Civil)
TANKERS   Name of Tanker
ENGLAND

The important part of this heading is on the left of the card and all tankers flying under British flags are brought together and filed by production number rather than by name of tanker. A researcher looking for a shot of a British tanker would be able to locate one quickly, but it will also be useful for him to know which tanker he has located. Therefore the name of the tanker is included in the heading. All parts of the heading are relevant and can be used in filing. Stockshots can also be filed on a similar principle in a general library, e.g:

STOCKSHOTS   London
ENGLAND   St. Paul's

Initials in subject indexes. It is easier to spell out organisations in the subject index and refer from the initials especially as now several different organisations may prove to have similar initials and different philosophies, e.g. OAS is either the Organisation of American States or the French-Algerian terrorist group.

Subject index cross-references. In the subject index two types of references are used. The *see* references refer the user from a subject heading which has not been used to one that has, e.g:

ARTIFICIAL SATELLITES *See* SATELLITES, Artificial
FLOODS *See* DISASTERS
            FLOODS
SOLDIERS *See* MILITARY PERSONNEL
FARMING *See* AGRICULTURE

These include synonyms, reversals and preferred terms. No entries should appear under the first of each of the headings above except the reference card.

See also references refer the user from one part of the catalogue to related subjects and in this event material is found under both the original heading and all those which are referred to by the *see also* references. Only those subject headings which are actually in use should be referred to with this reference, a user does not want to be referred to a subject heading which is not yet in use. A subject search is aimed to locate information about something, but relevant material may be found in films dealing with related subjects. If the index does not refer the enquirer to these related subjects it is failing in one of its main purposes.

A subject index is therefore a network of terms closely

connected by cross references so that when one term is selected at the beginning of the search all other relevant terms will be automatically retrieved. This aim calls for a multitude of references and it is seldom that an ordinary subject index can cover all possibilities. This requirement of an almost infinite number of cross references needed to cover all the possible terms which may be used to approach the subject headings is a serious disadvantage of alphabetical subject catalogues and many additional schemes have been tried to overcome this problem. Thesauri of terms for use in special subject areas have been used experimentally as well as KWIC (Key Word in Context) indexes, but as these are designed more for mechanised retrieval than alphabetical subject indexing the results have not been helpful. They engender many irrelevant headings and the number of cross references reaches astronomical proportions. A thesaurus of terms would have to be very comprehensive to cover the subject area of newsfilm and KWIC indexes may not have a sufficiently succinct title or abstract to work from.

Further disadvantages of the alphabetico classed system include a certain inflexibility and a lack of compatibility with other systems as a base for national and international co-operation schemes.

Filing problems in alphabetical indexes. Filing in alphabetical indexes, including the dictionary catalogue, is sufficiently specialised to warrant separate consideration. A standard set of rules is essential to help to try and avoid the double filing of entries. Misfiled cards can start up new sequences in an alphabetical arrangement of subject headings or in location and personality indexes.

Subjects are filed alphabetically as the other indexes, using one line of the heading at a time until filed through and then using the title or production number to sort within a class or subheading.

The filing is most convenient in this index on a word by word basis. This assists in keeping the subheadings in order and closely related subjects together. Filing word by word means arranging the entries first by the heading word; if the first words are the same, then file by the next word and so on. Thus the following arrangement would be made:

AIR	*Not*	AIR
AIR FORCE		AIRCRAFT
AIR OPERATIONS		AIRCRAFT INDUSTRY
AIR ROUTES		AIR FORCE
AIRCRAFT		AIR OPERATIONS

AIRCRAFT INDUSTRY   AIRPORTS
AIRPORTS   AIR ROUTES

The latter arrangement is a letter by letter arrangement and is not immediately clear to the user.

Thus it is possible to have the two principles of filing operating in the same system of indexes, but not, it should be noted in the same index or dictionary catalogue. The principles are used where they are most appropriate and easy to understand, and as long as the two principles are kept separate and not both used in the same index they should remain easy to use. The difficulties occur when word by word and letter by letter arrangement are used in the same index, double filed headings appear and mistakes in alphabetisation which result in film being overlooked or lost to the user.

The subjects will probably have been subdivided by a variety of methods, such as two line headings, commas, colons and brackets or other punctuation marks, e.g:

ANIMALS
LIONS
KENYA

SATELLITES, Artificial
PRISONERS, Released
CRIME : MURDER
POLITICAL SCIENCE : GOVERNMENT
AIRCRAFT (Civil)
CONFERENCES (International)

The filing order of the punctuation marks can be decided from existing filing codes, and it is usually taken to be:

Two Line Headings
Brackets
Colons
Commas

MACHINE BASED RETRIEVAL SYSTEMS

The nature of some film libraries complicates the question of mechanised retrieval systems in several ways. The wide ranging and complex nature of film subjects and current affairs means that any effective thesaurus of terms needs to be complex, capable of infinite expansion and universal in its selection of terms. The number of subject entries needed for each film could be coped with but the number of credits and personalities would not be easily incorporated. Credits and personalities are disparate entities which cannot be related to one another and no hierarchy of terms can be applied, so that one would need a separate 'term' for each of thousands of names.

Film library searches are of several types depending on the type of library. Distribution libraries use computers but not necessarily for subject retrieval, rather for housekeeping routines, bookings and film availability. Archive research is of several different types aimed at retrieval of specific terms or research into the development of the art or history of the film, or the development of particular careers which require general retrieval. Other researches can be detailed research for projected programmes, or the 'one-off' type of question. The question may be 'What have you got on the actual disaster which occurred on the 25th May 1965?' rather than 'What have you got on a certain type of disaster?' Also the answer may be required immediately. There can be no batching of enquiries to reserve computer time. Several thousand entries may have to be searched for one item, and no matter how quickly this is done the end product does not justify the expense involved. Film library catalogues should be designed to answer the questions asked quickly and correctly without the use of a computer.

Most film libraries in current use have large collections of both older material and current additions. To put the material on to punched cards or tape takes a great deal of staff time and requires considerable expertise. At present most film library staffs are working at full capacity and there is no time available to set up alternative systems of cataloguing for minimal or doubtful benefit. One film library which studied the problem in practical terms in England is the Imperial War Museum. Experiments are still at an early stage but the initial process of viewing and classifying film began and a thesaurus of terms and features was built up as the system developed. The film was indexed by subject sequence rather than shots. Abstracts were written for each film and these were used in the indexing. All features were pulled out and coded according to the thesaurus. The cards were punched, as many cards as necessary, and the abstract was included in the sequence.

This is a punched card retrieval system. The search questions are reduced to the coded feature terms. Large feature cards are used on an optical coincidence viewer to discover the relevant sections of the 'catalogue' to search. The card sorter is run and the abstracts which answer the researcher's questions are withdrawn from the system. One advantage of a punched card system it is claimed, is that enquiries do not have to be batched as they would with a computer, but can be answered as required. Despite the claims for this system it appears to be a long, slow job. The eventual saving in research time over a manual index is not significant. Similar thought and effort applied to improving conventional catalogues might have a wider application and usefulness. It is certainly more useful to stockshot and newsfilm libraries where the changeover from their current systems presents almost insuperable difficulties. The amount of material to be catalogued and the lack of staff time to devote to this job are major obstacles.

The other possible application of machine retrieval of information for non-print media which is being discussed at present is the use of MARC tapes. These tapes are already being used experimentally for books by the Library of Congress in the USA. The Library of Congress and the British National Bibliography are co-operating to make the scheme available to Library of Congress subscribers in the USA (based on the LoC classification) and British National Bibliography subscribers in the UK (based on Dewey classification). Film librarians have long been interested in the LoC through the Cataloguing Rules for Motion Pictures and the trend is now towards establishing a machine-readable record for all media, not restricted to books.

Discussions and feasibility studies are in progress. Unfortunately some film libraries, especially those with large numbers of short films or stockshot material, are already having difficulties including all their material in conventional national catalogues because of the amount of film produced each year and the fundamental differences in cataloguing many short films, newsfilm and other types of film. The MARC system will probably have more application and usefulness to other film libraries than to those dealing with stockshots and newsfilm, although of course all developments should be watched closely to see if any agreement and systems of reference can be found.

SYSTEMS IN USE

Film libraries in the UK favour the use of classified subject indexes except for newsfilm libraries which prefer the alphabetical subject index. Major companies such as Visnews, British Movietone and Pathe News all have alphabetical subject catalogues. Of the television libraries BBC TV news uses the UDC system which facilitates reference between the News Library and the Film Library, and ITN use an alphabetical subject catalogue. Other film libraries which have collections of newsfilm material included in more general collections and do not deal exclusively in newsfilm use other types of subject catalogues. National Film Archive use UDC and the Imperial War Museum are experimenting with machine based indexes.

9

STORAGE AND PRESERVATION

A MAJOR CONSIDERATION in deciding the type of storage conditions is the purpose of the library involved. The library has to achieve adequate storage which will match the calls made on it rather than allow the storage conditions to dictate the working of the organisation and the quality of the service offered to the user.

An archive, a distribution library, a stockshot and a newsfilm library are all different in purpose and this will be reflected in the storage conditions used by each.

The aim of archival storage is the permanent preservation of film and to this everything else must take second place. The conditions necessary for permanent storage preclude the constant handling and use of the material. Changes in temperature and humidity from the storage area to the outside world are such that once stored the films can only be withdrawn slowly and under strictly controlled conditions to ensure the continued preservation of the film.

Archive preservation copies are used only to make additional duplicates or projection prints when those in use become worn or damaged. Ideally there should always be a duplicate copy or print of each archive film available. The original copies should be stored under the best possible conditions and withdrawn at set intervals for rewinding and inspection. Any deterioration can be dealt with as it appears.

In other types of library different conditions and usage are necessary and material has to be readily accessible and speedily prepared ready for reuse. Ideal storage conditions work against the accessibility and speed of preparation. Colour material stored in ideal conditions, for example, can take up to 24 hours to 'warm up' to a handling temperature. Often there are insufficient funds to provide duplicate copies of all material held so that the library frequently has to use original material for viewing and printing. The use of originals in a film library is a compromise solution to a difficult problem. The risk of damage by handling has to be

177

weighed against the cost of providing a duplicate. Duplicates may be made as a matter of policy for much-used film, more important pieces or more obviously valuable material, but unfortunately this solution is not widely accepted at present and funds are not readily available for duplication.

The treatment of colour film provides a good example of the difference between the purposes of archival storage and current usage by other film libraries. An archive will store colour in separation negatives at low temperatures to retain the original colour values, and this means printing and storing three pieces of film as opposed to the one colour film. Printing takes longer from separation negatives to the original colour prints and as already stated time has to be allowed for the material to reach handling temperature. Other film libraries would find this method both expensive and inconvenient, because it would interfere with the fast service on which much of their success depends and the libraries would also have difficulty in finding space to store the additional amount of film. In some cases it may be necessary to store a proportion of films in separations, but this policy will have to be very selective because of the cost involved.

Many commercial film libraries, due to their methods of work will often arrive at a compromise between ideal and workable storage conditions. The archives will provide the industry with standards for ideal storage conditions even if only in theory, and the commercial libraries will have to adapt these conditions to their own requirements.

STORAGE PRINCIPLES

The type of storage provided is to some extent dictated by the sort of film it is intended to store, i.e. nitrate or acetate, positive, negative, colour, magnetic tapes, video tapes, etc.

Separate-storage requirements. If both nitrate and acetate film are included in the collection, it is essential to store them separately, because the gases given off by nitrate film have an injurious effect on acetate film. Nitrate film is also subject to stringent precautions against fire, and regulations require that the film is stored in closed vaults with adequate blast openings in the design of the vault to prevent serious fire and explosion. Once a fire has started in a nitrate vault it will run its course in that particular vault and nothing can be done to save the film. But if the vaults have been properly constructed a great deal can be done to prevent the fire and consequent explosions from spreading to other vaults and the rest of the collection. Nitrate should be stored in small vaults and the construction of storage vaults for nitrate is more expensive than for acetate. As there will not be much nitrate film left in future, it is worthwhile for a company which acquires a nitrate collection' to consider transferring the film to acetate stock with the funds available, rather than building new vaults for the nitrate material.

Negative and positive film can also be stored in different vaults, although this is not essential. It serves as an additional safety measure if one vault of film is lost and the library has both positive and negative of the same material, at lease one record of the film will be retained. Cut stories and uncut stories of the same material should also be kept in separate vaults for convenience as well as a safeguard. If there is an accident one copy might be preserved and a new cut story can always be remade from the uncut.

Magnetic tapes and recordings. Because of the somewhat unstable nature of magnetic materials for recording and storage (including the danger of wiping by a magnetic field, or purely by accidental handling, the possibilities of print-through. ghosting or copying effects), the safest way of ensuring their preservation is to print them on to optical film, either in a composite print with the picture image, or on a separate sound track. The magnetic tapes could be retained in a separate storage area for recopying. Although tape sound is usually better quality than optical sound, it is less convenient to store and use with the film stock. Tapes when they are retained and stored should be kept separate from film in similar temperature and humidity conditions.

CONSTRUCTION AND USE OF VAULTS

Before considering storage conditions, a basic decision has to be taken as to what sort of vaults will be employed and additionally how the material is actually filed in the vaults, i.e. horizontally or vertically.

Nitrate film must be stored in closed vaults with a maximum capacity of 500 cans holding 1000 feet each in England (in other countries regulations may permit up to 1000 cans to be stored in any one vault). The vaults should have adequate blast openings in the roof so that if explosion occurs it blows upwards, not outwards. The construction should therefore be single storey and with thick walls, preferably with an air passage between the outer wall and the individual vault walls. This will assist any air conditioning unit to be more efficient and will ensure that the walls of the vaults do not overheat. The vault doors should be kept locked and must be well fitted to prevent blast from explosions blowing out through the door and thus spreading the fire.

Open racking can be used for the storage of acetate film. This means that a greater area is available for filing and storage than if vaults have to be constructed in the same space. In open areas fire precautions still have to be taken as well as precautions against dust. In a large area dust is easily raised and can damage the film if wound in to it. The film handling area is also subject to dust and in both areas measures have to be taken to keep it down or extract it.

Filing methods. Once vaults and open racking have been constructed and containers for holding film decided on the next question is how to store these containers on the shelves, i.e. horizontally or vertically. Horizontal storage is always recommended for archives. If film is permanently stored in a vertical position, with the larger reels of film, the whole weight of the reel is always on the lower part and damage and distortion result from pressing the lower layers together. Horizontal storage is not a space saver, but should be considered for large reels which are not going to be used and moved frequently. It can also be inconvenient for quick retrieval if cans are required at the bottom or half way down a pile. All the others have to be moved and put somewhere while the required can is extracted and then returned to place. When the can is replaced the same procedure is again required. Archival vaults are often constructed with a separate compartment for each can of film to be stored horizontally. This is impractical for commercial libraries.

Vertical storage of film is more frequently employed by commercial and other film libraries where cans are continually being withdrawn and opened. Using 16mm film there is less weight to contend with, and in, for example, newsfilm libraries the film is usually of short length and does not present the same problem of weight as 2000 feet of 35mm film. A can in a newsfilm library contains several pieces of 16mm film which are in frequent use. The film is often moved around in the can and it does not rest on one section of the reel for long periods. The main danger in such a system is caused by overfilling the can, for if the film is squashed in it will become distorted. It should be standard practice not to fill a can of film completely, but have a certain amount of space for movement.

STORAGE CONDITIONS

The most important storage conditions are concerned with the temperature, humidity and ventilation in the vaults.

Temperature. When film becomes warm it expands and when it cools, it shrinks. If there is constant movement of film between different atmospheres damage to the film results. Taking film out of a cold store area into an overheated office atmosphere where it is rewound and run on a projector without allowing the film time to readjust will probably damage the perforations and cause the brittleness in the film which cracks the emulsion.

Optimum storage temperatures have been cited in a pamphlet published by the International Federation of Film Archives called 'Film Preservation'.

Nitrate film should be stored at a low temperature for best results, the optimum is $35°F \pm 3°F$ ($2°C \pm 2°C$). A higher temperature, e.g. $64°F$ results in acceleration of the normal process of deterioration and more rapid disintegration. It is worth noting here that the National Film Archive, in order to save the cost of air conditioning, have deliberately chosen to store their nitrate at $55°F$ ($13°C$) arguing that air conditioning and maintenance of a lower temperature would only extend the life of the nitrate film for a very limited period. This temperature is easier and less costly to maintain and has the added advantage for other libraries that the film is relatively accessible.

The maximum temperature for the storage of *acetate film* is recommended at $54°F \pm 3°F$ ($12°C \pm 2°C$). There is not the same problem of disintegration of the base as with nitrate, but the emulsion is also dependent on temperature and humidity. A high temperature reacts with the humidity value. If humidity is also too high it encourages fungus to grow in the emulsion until it destroys the image. Alternatively it accelerates the process whereby the gelatin in the base becomes sticky until the emulsion is stripped off the base.

Colour film has added another problem to the list in recent years in television libraries, although it has existed for many years in feature and production libraries. The difficulty is one of preserving colour film and still keeping it available for immediate use.

There is no broad agreement on the optimum conditions for the storage of colour film, e.g. Kodak gives $0°F$ ($-18°C$) while Agfa considers $59°F$ ($15°C$) acceptable. (Archive preservation of colour is best achieved with three black and white separation negatives or prints, that is one for each basic colour image, yellow, magenta and cyan) but expense and access rule out this method for the commercial and newsfilm libraries.

Colour film is less durable than black and white and when it begins to deteriorate the colours bleach out one at a time. The colours fade most rapidly when temperature and humidity are too high.

With this information in mind the film librarian now has to decide on the conditions which will apply in his own vaults. If his film is not for archival preservation, but he wants to keep it in good condition for as long as possible and maintain it in an easily accessible store without risk to the film he has to select a temperature range which does the least damage to the whole range of film stored and yet is not far removed from the outside temperatures. This enables film to be removed from the vaults, rewound, sent for processing or viewing as quickly as necessary to the user. In many film libraries, especially newsfilm and television libraries one is unable to achieve optimum storage conditions because of the nature of the call on the material. The film, all the film, has to be in a constant state of readiness. A compromise is the only reasonable solution and this compromise can be achieved in the temperature of the storage area. Taking all factors into consideration, if nitrate, acetate and colour stock is to be stored in the same system of vaults a constant temperature of 55° F has been recommended. This is, in England, not far from the outside temperature and fairly easy and economic to maintain with air conditioning. The film does not have to go through a long warming process to a useable temperature.

Humidity. As humidity is relative to temperature, once a constant temperature has been decided on the humidity ratio is selected to fit the circumstances.

Gelatin in the film base readily absorbs moisture, swells and becomes sticky. Eventually it strips off the emulsion from the base. If the atmosphere is too dry the plasticiser which keeps the film elastic and the moisture in the emulsion evaporates — this occurs in both nitrate and acetate film. When the moisture and plasticiser have gone the film becomes brittle and shrinks, the distance between the perforations alters and if the film is then projected or processed, the perforations are likely to tear. If the film becomes brittle there is very little that can be done — it is possible to restore elasticity to slightly deteriorating film for a short time, but only long enough for a dupe to be taken, and as stated only for a small proportion of film which has become brittle.

High humidity (over 60 per cent) encourages both the swelling of the gelatin and the growth of fungus, while low humidity (under 40 per cent except where a low temperature is also operating) encourages shrinking. Therefore a level somewhere between these two figures would be the optimum. Having selected a fairly high temperature, a humidity of 50—60 per cent is a reasonable figure. Finally it is important to maintain this humidity at a constant level to avoid damage.

Ventilation. For nitrate film god ventilation is essential, whereas acetate requires only normal room ventilation. Air should be changed every three hours. Automatic air conditioning plants guarantee the best storage conditions but are very expensive. However acid gases and pollution of the air should be warded off in any circumstances as these attack the silver image and destroy it, and this may call for a filtration plant in a heavily industrialised area.

STORAGE EQUIPMENT

The main items of equipment are racking and cans, wrapping material, bobbins, spools and leaders.

Racking. Shelving in the vaults should be of ordinary steel construction. Wood warps and will not take the weight of film cans. It is also an additional fire risk and cannot be used in nitrate vaults. The distance between shelves is based on size and type of can used. If square or rectangular cans are used a little extra room is required at the top of the shelves. They should not be a tight fit but should allow for easy access and slight variation in the size of the cans supplied. Round cans need a little more room when they are stored vertically by dropping down between front and back shelves to hold them in position and this distance below the shelf needs to be allowed at the top to make for easy withdrawal. It is inefficient to have to remove one or two cans in a shelf every time a third is needed, because the space is too small and cans have to be turned at an angle to get them out. Shelving in a closed vault should not be constructed so that it is provided in corners. Accessibility of all cans should be maintained. The racking should also be adaptable and capable of alteration to allow for reracking if it becomes necessary.

Cans. The normal method of storing films is in cans. These cans are made to the individual specifications of the library concerned, for example, a production or documentary or newsreel library which is dealing with 1000 or 2000 foot reels will order cans to fit the size of film normally stored, whereas a stockshot or newsfilm library which deals with shorter pieces of film may find that square or rectangular cans are of more use. A disadvantage of cans for storing film is that being metal they tend to rust and this has a destructive effect on the film stored in them. Rust causes very rapid deterioration and when metal cans are used they should first be cleaned (some firms use benzine for this) and examined very carefully for any traces of rust before being put away. Frequent examination of the cans is desirable to determine if rust is forming, and once it is detected the can should be changed immediately.

Metal cans are also subject to damage from acids, some of which may even come from the film itself. Experiments are being carried out in the USSR with plastic containers for film storage. These when fully developed would have advantages over the widely used metal cans, for they would not rust, would resist acids and stains and could be manufactured at similar cost to metal cans. Additionally they could be made airtight or with ventilation according to the type of film to be stored in them. Research by archivists in this direction will be of interest to all film libraries, but problems such as the composition of the plastic and its relationship with the type of film to be stored as well as condensation will have to be overcome before plastic becomes a film storage material. Plastic cans are now widely used for non-permanent storage and by many distribution hire libraries dealing with 16mm film. An added advantage is that plastic spools and cans are lighter than metal and can be mailed more cheaply. Also metal cans once they become damaged or battered can prove very difficult to open.

Other materials used for storing film include stainless steel and cardboard, but the use of stainless steel cans is precluded by the expense in most libraries. Cardboard boxes should not be used for permanent storage of film — cardboard absorbs moisture and deteriorates the film. It is also not as long lasting as metal.

Wrapping material. Film is sometimes wrapped in polythene bags before being stored in the cans. This has the advantage that until the piece of film is needed for viewing it is not handled. When required it is taken out of the bag, but until then the polythene serves as a protection against dust and sticky fingers. Some libraries rely on the leader attached at the start and end of the film to protect it from handling damage. Polythene, while it protects the film from handling damage, might produce condensation which could damage the film in storage. Care has to be taken to ensure that no moisture is inside the bag when it is put away, and that the film is not subject to sudden changes in temperature when stored in the bag. Storage in polythene is airtight and therefore should never be used for nitrate film.

Wrapping film in paper, tissue or waxed, is not good practice. The paper tends to deteriorate and to produce the dust which it is supposed to be keeping from the film. Paper can be used for short periods to protect prints in transit from laboratory to customer, but it should not be used for storage.

Bobbins. Film should always be stored on a core or bobbin whether for permanent archival storage or continuous use storage. Cores will help prevent the film from curling at the inside, make for easier handling of the film and allow for rewinding without damaging the inner part of the film. The core can be made of wood, plastic or stainless steel. Wood cores are used when some form of identification is marked on the core itself as well as the film, e.g. the film number, location number and stock. One practice which should be discouraged is of removing the cores and winding the film small to save space. This scratches the emulsion, makes the film brittle and could even crack the emulsion.

Spools. Film is not normally stored on spools, which is an expensive way of storing it and also takes up space. However in some circumstances it will be kept on a spool for easy retrieval and hire to allow for immediate projection. Spools can be plastic or metal and a variety of designs are available. Split spools may be used for convenience of projection for film stored on bobbins. These are of sturdy construction and usually made of metal.

Leader. No matter what core the film is wound on to, it should be supplied with leaders at head and end. Leaders are important in storing film both for identification and protection. They help to protect the film from scratching on the core, on other films, on the tape or sides of the can. The number of the film is usually scribed — that is scratched with a special sharp instrument — on the leader as close to the picture as possible to prevent the laboratories from removing the number. (With colour film, scribes will not print through, and the number has to be marked on the leader with a felt pen — a less permanent method than a scribe). When film is printed the laboratories print several pieces at once in large rolls. These prints and the originals have to be broken down and it is of great assistance to have the identification number at the beginning of each separate piece of film.

FILM PRESERVATION AND MAINTENANCE

No matter how much care is taken in storage, film will require some maintenance or restoration, either major restoration as in duping or minor surgery as in repairing a few perforations, or treating small marks on the film. Nitrate film will eventually and inevitably deteriorate and have to be restored to a usable state. The life of nitrate film made before 1920 is now likely to be in a state requiring restoration and duping. (This figure of fifty years for the life of nitrate is the norm; there will obviously be some exceptions, some having a longer life and some deteriorating more rapidly.)

Irreparable damage. Some damage to film is irreparable, and this is manifest in the following circumstances:

1. When film reaches the last stages of deterioration the emulsion softens and blisters. The film sticks together and the base disintegrates.
2. When film loses flexibility and breaks on rewinding. This film is incapable of projection and therefore of duping.
3. Where colour fading has reached an advanced stage — the image has bleached out.
4. When film has been attacked by fungus and the image 'eaten away'.

In all these cases the film is irretrievable and must be destroyed or may destroy itself and many other films with it. If fungus attacks one piece of film in a can, for example, it will probably spread to other films.

Reparable damage. Other damage is reparable, such as dirt on the film, spots, brittleness, scratches, tearing of perforations, stickiness and bleaching of the silver image. Dirt is removed with chemicals and can be done mechanically on an ultrasonic machine. This harms the film less than other methods of cleaning, but the conditions under which any treatment takes place should be comparable with the conditions under which the film is stored. Removing film from regulated temperatures in vaults and subjecting it to the different temperatures of handling area and processing laboratory may have an injurious effect which overrules the wisdom of having the material ultracleaned. For nitrate film, probably the most sensible expedient is to ultraclean the film and then dupe it immediately. One library which had its film ultracleaned to improve the quality and that of the dupes from it, found that the film began to deteriorate much more rapidly than would have been expected in normal usage. Whether this deterioration was due to the process of ultracleaning reacting on the nitrate film, or whether it was just a matter of changes in atmosphere has not yet been established.

Small spots on the film are removed chemically by hand, while scratches can be removed when they are not too deep, either by polishing the celluloid, or swelling the emulsion and then drying the film to 'absorb' the scratch. These methods are used according to whether the scratch is on the celluloid or emulsion side of the film. Where a deeper scratch exists a thin layer of wax can be applied which will fill the scratch. An anti scratch process can be installed in processing machinery before the film enters the printing gate. This coats the film on both sides with a liquid which has exactly the same refractive index as the base. When the film is printed the scratches do not transfer to the copy because there is no deflection of the printing light's rays by scratches or dirt. This process is probably the best solution, but is expensive and needs an organisation with considerable resources and a laboratory especially equipped for the purpose.

When film becomes brittle it is generally useless, but a temporary reversal of the brittleness can be achieved provided it has not reached an advanced stage. The film is put in a 'filmostat' which enables it to absorb a certain solution which has the effect of replacing the plasticiser. When the film has acquired a certain suppleness it has to be duplicated immediately and the original treated material destroyed because it will only become brittle again and quite irreparable. This is an interim measure designed to retrieve film long enough to have it duplicated.

Shrinkage is normally dealt with by using a step printer in printing a duplicate so that only one frame is printed at a time. Because the film is not being moved automatically by use of sprockets in perforations it can be printed without tearing the perforations or moving the film out of rack.

Shrinkage is irreversible but, although it is obviously a time-consuming process, shrunk film can be replaced. It is naturally best to duplicate film when it has shrunk only to a small extent, rather than leaving it to shrink further and increase the problems of restoration. This maxim applies to all the restoration of film: if trouble is rectified as soon as it is discovered, further deterioration and damage will be averted and expense spared in restoring the film.

Stickiness is dealt with by rewinding the film under water and then putting it through a drying process to get rid of stickiness. With nitrate film where the stickiness indicates deterioration other steps have to be taken to dupe the film and destroy the original.

Where the silver image has discoloured it can be restored in some cases by bleaching and then redeveloping.

Torn perforations can be repaired by cementing new perforations on to the film, or a product called Permacel may be used to cover the entire film for long pieces of damage. Permacel is used effectively only where the perforation intervals are standard, i.e. no shrinkage has occurred.

PROBLEM AWARENESS

One of the major difficulties that film librarians face in achieving and maintaining good storage conditions and preservation policies is the lack of awareness and consideration of the particular requirements of the library by the administration. It is generally considered to be part of the function of an archive to preserve the film held in the collection for future usage and as a result archives include storage and preservation costs in budgetary requirements as a matter of course. However commercial companies tend to view the matter from a different point of view and in these organisations if management cannot be made aware of the problems and the need for consistent policies there will not be allocation of the necessary funds to put the policies into practice.

Without a consistent policy when material begins to deteriorate it cannot be saved in many instances before complete destruction of the image has taken place. It is necessary also to have a continuing policy so that deteriorating or damaged film is located, recognised and a system of selection is used to gauge the usefulness of the film and take steps to preserve it if required.

When there is film which is likely to deteriorate in the collection a sum of money should be set aside in the library budget, or a special sum allocated to the library for preservation purposes.

When it is a question of repairing film to make it usable, in the case of more recent acetate film, another sum should be set aside for 'running repairs'. Some film companies cannot be easily persuaded that recent film needs the same care in storage and preservation as the older material, and budget allowances do not include repair costs. Distribution libraries are most aware of this problem and examine film after each hire period and effect any repairs necessary. They may budget for a certain amount of fair wear and tear or they may claim from the user for more extensive damage necessitating expensive repair or replacement.

Film companies, especially commercial film companies today tend not to be fully aware of the problems. Specifically:

1. There is not enough realisation of the deterioration factor in nitrate film.
2. The extra storage space and finance for second, unused, copies of material for preservation policy is not forthcoming. The argument against this need is that because of the shortage of storage space, all material should be used if it is to be a source of income.
3. The potentialities of early film are often not realised. The film companies may be exploiting the material in the wrong places, that is concentrating on television documentaries and ignoring the educational field.

A film library has to be established as a separate viable department with its own systems, finance and independent customer list. Whatever the organisation's concerns are the library has its own separate function as a historical store as well as a store for current production material.

The librarian is greatly helped in bringing the administration to recognise this separate function if he can present the company with a viable or potentially viable entity. A collection which has been proved to have wider applications and a wider range of customers than the current production service will have greater opportunities and more powerful arguments for acquiring financial assistance to carry out its policies of preservation and achieve good storage conditions.

Several policies for preservation and storage have been tried and many more discussed. They range from the individual efforts of companies to co-operative schemes on a national basis.

COMPANY PRESERVATION POLICIES

Because of the expense involved in preserving and restoring film, many decisions have to be made on the basis of cost. Some film of value may have to be destroyed because it has deteriorated beyond repair, other film may have to be destroyed when alternative shorter versions are available because of the serious lack of storage space for new film subjects and stories. Limited funds may mean that a cut story is preserved as opposed to the uncut or unedited version because it costs less to duplicate. In deciding which film to preserve when it begins to deteriorate or when extra storage space is required and a weeding process is undertaken, other principles of selection are applied to preservation. The content of the film is of prime importance and normally the edited version of a film is preserved because it is better documented than the uncut version, contains the best material taken from the uncut original, takes up less storage space and costs less to dupe and preserve.

Where a film has become damaged through scratching, it is better to repair the damage as far as possible and then dupe the film if an original negative does not exist. 'Filling' scratches, restoring elasticity, repairing torn perforations are all to be regarded as temporary measures to improve the quality of the image for a short period so that duplicate copies can be made of the restored print. Scratches will appear again, elasticity can only be restored temporarily and repaired perforations are always a source of weakness in the film. Film should be preserved in as good condition as possible and therefore a duplicate of a repaired film should be preserved rather than the original damaged film.

After the decision is taken to preserve a film the question arises as to the form in which it should be retained. When the film is beginning to deteriorate, duplicates have to be made to ensure preservation, but the most useful form of duplicate has to be decided, that is whether it is to be a duplicate negative or a fine grain print. The original stock available influences the decision, for a duplicate negative can be taken in one stage of printing from a positive original while a fine grain print can be taken in one stage from a negative original. A preservation duplicate is usually taken to the first stage of printing from the original to save further expenditure.

If the decision is between different forms of the same story it is taken on the basis of future usefulness. If there is a choice between nitrate and acetate, however, acetate is obviously selected because of the inevitable deterioration of nitrate. If negative and positive film exists for the same story and one version has to be junked the negative should be retained for future printing purposes. A fine grain positive can also be used for further printing but it is usually less useful than the negative. However the negative is not particularly helpful for viewing purposes and whenever possible a negative and a positive should be retained, the negative for printing and the positive for viewing.

The choice of the type of sound track to be preserved depends on the other systems in use in the organisation and the amount of storage space available. If current storage is of greater importance than a slight reduction in quality, combined optical prints are more useful than film with a separate magnetic track. Magnetic sound can also be laid on to the film, but there is a loss of quality from the separate magnetic ¼in tape and the greater ease with which optical sound can be handled and stored makes it better to store the sound in this way if separate tracks are not feasible.

Colour preservation and storage present additional problems. Colour prints are easily damaged in handling and viewing and extra measures have to be taken to preserve them. The most satisfactory method of preserving colour is by the use of separation negatives. This is too expensive a method for most commercial film libraries to contemplate, although it may have to be considered for a few particularly valuable stories. The cost of making two colour prints is prohibitive for any library which contains large numbers of short films or sells stock footage. Black and white prints taken from the colour stories form the most feasible solution found to date. They are the least expensive copies to make and save the colour from constant handling. Prints take up storage space but the benefits of having them can be set against this factor. Also it does not take up as much space to preserve the original colour and a black and white print as three separation negatives plus a black and white or colour print.

Any decision on the form of the preservation copy has to achieve a balance between the costs to the library, the quality of the material and the customer requirements.

The foregoing has considered libraries which preserve original material and use it for viewing and printing. Another policy which helps to preserve the originals is often used, that of printing show copies from the originals. Many film libraries do not allow their originals or master copies to be viewed, but retain them only to make additional viewing prints as they are required. This is similar to archive policy. Some production libraries allow only show copies to be projected. Distribution libraries are the most obvious example of the use of show copies — they do not lend original material, only a show print of the original. Newsfilm libraries are not in the same position. The number of films entering the libraries precludes the printing of viewing copies for all film for economic reasons. A newsfilm library which show-printed all incoming film would have no funds available for other functions, e.g. staffing, equipment, etc. Also many of the films coming into a newsfilm library are not worth the expense of show copies, either for technical quality or subject interest. Nevertheless there is a strong argument for making show copies of some of the more valuable or widely used film (the two are not synonymous), but a strict control has to be kept on the amount of film being printed for this purpose and it should be a continuous policy with a definite budget. A fund could usefully be set aside for this purpose each year.

CO-OPERATIVE SCHEMES

Is it then wise for individual organisations to attempt to preserve their own film on their own premises, or would it be better for a co-operative bank to be set up for the permanent preservation of important items? Putting aside what is or is not important, would or could this concept work? There is an inevitable conflict of interest here. A central preservation area might not accept ordinary deposit prints for permanent preservation on the basis of quality, although a fine grain print from the original negative should be acceptable. In addition, most companies could not deposit original material. Firstly, it is required by them to carry out their own functions and, secondly, they often are not working with original material, but prints provided by overseas companies or sources. Companies with a reputation and facilities for speed of printing do not want to go to outside sources for printing original material. In spite of all these objections, if the companies were to co-operate in such an effort the film could be preserved under ideal conditions for the benefit of the companies involved. Finance would have to come from the participants in such a scheme, but it would probably prove less expensive than the piecemeal preservation which is going on at present. The National Film archives were designed to do this sort of job most effectively as they have the facilities to store and preserve film, but they would need considerable financial support to cope and staffing would also have to increase. The participants in such a scheme would help finance this project for their own benefit as a repository for good quality prints or negatives of their more important film. They would retain all rights in their own film and continue to print and supply copies from their own libraries. The national repository would act as a central point of research in film as it does now and additionally provide a safeguard for the companies who deposit material. Unfortunately it is doubtful if such a scheme could ever be put into operation given the conflicting commercial interests involved.

The alternatives are therefore:

1. Individual efforts and expense by separate companies to preserve and store originals or duping copies separately from show copies.
2. More deposit in the National Film Archive with the constant reminder that a committee at the archive could reject material which had been offered for storage. This would leave the owning company with the original problem of endeavouring to store its own preservation copies.

10

STAFFING

THERE ARE three types of work to be carried out in a film library of any size and the staff needed for each type is different both in qualification and ability. The division of work can be summarised as:

1. Administrative including framing library policy, overall control of staff and staff training, exploiting library resources and contract work.
2. Clerical and routine, including keeping records, filing, shelving, typing.
3. Technical and professional, which includes staff dealing with:
   (a) Film processing and duplication, ordering, preservation and repair.
   (b) Film acquisitions and selection, cataloguing, classification, indexing, enquiry and information service.

ADMINISTRATIVE STAFF

The administrative staff in a film library are responsible for framing the library policy and carrying it out within the terms of reference laid down by the management of the whole organisation. They are also reponsible for current layout and future planning of the library. New buildings may have to be designed and this should be done by the librarian in consultation with the architects.

Library promotion and sales are an administrative responsibility as well as contractual work which results from sales. Reports and statistics on library sales and contracts also come from the administration department.

Staff recruitment, control and training are organised by the department as well as working conditions such as hours of work, shift rosters and overtime.

The administrative staff is sometimes limited to the librarian, or in larger organisations to a librarian, a deputy and a personal assistant.

The qualities needed in such staff are an organisational ability, an economic sense and an ability to deal with people, both customers and staff. In addition to these administrative abilities the film librarian needs a basic understanding of the nature of the material he is dealing with, i.e. film. He should be aware of the optimum conditions for storing the film, the best ways to handle it and have a wide knowledge of general library techniques which can be applied to film work. Also a knowledge of film production methods and laboratory processing techniques are needed. The librarian does not have to be a film technician but should be aware of current developments and how they are likely to affect the library's work.

The librarian should also be informed on legal requirements and cinematograph regulations which apply to the work of his department. Legal points have to be observed in sales and contract work and also in the more technical storage and handling of film.

CLERICAL STAFF

There are two types of clerical staff to be considered.

Secretarial staff are needed to cope with correspondence and contracts. They should have good typing ability (shorthand is desirable but may not be essential) and some bookkeeping ability to determine royalty payments and laboratory charges. The secretarial staff are also required to maintain statistics of library workloads, income and expenditure.

Other clerical staff are needed for filing records, typing catalogue entries and maintaining film movement catalogues and other records.

The sorting and filing of the shotlists where these are produced can be done by a clerical assistant as well as the retrieval of these documents for reference and use by other staff and outside customers.

A clerk/typist can be employed to type out catalogue entries and headings and for sorting these entries for filing.

Filing clerks may be employed in large libraries to maintain records such as the film movement record and even the catalogues. Many cataloguers prefer to file their own references but clerical staff can be trained to file in even complex catalogues if they are working to set rules. They need accurate sorting ability, tidiness and a sense of order. Spelling ability is also important and an ability to recognise errors and correct them. The filing clerk should have sufficient ability to check the entries she is filing, and the filing process should not be allowed to become an automatic unthinking one. Speed of working is important and desirable in a busy organisation, but accuracy is more essential for a catalogue filing clerk.

TECHNICAL AND PROFESSIONAL STAFF

The technical and professional staff in a library are considered together because normally the two aspects of film library work are interchangeable. The same people who shotlist and index the film may show it to customers and prepare film for the laboratory. Selection and enquiry work is also undertaken by these members of staff. It is difficult to make a sharp division between the two categories. Cataloguers and selection staff need to know how to handle film in order to view it, how to use the viewing machines, how to edit the film in selecting from cuts and they should have a knowledge of photographic quality for selection purposes. The selection staff need to have a greater knowledge of film handling than the cataloguing staff, but again the two jobs should wherever possible be interchangeable. A cataloguer who knows the material from the indexes is in a good position to select material which is relevant to the collection.

Bearing these points in mind the technical and professional jobs in a film library can be divided into the following for consideration:

1. Technical staff
2. Selection and acquisition
3. Enquiry
4. Cataloguing

Technical staff. The technical staff can be further subdivided into those who deal with the storage of the film in the vaults and the handling staff who deal with customer requirements and laboratory preparation.

Vault staff includes vault assistants, vault keepers and preservation officers.

Vault assistants are needed to manhandle the film into and out of cans and vaults under instruction from more senior members of staff dealing with library or customer requirements. Archive staff who do this job have to be more specialised in order to understand the storage and preservation problems and be able to recognise signs of film wear and tear and rectify it. In large commercial libraries the amount of physical filing and retrieving of film is greater — it becomes a full time job and should not be done by a member of staff with greater abilities than it warrants. Junior members of staff are used, but the importance of the task should remove any 'menial' aspect. It should not be regarded as a dreary chore by juniors and it is often useful to vary the job with two or three other handling tasks. If three or four assistants are employed several tasks can be alternated and the assistants given experience in each, such as intake of film, canning up, filing and retrieval. If an assistant is doing more than one job in turn he will also have more opportunity to see the reasons for doing each one. He will see that accurate filing is important for speedy retrieval and how inaccurate filing can result in the loss of film. The filing of large quantities of film as with quantities of any other material is subject to human errors, numbers become transposed, can numbers are used as production numbers and film is filed in the wrong year.

A vault assistant is therefore a junior member of staff. He should be an accurate and conscientious worker to prevent the sort of error mentioned and needs to have a flexible approach to the job. Anyone handling film and film machinery also needs to have a certain mechanical aptitude. Film is fragile and awkward to handle. An awkward handler on top of this factor can have disastrous results.

Finally when a vault assistant is appointed he should be given a clear indication of his likely progress in the department. If he has a goal to aim for and is given to understand that he will receive promotion or an alternative job if he does the current one satisfactorily he will, or should, have more interest in his work than in a job with nothing to aim for. This is also helpful to the film library which tends to lose junior staff to film editing or production because no career is mapped out for juniors in library work.

Vault keepers are responsible for the storage of film and are normally placed in charge of the vault assistants. The vault keeper has to have a knowledge of correct storage conditions and how to achieve them, and an organisational ability to keep the film accessible.

In an archive, on the other hand, the vault keeper should be a highly skilled technician with a great deal of responsibility for storing, preserving and restoring the film. This post is usually referred to as that of film preservation officer.

Large commercial film libraries also need film preservation officers to check through the older film and arrange for duping where it is deteriorating. The preservation officer also repairs and restores any film which requires it. He must therefore be a skilled technician with all types of film handled in the library.

Handling staff prepare the film for viewing, view it with potential customers and prepare the film for laboratory printing and the prints and material for customers on its return from the laboratories. They are concerned with breaking down prints, matching prints, cutting negatives for various purposes including making stockshots, and ensuring that the film sent out is the same as the order. They need to have a basic knowledge of photography and film production methods as well as laboratory processing techniques. Film handling staff usually work their way up from more junior posts in a library and are given training in film techniques within the organisation.

Another section of the technical staff in a film library may include microfilm operators. They should be technically able to deal with the microfilm machinery, have a basic knowledge of photographic techniques and enough competence to be able to sort out the material to be microfilmed. The job can be very repetitive, but junior members of staff are not normally adequate for the job and all their work has to be checked by another more senior member of staff.

Selection and acquisition staff. Selection staff need to have a knowledge of photography to recognise the quality of the material. Also a wide knowledge of the collection in order to judge the relevance of the new material. Acquisition staff employed in distribution or educational film libraries need also a knowledge of customer requirements and the type, subject, age or ability level of the material likely to be required by the customer. In archives a knowledge of film history is essential as well as a knowledge of television production in more recent years for the acquisition of televised material. Some archives separate the two jobs and employ both film and television acquisitions officers. Staff who are employed to obtain current affairs or new material should have a background interest in current affairs and recent history in order to judge whether the new piece of material is sufficiently important or useful to be retained. Some writers claim that selection staff in newsfilm libraries should have a flair for news, but this is of less importance than having a flair for knowing the type of film which will be reused in all sorts of programmes and by all types of user. In highly specialised libraries selection staff may be employed with suitable training, e.g. scientists or historians to deal with particular types of film.

Acquisition and selection staff may also have to have film handling ability to select material from cuts rather than try to hand this job on to some other person. The delay in explaining requirements to another member of staff may not be justified if one person can select and process the cuts at the same time. In a stockshot or a feature production library however the actual job of negative cutting for stockshots is usually handed over to a specialist member of staff. As selection is such an important part of the library's work it follows that selection staff should be among the senior members of the staff. In small libraries the librarian may well undertake to do the work as he is the person responsible for the collection and therefore the material which is retained in it. Otherwise a senior staff member with wide general knowledge and film handling ability is needed.

Enquiry staff. The enquiry staff may have to cope with different types of enquiry from outside sources. Some enquiries require a detailed specific knowledge of the collection, e.g. stockshot libraries. Others need a wide general knowledge of the art or history of the film, e.g. archive staff. Others need a wide knowledge of the sources of film, e.g. distribution or educational film hire libraries where enquiries are often made for film not in stock and the librarian has to be able to locate and borrow film copies for the user or suggest suitable alternatives. Television library enquiry staff need a knowledge of both the collection to hand and a general ability with reference material as well as familiarity with current affairs. In a newsfilm library which serves news and current affairs programmes the enquiries are generally specific, a certain piece of film shot on a particular day showing a definite event or personalities. This type of enquiry can be answered by any member of the library staff who is competent to use the catalogues. If most of the enquiry work is of this type a specialist staff may not be appointed, but several other members of staff will answer enquiries in addition to or as a complement to their other work. In the larger, more general libraries which receive a number of enquiries daily, members of staff have to be allocated to enquiry work. Enquiry staff have to be quick workers in film libraries, intelligent, have a grasp of the contents of the collection or their specific subject and be able to translate garbled or woolly requests into intelligible search questions. They need to have a flair for looking in the right place for information. For quick answer enquiries the staff need to have a knowledge of film processing and handling in order to take urgent requests for printing material, instead of handing this part of the enquiry over to others. Enquiry staff need to know when a particular printing request is either impossible to fulfil or will take longer than the enquirer can wait. The enquirer often asks the impossible and should be informed of any difficulties immediately.

Other enquiries require more detailed research and here again depending on the volume of the requests specialist enquiry staff may be appointed or the work may be passed on to particular departments. The cataloguing department are in a good position to deal with these more detailed requests. They know the material in the catalogues and should know the relevant places to look for information.

Where a specialist enquiry staff is employed the researchers can select material and cut down on the incessant viewing of film. They build up a knowledge of the collections and can fill customers' requirements more efficiently than a non-specialist staff. The film researcher in fact becomes equivalent to an information scientist. The researcher needs a precise knowledge of customer needs and for this has to be trained in asking the right questions and translating the customer's answers into relevant terms. The research worker has to find out how much film the customer will eventually use, exactly what is required, e.g. specific titles, scenes, sequences, actuality, aftermath, close up, general views, personalities and establishing shots. Also how the material will be used in the final product, whether for information, atmosphere, to create period or establish locale. Next the research worker explores appropriate parts of the catalogues, eliminating obviously unsuitable film. The final product will probably be a short list of film for viewing which fills the customer's requirements and does not confuse him as much as the current practice of viewing everything on wide topics in the hope that a more specific topic will emerge.

Television companies and others sometimes have their own research or production assistants, often attached to a particular programme. In such cases it should not be necessary for them to pay an outside research worker to do the job they already employ a member of staff to do. Film agencies may make research facilities available to customers. This happens when the library devotes all its energy to putting the collection in order and staff are not available for research for outside customers. Providing the catalogues are accessible, reasonably coherent and accurate, outside research workers can use them. But a library has no control over the quality of the outside research workers and library staff are still required to guide the research workers and prevent 'blanket' viewing which does not use the collection to best advantage.

Cataloguing staff. This staff should consist of trained and experienced librarians with a particular interest in film. General training for library work assists them in standardising procedures and rules for cataloguing and classification, but they need to take account of the particular nature of film to carry through these general principles. Without a basic library training much time and effort is wasted in learning even simple cataloguing rules and without an understanding of film much time is wasted in making wrong decisions. Unfortunately there are few trained librarians in the UK who have a knowledge of film handling and no courses which specialise in the work. It may be argued that film librarianship is a very small and specialised subject, but more libraries are now having to cope with several audio visual media and more attention should be given to this aspect by those responsible for training librarians.

A film library cataloguer needs to have a training in general cataloguing principles, and a further training in the nature of film to enable him to utilise these principles in the particular medium. He also needs a wide general knowledge of current affairs and the techniques of film making to assist when shotlisting and indexing the film, as well as the usual attributes of any cataloguer — a tidy, accurate and systematic mind.

PLAN OF STAFFING

The normal plan of staffing and hierarchy in a large film library could be as shown on page 201.

Most film libraries have at least part of this staff layout, although few have as comprehensive a coverage at present. In commercial libraries with a large intake and output of film the library tends to split clearly into two departments presided over by an administration department. The technical processes of handling film, acquisition, storage, preservation, filing, retrieval, preparation for viewing, laboratory processing and despatch become separated from the department which deals with cataloguing the collection, documentation, enquiry and information work.

PROFESSIONAL AND NON-PROFESSIONAL STAFF

The ratio of technical and professional to non-professional staff is dependent on the type of the collection, the size and the state of indexing as well as the usage made of the collection. If the collection is large and well used there is greater need for

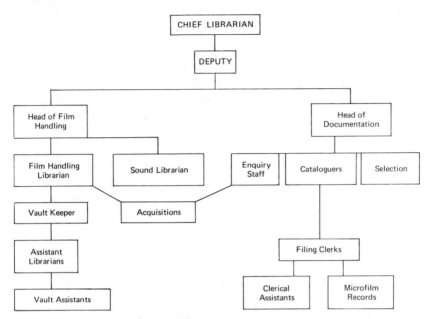

Plan of staffing and heirarchy in a large film library.

non-professional staff to keep the business flowing, that is to file and retrieve film, prepare it for viewing or processing, maintain basic records, such as those for film movement, and maintain bookkeeping and other clerical work concerned with charges and royalty payments. Archives employ a greater proportion of research staff than others. Enquiry and information services are more developed in some libraries than others.

If there is a large backlog of film to be indexed, a large proportion of the staff may be engaged on cataloguing. Selection, where it is a prominent part of the work and enquiries done within the library also need more professional staff and the ratio of professional to non-professional is more evenly balanced. The work allocation also influences the ratio of staff. If all members of staff do similar work or something of everything, higher grade staff are needed than if some are doing all clerical work and others professional.

FLEXIBILITY OF STAFF

Flexibility in terms of staff abilities is useful. Cataloguers who index the film can progress to the more searching enquiry work for customers, or they can also be used in selection work.

It is probably better to have a smaller group of higher grade staff than a large group of unskilled staff. In a large commercial film library many routine tasks can be carried out by unskilled staff, although not as accurately and quickly as trained staff would do the job. The balance has to be struck between consistently using a highly skilled person to do an unskilled job to the detriment of his skilled work, and using him to do a small proportion of unskilled work more efficiently than unskilled workers.

Older more experienced staff can undertake the whole range of necessary duties. Speed, accuracy and an overall grasp of the work and its purpose are not qualities to be picked up in a few short weeks, or by inexperienced juniors.

The use of specialist staff may bring additional factors to bear on the jobs carried out by members of staff. Specialist staff often prefer to follow through their own decisions, e.g. a classifier may prefer to file his own index entries. This brings the additional problem that certain areas of the index become the property of one person, a classifier becomes a law unto himself and it proves difficult for enquiry staff to retrieve information in certain areas. Specialists are valuable, but should never be the sole source of information on particular topics. The information has to be put into a general pool easily retrieved by all information staff. The value of specialists does not lie in their becoming walking indexes or the only staff capable of retrieving specific items of information.

Many organisations require flexibility in the staff, and each member is trained to carry through all jobs. This means that all members of staff have to be able to handle film, index and shotlist it, deal with customer requests and ensure that correspondence, contracts and royalties are notified to central records and finance offices. The advantages are that periods for holidays and sickness or terminations of employment do not disrupt or abruptly stop certain work and the staff have an overall grasp of the work and the purpose of an organisation.

SIZE OF STAFF

The size of staff depends on many factors, including the size of the organisation, the size of the collection and its projected use. The size of the parent organisation is important. If it is large and producing or acquiring large amounts of film it needs a large library staff to cope. If small, the library staff can be proportionately small.

The size of the collection is also a determining factor. The amount of film being acquired, the original size of the collection and its state of indexing and documentation indicate the number of staff needed to work on it. If a large collection of film is acquired by donation or purchase, and the accompanying catalogues and documentation are minimal, extra staff will be required to view the film, index it and instigate preservation procedures. Even if adequate cataloguing and documentation exist it may be necessary to amalgamate the new collection with existing systems, although most film libraries suffer from a lack of documentation rather than a surfeit.

Another factor which governs the size of staff is the use or projected use of the library's collection. This also determines the type of staff required. If the library is frequently used more staff are required for film handling, answering enquiries and dealing with requests. If projected use of the library and future exploitation can be measured, a delicate balance in staff is needed to ensure that the collection is in a state to sustain greater use both in the quality of its documentation and the necessary handling facilities. As a practical example, consider: A collection of some 26 million feet being added to at a rate of 12,000 items a year, i.e. with black and white, colour footage and cuts, some 1,124,000 feet per annum. This is part of a busy newsfilm agency supplying some 500 customers with 1,151,113 feet of film or 19,318 issues per year and coping with 300—400 enquiries per week. The library would need a staff of approximately 25 using conventional methods of indexing and handling the film. Of this number a chief librarian, a deputy and a personal secretary are administrative, 13 staff members are employed on film handling duties and customers' enquiries and 9 deal with cataloguing and documentation.

SALARIES

It is difficult to generalise about staff salaries as each library has its own particular structure and recruits and pays staff accordingly. But some factors should be considered when the salary structure is formulated. Salaries should be commensurate with responsibilities, experience and age, and special qualifications required.

Responsibilities. The salary structure generally follows the same hierarchy as the plan of staffing. The administration staff have the greatest responsibility. The heads of documentation and film handling departments have responsibility for the work carried out in their department and should receive a salary which recognises this. Barbara Kyle in the *Handbook of Special Librarianship and Information Work, Aslib 1967*, suggests that a deputy should receive some 66—75 per cent of the chief librarian and other senior staff some 50—65 per cent. In practice film libraries pay at the top of these ranges and the heads of department probably receive similar grading to the deputy librarian if there is one.

Experience and age. The more experienced members of staff should receive recognition in higher salaries than others within the same grade. This can be achieved by having a salary scale within the grades and appointing experienced people higher up the scale and inexperienced people at the lower end. Many of the staff in film libraries at vault assistant and clerical level are very young and they are paid a percentage of the full rate for the job until they reach an age at which the full rate can be paid.

Qualifications. This is an extension of experience, but whereas experience is concerned with proven ability in a particular job, qualifications are concerned with probable aptitudes for a job. Film handling and documentation or cataloguing staff are expected to have special skills associated with their work and should be compensated for having acquired these skills. Film handling staff are expected to have technical expertise in film processing, development, storage, matching film, etc., and cataloguing and enquiry staff have had previous training in librarianship, or information work. Again there are several salary grades within these two main sections, depending on the type of work performed and responsibilities.

Qualifications are not normally required for junior vault staff and clerical assistants, but vault staff are required to handle film which puts them into a technical grade. As the type of work is comparable, comparable rewards should be given. If this is not done the library will be unable to recruit staff to the less well paid post. The vault keeper in a commercial film library should receive a salary somewhere between the junior and senior film handling staff.

Salaries paid within a library should be comparable to other salaries within the organisation and those outside the organisation. The administrative staff, that is the chief librarian, should have a salary grade equivalent to other heads of departments within the same organisation. His responsibilities are as great, if not greater, and of the same type, i.e. policy decisions, supervision of work and staff.

The salary structure of film handling staff can be compared with that of editing and cutting room staff.

Within an organisation, parity of salaries between different departments may be difficult to judge, but discrepancies in skill and experience required, amount of work expected and the salaries awarded are a serious source of unrest. Additionally it is difficult to retain staff in the departments which offer less remuneration. The library is often regarded as a training ground for all staff. They receive grounding in library work but once trained go elsewhere for higher salary gradings and further prospects of promotion. This means that the library is wasting time training a recruit for other departments and cannot achieve the benefits of continuity. If the salaries were evenly balanced the library would be in a better position to recruit, train and retain useful members of staff. It should be part of recruitment policy to appoint, not general film assistants, but people with an interest in library work, and the salaries offered should encourage the person to remain in the library and not seek employment in other aspects of film work.

Salaries outside the organisation also have to be considered. In a film library salaries in other film libraries, film production work and general library work should be taken into account. Film librarians with library qualifications should fall into the scales recommended for special libraries. Film handling staff are graded on the current union agreements for film production work.

Union agreements in British film libraries are usually the basis on which all salaries are considered. Film technicians' unions such as ACTT and NATKE or staff associations like the BBC's ABS (Association of Broadcasting Staff) negotiate agreements with individual companies and lay down salary grades and minimum rates. Clerical workers may not be covered by these agreements but should be paid at equivalent rates for the type of job and experience needed. These union agreements are normally short term and do not have incremental scales for some of the posts. This makes it necessary for constant renegotiation of the salary scales.

WORKING CONDITIONS

Normal office hours and working conditions apply to many of the posts in film libraries, but in television libraries special hours may have to be worked to fit in with television schedules. Newsfilm agencies which work 24 hours a day have to have extended hours in the library to keep to television and airline schedules. Also, in a newsfilm or television library members of the library staff should be on hand to obtain film and provide information quickly when major news stories break. If they are not there, film may be withdrawn by other people in the organisation and this does not assist either the library system or the continued preservation of the film. It should be a rule in all film libraries that library film is taken from the vaults only by library staff and the department must have sufficient staff for the purpose.

Working shift hours in a library also means that a larger number of staff can be employed than the premises will carry at any one time. In film libraries essential equipment is bulky and takes up space needed for staff. Staggering the hours of work increases efficiency and the amount of work it is possible to do.

It is however not necessary or desirable to have all members of staff on shift. It is important to have administrative staff on a normal five-day week to cope with day-to-day contract work, contact with customers, exploitation of the collections and control of staff.

It is useful to have some of the cataloguing staff on a five-day week. They will then be aware of all material which is finding its way into the collection. Some stories and film never come to the notice of people on shift, no matter how rigorous the handover practice is. If the cataloguing staff are part shift and part non-shift, the non-shift workers can be made aware of film by checking the work done during the shift hours and filing the material.

Major research can be carried on either during shift or five-day week, but quick enquiries are dealt with by shift workers.

UNION AGREEMENTS

The film technicians trade union, the Association of Cinematograph, Television and Allied Technicians (ACTT) controls many of the agreements made between management and employees concerning salary grade and conditions of work. These conditions and salaries are not uniform throughout the industry but depend on current agreements. Entry into the film industry can prove difficult at present, owing to underemployment of union members, but where entry is obtained on production of alternative qualifications, as with library staff, union membership is often obligatory. Membership of the unions may be irrelevant to the staff who are recruited for their librarianship qualifications, rather than their technical qualities. For example, it is seldom necessary for a qualified librarian to have union membership in order to move around in film libraries, for only a few existing film libraries are bound by union agreements, mainly the production, news or television film libraries.

Librarians recruited into the industry on the basis of their qualifications and experience can obtain union membership after a period of time, but it is nearly always a matter of convenience rather than necessity.

STAFF TRAINING

As the staff of film libraries are seldom librarians in that they have acquired formal training and qualifications in librarianship, staff training assumes an importance. Film library work requires additional technical skills concerned with the handling of film. Many film libraries recruit their film handling staff from other departments in the parent organisation, thus side-stepping the problem of training staff in the library itself. Other recruits to film libraries are young junior staff with no training in film handling or library work and staff for the cataloguing or information departments where formal training in librarianship is useful. The main problem of most film libraries today is coping with the overwhelming flood of film pouring in, and basic principles of cataloguing, classification and information retrieval apply to film libraries as much as to any other type of library. There should be no need to train staff in these principles during working hours and they should be recruited on the basis of suitable qualification for the particular task. Special training should be required only for the nature of the material handled.

At present many film libraries neither actively recruit such staff nor do they accept the responsibility of training their unqualified staff.

Basic film handling techniques are important for all members of staff who come into contact with film. This is a positive measure to ensure the all-round usefulness of members of staff. The other and most important reason for basic film handling training is as a preventive measure. Film is an expensive and non-repeatable medium, especially newsfilm where an event occurs only once. Damage to film in rewinding, filing and storage, viewing or preparation for printing and use is extremely likely, but can be avoided if its properties are understood and care is taken in handling.

Current training methods. At present there are no sources of training for film librarians. There is no school of cinematography in Britain which is recognised by the industry or whose diploma guarantees subsequent employment. The normal method of entry into the film industry is by obtaining a junior post in a film-making organisation. Some technical colleges have part-time courses in film making or photography, while others have full-time courses, for example the Slade School of Film Technique and Hornsey College of Art, but neither of these produces a student willing to start in junior vault assistant grades in film libraries. The training given is in most cases irrelevant to film library work and concentrates rather on actual production or editing work. Other organisations have run short courses for film librarians, for example ASLIB, but the response was not encouraging. This suggests that training within organisations is so poorly regulated that interest is lacking in trying to solve the problem by interlibrary co-operation. The Aslib courses were more in the nature of introductory seminars on different methods in film libraries, not practical aspects of the work involved.

The ACTT and the ITC (International Television Council) announced in June 1968 a training scheme for entrants to the film-making field in general which was a step in the right direction of training people at the beginning of their careers instead of trying to train them on a particular job. But again the emphasis of these courses is on film production rather than any library techniques.

The possibilities of some form of training for film handlers in libraries include a short crash course by an outside source on film handling, e.g. a summer school, or a short course specifically aimed at film handling by one of the unions concerned, e.g. the ACTT/ITC scheme quoted. The other possibility is a short period of training within a film library, i.e. in-training before taking up the specific job. This latter is the most feasible, and is in the interests of the organisations concerned until more formal training can be organised. But too often because of staff shortages there is insufficient time for a new member to be spared for training. Additionally the senior staff are unable to spare sufficient time to train a new recruit. Where training is possible it should be undertaken by a senior member of staff with aptitude for the task as well as the necessary knowledge, and one who can be spared for the whole of the training period rather than one who is trying to train staff and carry out his normal work at the same time.

Extent of training required. Staff should be introduced to the aims of the organisation as a whole, how the library fits into the pattern of activity and how any particular job fits into the pattern of the library.

Basic training in film handling should include elementary points like not touching the film and emulsion surface to prevent dust or grease scratching or damaging the emulsion; how to wind film so that it is not too loose and rubs on itself causing scratching, or too tight so that it snaps. Recognition of stock used in the film industry generally should also be demonstrated (safety and nitrate film, 35mm, 16mm or 8mm) and any special handling problems involved, e.g. special handling and storage of nitrate. A junior vault assistant must be able to recognise deteriorating film. Additionally recognition of negative or positive stock, type of track (optical or magnetic), type of print (combined, mute, duplicate material, colour masters and prints or internegatives etc.). Where in-training is being given it is necessary to go over the viewing machines available to the librarians and their use together with any other machines available in the organisation which may have to be used.

A short introduction to the laboratory and printing processes is necessary as well as editing principles to give recruits an idea of how film and sound can be used.

Cataloguing staff need training in film handling principles, particularly where they are required to view the film material and use the viewing machines. They should also be able to recognise stock for use in collating details of the film. A period of time training cataloguers in film handling techniques prevents expensive and irrevocable mistakes. It also improves the cataloguer's experience and general usefulness.

Finally, short one-day refresher courses are useful to remind the trainee of other types of material and machines which he may have to use. These afford opportunities for employees to widen their experience and improve staff relations, showing that management is sufficiently interested in their staff to help them gain experience.

There is currently a move to introduce more consideration of audio-visual materials in the general training of librarians. This inclusion will not be before time, but there are several points to bear in mind. The introduction of audio-visual librarianship should be throughout any syllabus and not restricted to one or two papers or sections of a course. More and more librarians are finding that they have to deal with information packaged in several media within the one library. Libraries are tending to become centres for the storage and exploitation of all materials including books and a greater number of these will undoubtedly emerge than those limited to one physical form or medium. This means that even when audio-visual librarianship is included in library school syllabi as a matter of course consideration of each physical form will be restricted to the general rather than the particular or detailed familiarisation with a material. Film libraries will have to continue with in-training programmes, or short courses, or extra-mural courses provided by external bodies concerned with film librarianship only.

II

LAYOUT AND PLANNING

A S A FILM library expands, its functions increase, staff increases, more storage space is required and a larger working area is always being sought. The accelerated growth of the television and newsfilm industries in particular, together with the haphazard way in which many film libraries have been developed in the past, means that they have outgrown their existing premises and there are few if any that can be cited as ideally or even tolerably well designed and equipped. There are two alternatives when existing space becomes inadequate: the library can either seek new premises or acquire additional space within the present building and reorganise within the new area. When the library acquires new premises even more careful planning is required and the opportunities for planning are greater.

Preplanning is an important phase in any system of reorganisation. The objectives of a library, the services which are planned, the space required for storage, equipment and staff to work can all be drawn up and considered and basic requirements decided before the space is allocated or the accommodation built. During preplanning the function of the library has to be considered in relation to other parts of the main organisation as well as to outside users. Alternative plans and systems can be drawn up and examined and, if time allows, some practical experiments can be made in specific areas to help decide the most helpful solutions to the problems encountered. These measures should help to prevent expensive and unworkable mistakes being made.

RESPONSIBILITY FOR PLANNING DECISIONS

The responsibility for providing the functional unit is the librarian's. He should be responsible for planning and the layout of his own department in order to make it work efficiently. It should not be left to the administrative staff of the company, because they are aware only of the broad outlines of the services and functions of any one department, not the detailed running and requirements. A film library has special requirements of storage, issue and retrieval of film. The planning of the actual layout is done in close consultation with the architectural staff who can advise on what can and cannot be done within the general design, but flow patterns and inter-relation of jobs within the library can best be supplied by the librarian.

A film library has to be planned with its functions firmly in mind. Existing services should be taken into consideration as well as any anticipated changes and expansion in the stock or type of user services. Film libraries which serve the main organisation and only a small percentage of outside users, are planned in relation to the company offices. Alternatively the library may serve an extensive range of outside users with only a limited type of service to its own company and in this case the department can be planned to be more independent of the main organisation. The company is regarded as one more user of the library in the latter case, but it also serves as the storehouse of company film and helps to exploit the film commercially.

PLANNING FOR THE FUTURE

In planning any layout, future needs have to be considered. To design a unit that will fit current requirements is mere expediency, not planning, and any library, by its nature, has to allow for expansion. However this should be done realistically. In a rapidly growing library, where storage space is at a premium, the temptation is always to ask for as much space as possible, on the basis that it will be needed in several years time. But even in a library it is possible to overestimate the amount of space required and it is wiser to plan for the foreseeable future. If plans are made too far ahead, developments in the film industry (as well as techniques in other libraries) may outstrip today's knowledge and the planner may find that he has provided for materials and functions that cease to exist in a few years' time.

Nevertheless it is difficult for a film librarian to work out how much vault space will be needed in 5–10 years' time with a rapidly expanding collection and the diversification of functions of the parent company. A company tries out new functions, e.g. a production company may increase its stockshot collection to the extent that it begins to sell material outside the firm, or a newsfilm company may compile documentaries, find that they are useful and expand this side of their activities. All this film and its documentation has to be housed, and may begin to use up space needed for the original film. In planning for expansion therefore the librarian needs to be aware of all aspects of the parent company and its future policies, so that he can allow for adjustments in emphasis and provide functions and space to deal with it.

SITE PLANNING

Film libraries attached to production companies need to be sited near the company's main production offices and the studios. Distribution and educational hire libraries do not need to be attached to any one studio and can be cited centrally to cover as many users as possible in a small radius. Other educational film libraries attached to particular colleges or which form the central core of a circuit should be in the institution concerned or again centrally placed to the circuit area.

Television film libraries are normally sited in the television station or, like the BBC, in an area which is situated within easy distance of the studios. A large television film library takes up a vast amount of space and it may not be viable to house it in the station offices.

Newsfilm agencies and the libraries related to them are best served by being close to the film movement routes, e.g. airports for shipping the film and the television transmission stations for telerecording facilities and an outlet for film. If the agency is connected closely with a particular television station, it should be accessible to that station. Future developments in television could in time eliminate this necessity by the use of coaxial cables, closed circuit or telecine techniques for the transmission of film.

Once a site is chosen the library requirements have to be considered and special consideration has to be given to the siting of the film store and the library department in relation to the rest of the organisation.

Vaults. Major consideration should be given to the storage of film and special vaults may have to be built. The essential features of these vaults are discussed on pages 179–80. The vaults should not be exposed to much sunshine to prevent overheating, and should therefore be built either in the shade of other buildings with air passage on all sides, or behind natural sunbreaks or trees. An air conditioning or ventilation unit should be installed in any new vault building, but there is no point in increasing its workload when simple precautions about siting can be taken. Vaults should also be above water or flood level and have adequate drainage installed around them to ensure they do not take in water. Finally the vaults should be as close as possible to the library in any busy organisation where fast movement of film is needed, preferably with covered way access, and this access should be direct from the library, not through other departments.

Library. The library should be placed so that it is accessible within the organisation concerned, and close to the services it deals with most. It should be placed next to the vaults for speed of film retrieval and efficient running of the department. Many factors work against this condition, but splitting the library and film store should be avoided if at all possible. A library within a film organisation is usually most closely connected with the technical processing department, e.g. laboratories, cutting rooms for easy receipt of film and traffic for external services. Some services within the company may require easier access to the library film than others, for example any departments producing background features using library film. These departments often have quantities of library film out at a time, and if the library needs any for supply to other users, the departments should be accessible.

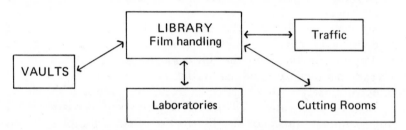

Direction of services — a consideration in the placing of the library within the organisation

The library is best sited on the ground floor to save carrying film up and down stairs from the vaults to work area, and as far as practicable library services where interdependent should be on one level to improve efficiency. Some departments may be placed on another level, e.g. microfilm units, administrative staff; but in general film, documentation, catalogues and the staff which cope with all these plus the enquiry staff should all be easily accessible to one another.

It is important to have all departments under one roof. This makes for greater ease in working and eliminates unnecessary delays and risk of loss of film in transit. If the vaults are not in the same place as the offices, the library is unable to provide the fast service required for meeting television news deadlines. Some film libraries have been forced to store their film at considerable distances from the main offices and information centres. The reason is usually that main offices are in an urban area and the fire regulations insist film is stored in an area where there is less danger from fire and explosion. Transporting the film from the vaults to viewing offices or laboratories can take considerable time and the service to users has to be organised on a different basis. Sometimes viewing facilities can be made available at both main offices and vault areas, some 'viewing' copies may be made on videotape and transmitted from one area to another.

RELATIONSHIP BETWEEN UNITS

Once the site of the building and the library are decided, the next step is to analyse the relationships between the functional units within the library and the special needs of each unit. Once the departments are gathered together, the library can be planned with reference to the interrelationships between departments of the library. The two main sections of a film library deal primarily with film handling and the documentation of film. A typical division of labour in a large film library includes:
1. Administrative and secretarial staff.
2. Film handling staff, including the intake of film, viewing and preparation.
3. Documentation staff including the intake and filing staff, cataloguing and classification.
4. Enquiry staff.
5. Selection staff to be accommodated, and also several services have to be allowed for such as:
6. Customer viewing facilities.
7. Other services such as photocopying.
8. Microfilm.

Administrative and secretarial staff. This includes supervisory staff, and those connected with sales, copyright, contracts, general policies of the library and staff relations. It is not essential to have this department in the thick of the work area. It is connected with all other sections, but is concerned with processing the work done by other departments, rather than having to use the services maintained by these sections. This staff could be placed at one end of the library area, or on a different level, but still with direct access from the main work area.

Film handling staff. They need to be in the central work area with winding benches for preparation of film whether for intake, permanent storage, distribution, viewing or laboratories. An adequate number of winding benches of the right or interchangeable size is essential to prevent queues and blockages forming. They should be close to the viewing machines for final checking or selection of material. The section of the library must also be close to the vaults with direct access to facilitate the continual movement of film to and from the section. The department should also be accessible to outside departments, especially cutting rooms and traffic for intake of film and supply to customers.

All work areas should be well lit and ventilated, but ventilation is of great importance in this area, particularly if noxious chemicals are in use or being handled, e.g. nitrate film, film cement. The area should also be kept as dust free as possible because dust damages film.

Documentation staff. Documentation staff deal with the intake of film documents, scripts, shotlists and background material. The staff should be in the same area as the material to facilitate filing and withdrawal for researchers.

Cataloguing and classification staff should have easy access to the shotlists, film accessions records, film and viewing facilities for shotlisting. The departments should be housed in a separate area to allow for the peace and quiet these tasks require. They will need to be in the same area as the main index for quick reference and other enquiries or research, but there should also be a separate room for the actual indexing, to allow for work undisturbed by the constant interruptions which occur in the main index room. Noise can cause mistakes and a mistake in information being fed into the catalogues may perpetuate itself. The cataloguing staff also need access to the reference library and information unit. Reference books, periodicals, newspapers or tape messages are all used by the cataloguing staff as well as the enquiry staff of the film library.

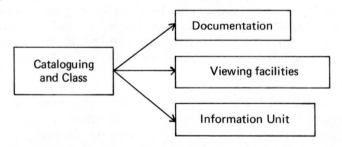

Access required by cataloguing and classification staff.

Enquiry staff. Staff engaged on enquiries should be close to the reference sections just mentioned and the main index. As this department probably makes greater use of telephones than others in the library the noise factor means that they should be separated from the cataloguing or selection sections where noise can be disturbing. They should also be separated from the film handling areas where machines are running as this noise will disturb them. It is not so essential for the enquiry staff to be near the film, as the enquiries are usually passed on after research to the film handling sections who withdraw and process the film for the customer.

Selection and acquisitions staff. Access to viewing machines which are not constantly in demand for customer and other requirements must be provided. Winding benches and film handling facilities or editing machines should be made available if feasible. The staff also need reasonable access to the catalogues for checking material for final selection against stock already held as well as access to the reference library, especially for acquisitions staff. If stockshot selection is intended the selection staff also have to have full projection equipment available for final selection.

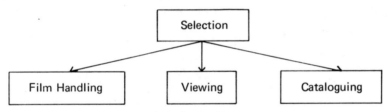

Access required by selection and acquisitions staff.

Customer viewing facilities. Viewing machines run by the film handling staff will be sited within the library, in quiet soundproof areas to prevent the transfer of noise either from the viewing machines or from other work areas of the library. The viewing machines should be accessible to outside users, not tucked away at the far end of the library where customers have to trail right through the work area. The machines should also be reasonably accessible to the vaults and film handling areas where the film is prepared for viewing rather than near the catalogue areas.

Additional services. If a separate print room is to be made available for photocopying, both for outside users and internal use, it should either be incorporated in the library or next to it if any of the library systems are geared to photocopying. Shotlists may have to be copied for supply with film, or lists may be compiled quickly by photocopying catalogue cards. For either of these purposes the photocopier should be immediately accessible to the library staff and they should do the work to prevent loss of shotlists or catalogue cards. If they are left to be reproduced by others the risk of loss is the greater.

Microfilm units if used are also generally sited in the library area concerned with documentation. One film library microfilms its shotlists and houses both the microfilm production unit and the storage cabinets plus viewers and print machines. The microfilm records need to be readily available, but the production unit or camera can be sited away from the priority areas which have considerable interchange of function and material. To benefit from the microfilm system the user needs quick access to the records and storage cabinets need to be kept at a central point near enquiry, research and cataloguing departments. A safety file can be cited elsewhere. Readers will be scattered at certain points in the system, near phones for research, in the cataloguing department, near film viewing machines for use when showing film, in selection areas and possibly also extra departmental viewers for use in other parts of the organisation. Print out facilities for microfilm can be placed in the unit for photocopying. This keeps the noise away from other departments and controls the unavoidable clutter of materials and papers associated with these copying processes. If reader printers are used the system will be organised differently, probably fewer machines, but they may have to be sited in the enquiry departments for efficiency.

SPACE REQUIREMENTS

When the various functions of the library and their inter-relations have been drawn up the amount of space each activity requires should be considered. Space is needed for all equipment and staff actually operating and allowance must be made for additional staff and equipment in the foreseeable future. Space is needed for:

1. Storing documents, i.e. film and shotlists.
2. User activities.
3. Staff activities.
4. Services (including architectural services, not library services).

Storing documents. In a film library the space use increases rapidly as film is constantly added and plenty of extra vault space should always be allowed. The amount can be calculated on the basis of the average amount of footage contained in a can and how many cans are stored on a length of shelving. An average number of stories and therefore footage can be taken per year and the amount multiplied by the number of years to be provided for.

Storage space for other documents includes shelving for reference books, box files, periodicals and pamphlet material, lateral filing cabinets for shotlists, filing cabinets for catalogue cards, and any special cabinets for holding microfilm.

Shotlists can be stored in box files on ordinary shelving, but this is a cumbersome, inconvenient way to file. Lateral filing cabinets take more material in a smaller area, but the cabinets themselves are large and take up space. The lateral files can be placed end on to the wall to save some space rather than backing on to the wall. The files do not have to be near the walls if the room can be utilised better, but the cabinets are so large that it is often best to keep them out of the centre of a work area. Mobile lateral filing cabinets take less room and require less access space. The storage space required for the documents may be reduced still further by utilising microforms or photocopying techniques. Cabinets for storing microfilm require only space for the cabinet and a double depth of drawer plus user space for consultation.

Other records in a film library include reference books. Depending on the function of the library these may take up an increasing amount of space, or may remain static in number if not in currency. Ordinary shelving or bookshelves built on to office furniture are adequate.

Other material needs to be stored, such as general film lists, lists of special subject interest, press cuttings, pamphlets, catalogues of exhibitions and fashion shows, technical records, production records, film movement indexes, library supply and costing indexes. Shelving or lateral filing can be used for all these records, according to which is available.

Filing cabinets for catalogue cards depend on the size of card used, which in turn depends on the type of indexing carried out. If a large card is used (8 x 5in) single-drawer cabinets are often better than double. Double-drawer types are sometimes heavy to withdraw and if more than one drawer at the top is pulled out, the cabinet can become top heavy and cause an accident by toppling forward. Other catalogue cabinets for smaller cards can be in single drawer form with a division down the middle to give two filing ranks. Filing cabinets should have drawers in accessible positions, not too high or too low. Some filing cabinets have drawers down to usable level with cupboard space underneath. In calculating the amount of space used by a card filing cabinet room has to be allowed for pulling the drawer out to its fullest extent and then some space for the user to consult the index.

User activities. The sort of user activities to be allowed for are research facilities and viewing facilities. The emphasis in film libraries is more strongly on staff activities for the benefit of customers, rather than direct customer activities. The staff constantly have to intervene between the customer and the film, withdrawing, preparing and showing it. Film is necessarily stored in closed access and any closed access system needs additional staff between material and user. Distribution libraries rarely need to cater for users on site as most borrowing is done by post, although preview facilities are often given and a viewing theatre is therefore provided.

In other libraries an adequate number of viewing machines will be needed (adequately staffed again) as well as facilities for research in the main index area, research desks or tables and chairs with microviewers for reading shotlists. As more staff become available for cataloguing and organising the collection and making it available for reuse, more users are attracted and more staff is needed to cope with user needs and additional equipment has to be allowed for.

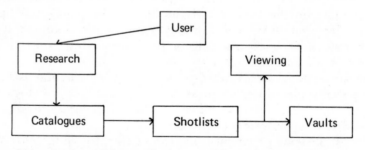

User activities, showing staff intervention between the customer and the film.

Staff activities. The space needed for staff activities grows much more rapidly than that for users. Additional staff in a film library need a large amount of space because their equipment is bulky, especially on the film handling side. The catalogue may also increase more rapidly than expected as the backlog is incorporated and new methods to speed the operation are used.

The film handling area should not be cramped but should allow for easy movement around the winding benches with enough room for trolleys to be used both for working on and transporting film. Winding benches are best placed around the walls, near to electric points for underlights and joiners, and shelving for holding film cans and records. Insufficient space for rewinding film results in damage and an insufficient number of winding benches causes queues to form and leads to confusion when trying to sort large numbers of small reels of film. The rewinding equipment should be fitted with interchangeable central spindles to allow for 35mm and 16mm film at any one bench. Upright winders can be used, especially for measuring film. They take up less space than a flat rewinder and can be mounted on narrower benches, but are not recommended for all rewinding jobs.

Film inspection machines are useful in any large distribution library handling a lot of film in and out each day, but manual or automatic bench rewinders should also be used for particular jobs in hire libraries. The film inspection machine will cope with all routine inspection, but major repairs or short films are best checked on a bench rewind.

Viewing machines are required by several sections of the library and can either be incorporated in the film handling department for checking purposes or in soundproof booths for the use of staff and customers. Sound proofing can be carried out in separate rooms or insulated curtaining can be used to divide a viewing area. Whichever method is used the sound proofing must efficiently stop the transfer of noise from one department to another. With efficient sound proofing the viewing area has to be large enough to allow for adequate ventilation and air circulation.

In addition to specialist equipment, a film library needs much of the usual office furniture like desks, chairs, stools, typewriters, tables etc. Office furniture for film libraries does not require any special features, but unit furniture is the most useful where the units can be built up into blocks of desks and tables to allow large surface areas for people to work on. This applies to any area where large numbers of news copy, shotlists, catalogue cards and film have to be sorted. Custom built furniture can be made, but most film libraries find it too expensive and inflexible. If the equipment is easily rearranged into new patterns as the library expands the furniture can be converted into new layouts to make full use of all the space available. As a library grows, additional equipment is taken in and areas of space change shape. If the basic furniture can be adapted to new shapes it will have a longer useful life.

Services. Finally, consideration has to be given to general services such as lifts, corridors, doors, cloakrooms, etc. All of these may already exist and the library has to be planned around them, but some may be left until the final layout has been decided. In either case this is largely a matter for the architects and it remains for the

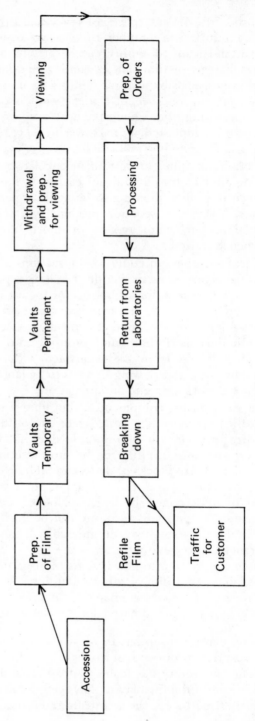

Film Handling Flow Plan

librarian only to ensure that all the available wall space is not used for electric points, radiators or air ducts and that the stairs do not turn up in the middle of the main work areas.

When all the information is gathered the librarian is in a position to begin planning the layout for his library. Systems analysis, flow plans and critical paths can all be used to determine the most useful layout for the department.

Given the flow plan and the site or area available, plans can be drawn up in close consultation with the architectural staff.

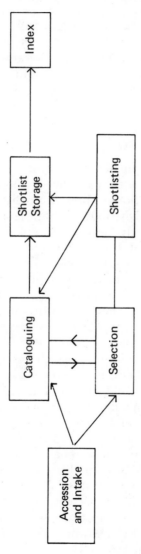

Documentation Flow Plan

12

ECONOMICS

T HE ECONOMICS of a film library can be divided into expenses and income. Expenses incurred by the library include film acquisition, salaries, laboratory and maintenance costs. A considerable outlay is also necessary for equipment. Film library income comes from the sale of copies of film and royalty charges.

FILM ACQUISITION COSTS

Many film libraries do not have to buy their films, unless one library buys a collection from another or there is an amalgamation of two or more collections. Films normally enter libraries from some linked activity. Distribution libraries acquire film from a general agreement with several companies. The production company is relieved of the setting up of an entirely separate department to hire copies of its own film. This is more important for small production companies who need existing resources to produce further film and rather than set up a very small distribution department they come to an agreement with an existing distribution library. The library is supplied with an agreed number of prints and then hires out this film and maintains the viewing copies. Distribution libraries charge for this service either by the print hired or a blanket agreement according to the number of films dealt with for any one company. Distribution libraries which deal with cinema distribution work on similar lines, but usually handle publicity and circuit bookings as well.

Educational libraries acquiring film from outside sources usually have to buy the film at full purchase price, or they may obtain educational discount. Unless the library has considerable funding or is acting as a co-operative store for several other institutions, setting up a collection of viewing prints can be extremely expensive. Most educational institutions in the UK tend rather to hire film for the one or two showings a year that are necessary.

The usual way in which a television or newsfilm library acquires film is for the film to be shot and edited for a programme or newsreel, and then the original negative is passed to the library for storage, preservation and indexing. Some film may have to be bought to supplement a collection but this is not normally a significant factor in the library budget. Copyright remains with the original owner of the film, and the purchasing library is not able to supply this film without royalty payments to the owner.

The film library's expense usually begins once the film has been acquired and passed through normal editing channels. In addition to all the edited and screened stories, the library is usually the repository for all the cuts from these edited stories together with a number of uncut stories which have for one reason or another not been used in the service. Some of the uncut stories may have to be bought by the library if selected.

EXPENDITURE ON STAFF SALARIES

Assuming that the stock (film) is incorporated in the library without payment, staff salaries are probably the largest overhead item in any film library of size, and salaries are also a continuing overhead. Equipment is initially expensive, but once installed expenses reduce, whereas the salary bill continues at the same level or rises as the staff gain seniority and experience, or grow in number, or benefit from pay awards.

LABORATORY COSTS

Laboratory costs are incurred by the library for duping film which is deteriorating or liable to become damaged from overuse. A spare or viewing print of well-used material is excellent insurance against damage, but usually has to be paid for from the library budget. It is advisable to set aside a sum each year for this purpose to enable constant replacement to occur rather than suddenly find a large quantity of film which is in urgent need of duping and nothing in the budget to pay for it. Other laboratory costs for printing material for library customers are passed on to the customer direct and should not affect the library budget.

MAINTENANCE COSTS

Maintenance costs should be allowed for in the library budget. With the increasing use of machines of different type, copying, reproduction of cards, microfilm, film viewers, splicing equipment and winding benches, constant maintenance by engineers is essential. In a film library, the maintenance of film machinery, inspection machines, viewers and winding equipment is generally done by on-site engineers who maintain all film equipment in the organisation. Equipment on hire or supplied by specialist firms, e.g. Xerox machines and microfilm equipment, needs outside attention, either preventive maintenance or in the event of a breakdown. Many firms have special all-in maintenance, whereby the user pays a certain amount each year and receives a number of services on the equipment and special concessions for the supply of parts.

COST OF SITE FACILITIES AND EQUIPMENT

The costs of a film library will include rental for the ground or office buildings, although these are usually absorbed by the parent company and not charged up to the individual departments.

The cost of creating good storage conditions for film, air filters, air conditioning and ventilation may be charged against the library and this is usually a large outlay.

A film library needs much of the usual office furniture like desks, chairs, typewriters and filing cabinets together with a range of specialised equipment to deal with the material handled. Filing cabinets are needed for storage of shotlists and catalogues and the cost grows with the growth of the collection.

A great deal of stationery is required, such as paper for shotlists, folders, catalogue cards, labels and guiding for the catalogues, and stencils for duplicating. Some of the stationery is obtained from normal suppliers, but much has to be custom printed, e.g. production records.

Copying may also have to be charged to the library, for example Xerox equipment, other photocopying equipment and microfilm.

Special equipment is necessary for the film handling department, e.g. film inspection machines, winding benches, waste bins, repair material and leader, as well as storage equipment, including racking for the vaults, cans, boxes and bobbins. Finally, viewing machines are needed and the number depends on the type of work carried out. Sufficient machines are needed for customers, staff checking, shotlisting and selection. Machines also have to be provided for each type of film used, i.e. sound (optical and magnetic), 35mm, 16mm or 8mm.

SOURCES OF INCOME

Income refers specifically to those libraries which sell film and the rest of this section is devoted to a consideration of the charges made by film libraries which exist to sell film for reuse by the user, whether this reuse is entire or only in short clips. Film libraries which fall into this category are principally stockshot and newsfilm libraries, but production libraries also sell short film clips and archives may well supply this type of service for producers of compilation films or programmes. In other libraries economics may be ruled by a set budget rather than an earned income and the following discussion is not applicable to their situation.

Because of the fragile nature of film and the expense of preserving more than one copy of short information film, many film libraries are not lending libraries. Stockshot, television and newsfilm libraries never are. Film is only loaned within an organisation for the compilation of background features or profiles. If material is required by other organisations or users a print or duplicate is sold on a fotage basis. The risk of damage and loss is too high to permit original material to leave the library or governing organisation. Film in this type of library is not normally reused in its original form except for complete programmes. Generally, a producer or editor re-edits and cuts the material. If the original film is cut it is no longer the same film and the library records no longer refer correctly to the film.

Some costs are passed on to the user of a hire library. Customers are charged set fees normally based on one day's hire or one viewing. The fees are set according to the length of the film, and whether it is colour or black and white, sound or silent. Postal or delivery charges are passed on to the customer and damage may also be charged if major repairs have to be effected. If the customer severely damages, destroys or loses the film, he may be charged for replacement.

Costs in commercial film libraries other than the hire libraries are passed on to the user or customer in three ways: a processing charge to cover the cost of the film stock and materials used in making the copy for the customer to work from; a royalty charge which helps to reimburse the library for the 'exclusive' nature of the film and goes towards the costs of running the library and storing the film material; and search and handling fees.

ANALYSIS OF PROCESSING CHARGES

Processing charges arise from the production of material from the library stock. They vary according to the number of printing stages involved, whether colour or black and white, sound or silent, etc., and whether external laboratory work is necessary.

Printing stages. The library supplies the customer with the material required, but sometimes material has to go through two or three stages of processing before these requirements can be filled. The customer normally pays for all stages whether he is supplied with them or not. In some cases the library may retain the intervening stages for its own use. If duping because of deterioration or shrinkage is necessary the library can retain the duplicating stage as its 'original' material for future printing. Other intervening stages which can be utilised by the library are reduction and blow up printing and spare colour material.

Technically, in normal printing, the tonalities are reversed so that positives are printed from negatives and negatives from positives. The exception to this is reversal printing, but the cost of reversal printing is correspondingly higher. The basic cost to a customer is a black and white print from a negative. If a duplicate negative and print for cutting purposes are needed, three stages are made from an original negative and the final two are supplied. The third stage, if it is not required by the library, is destroyed. The customer is charged for it but is not supplied with it because it is a duplicating stage and no use for transmission. Nor is it in the library's interest to supply the customer with duplicating material.

If the library film is positive and the customer requiries a print the film has to go through two stages: a duplicating negative and a print from it. Again the customer is charged for duplicate negative and print. It is important in this connection that the librarian knows the stock available in the library in order to quote appropriate charges to the customer. This information is therefore included in the film record, production record, or any other material related to the film.

Scale of charges. There is usually a set scale of charges for film processing by any one organisation and these scales are roughly comparable between organisations. The charges are made to the libraries by the laboratories whether external or internal to the organisation, and the whole charge is passed on to the customer. The library does not gain or lose from the transaction and makes no profit. Charges are made according to the printing processes involved, the materials used and the time taken to complete the printing according to the customer's instructions.

The library already holds the developed material, and one stage of printing is finished before the library has to handle the film. This developing charge is normally absorbed by the owning company. Straightforward contact prints are the basic cost to a customer and are the cheapest to produce. Duplicating positives, that is fine grain prints, are more expensive and duplicating negatives are approximately double the contact print cost. Development and printing for reversal stock is half as much again as contact prints.

These processes cover the most usual printing required, but should more complex steps be required using different processes and machines, the cost increases accordingly. Reduction printing is often necessary either to bring early film on to the same gauge as more recent film and to provide a uniform gauge for the film editor to work with, or the customer may have only 16mm projection equipment and any 35mm material will have to be reduced to make it available to him. Reduction printing uses a different type of printer and the cost for the process is increased. Blow up is an even more expensive process, and not always as successful as reduction in achieving a good quality image.

Often the customer does not require a print of complete films, if the footage is considerable, and may ask for certain sections only to be supplied. This means that the laboratory has to stop and start film printing at set points and maintain more supervision over the film as it goes through the printer than they would for a straightforward print. A charge is made to cover the extra work involved. The laboratory usually stipulates that a minimum footage run is ordered. Many will not print sections of less than 30 feet and the resulting saving on short pieces of newsfilm may not be worthwhile.

The cost of colour printing is considerably higher than black and white because the processes for colour printing take longer and the materials used are more expensive. The cost is anything from double to treble that of black and white printing. Inter-negatives which may have to be taken to preserve quality are also very expensive.

If sound is required the charges do not increase for optical tracks as the same process is used in printing film and optical track. Magnetic tracks can be supplied at low cost.

The printing of key numbers also incurs no extra charge, as again it is done in the same process as printing the film.

In some cases, either to ensure that film supplied is not transmitted or to assist customers who cannot attend for viewings, scratched prints are supplied to show the customer the film content. The customer returns the prints with his instructions for printing. These scratch prints are normal black and white prints chargeable at contact print rate, but have been scored through each frame to prevent misuse.

External laboratories generally charge more than a laboratory connected with the library through the parent organisation. These external laboratories have to cover their own overheads through subscribers' payments for that service. The charges are therefore passed on to the customer when it is necessary to pass work out, either because the firm's own laboratory is too full to cope or not equipped to produce the required material. In an expanding organisation one or two types of printing jobs are not initially available, e.g. special sound printing or transfers, reductions, blow ups, stills. In some cases it may always be necessary to use outside laboratories, e.g. stills, where the whole of the rest of the operation is concerned with film.

Charges for special jobs or rush jobs also have to be passed on. Many firms charge extra for weekend work, and speed printing where material is required in a matter of hours. Other laboratories charge only for overtime of particular crews where material is required quickly on the basis that they are fully operational for 24 hours a day, 364 days a year.

ROYALTY PAYMENTS

The customer of many commercial film libraries has to pay the libraries in consideration of the time and money spent in obtaining the film and its subsequent preservation by the library for his use. This charge is known as a royalty charge where the customer is paying the 'owner' of the film a 'copyright' fee.

If the library does not own copyright on much of its material the royalty charge has to be levied by the owner of the material. Archive film is often in this category. The archive notifies the user of the owner of the copyright and usually does not release the printed film to the user until clearance is given by the owner.

Hire libraries are not involved in exacting royalty payments. They do not sell film and the users may simply view the film hired, not copy it or cut it to their own requirements. If a user subsequently wishes to obtain prints of the material he has to approach the original copyright owner.

A company which controls and sells its own film or library material hires or pays a cameraman a fee, sends him, or arranges for him to attend events either 'exclusively' or in 'opposition' to other cameramen. The resulting film is syndicated and eventually finds its way into the library. The library on behalf of the company usually claims exclusive rights to film shot by its own cameramen. Additionally a library may have bought certain stated rights in other film, either exclusive or non exclusive, and acquired entire collections of film when other companies closed down, or contracted their activities.

CALCULATION OF ROYALTY CHARGES

The royalty charges are calculated by individual companies according to several criteria and the scales can become complex. The charges depend on the type of production the film is to be used in and the distribution rights required by the customer. Royalties are based on the amount of footage used in the final production rather than on the footage supplied to the customer.

This is normally done on the understanding that the customer destroys the remaining footage supplied. This prevents the customer from acquiring footage for his own use in future productions without paying royalty fees for it. Certificates of destruction should be produced for this excess footage.

Sometimes a customer may agree to pay a royalty charge on all footage supplied. The subscriber pays at the footage supplied rates and retains the film in his own library for future use at agreed rates. This means the customer pays more, but is able to do more with the film.

Libraries do not charge a special rate for film to which they have exclusive rights. The ordinary rates for royalty charges should cover exclusive and non exclusive film alike. If film is exclusive to one library, that library will be the only one able to supply it and payment will automatically go to the library.

Type of user. Production can be divided into television and theatrical or non-television productions. Television rates are lower than theatrical because of the amount of footage used by television, its non-repetitive nature and restricted distribution. Film shown on television is incorporated into programmes or news bulletins to illustrate particular events and these programmes are shown once or twice only at set times. Television reaches a wide audience but the monetary return to the television company is not based on one or two programmes, but their overall service. Television services are financed by government grants and/or investment by commercial organisations who buy advertising time on the networks. These arguments refer only to the short sequence used as part of a longer programme or in a compilation. Different conditions apply to the reshowing of complete programmes or feature films on television.

Theatrical usage of film is more directly related to monetary return. An audience pays to see a particular film or documentary and this payment is received by the distributor of the film. Films shown by theatrical distribution have to be shown many times over to different audiences in order to recoup their cost, and consequently library film used in these productions is being shown many more times than on television. Television programmes are retained and used in a small number of copies, a negative and a positive, but theatrical distribution prints are made in greater numbers and each print contains the library film which has been sold as one piece of film. The distribution of television film is often restricted to one television organisation and even if the programme is sold abroad the number of showings is restricted. Theatrical film makers sell film on a world wide basis, the number of prints increases, the number of showings and the returns received by the distributor increase accordingly.

Theatrical film can be feature or documentary. Feature films with wide distribution and costly production are charged at a high rate. The film they incorporate in their production is of very high quality. Commercial film companies and libraries expect to receive royalty rates for their film commensurate with the cost of filming the material by the production unit. Documentaries or theatrical shorts are not as costly to produce, usually have less wide distribution with lower returns and are not charged as high a rate. The distinction between features and documentaries may not be clear. In such cases the line can be drawn between the two types by a consideration of length. The library may set an arbitrary limit on the length of a short film, e.g. 3000ft, 35mm and regard anything over that limit as a feature, to be charged feature rate.

Films used for education purposes are charged at a lower rate than other types of film. The audience is a small special one and the films do not necessarily stand on their own, but need the intervention of a teacher. Distribution is not wide and they are not made for commercial gain. Educational films are increasingly being made and used both for school and higher education. Greater contact between the educational film makers and the film libraries is needed and should result in a general agreement on royalty and usage rates.

Other specialist groups have to be considered in royalty rates. For example a library may be given special facilities to film a new product or project by an industrial firm. A copy of the film may be supplied free for non-commercial use within the firm involved. But on other occasions a specialist group may see a process demonstrated and wish to obtain a copy of the film for study purposes in connection with their own experiments. Films of general use to staff conferences may be required for showing to small groups. These cannot be charged at the full rates as if the film were to be distributed and used for commercial gain. Special rates may be laid down for such circumstances, or the fees may be the result of mutual agreement by the parties concerned.

Advertising uses of film are another category where royalty payments are high. Such is the nature of advertising film that only small amounts of film are used in any one advertisement, but the number of showings is far in excess of any other types of film. Advertisers invest in particular programmes on television hoping that the programmes are good and popular and a large audience will be captured to see the advertisements for their products. Advertisements do not sell programmes; programmes sell or exhibit advertisements. Therefore because of the small amounts of film used and their frequent showing, high rates are charged. If an advertisement uses a recognisable piece of library film this piece of film may well become permanently associated with a particular product and be 'killed' as a piece of information. Adequate compensation is needed for this deprivation.

Type of usage. Film can be sold on a footage-supplied or footage-used basis. Footage-supplied rates are charged on all film processed for and supplied to the customer. Footage-used rates are proportionately higher and charges are only made for footage used in the final production. This applies only to the royalty charges; all processing charges are passed to the customer.

The film may be shown only once, or additional showings may be foreseen. A higher charge is made for continuing use if the film is going to be used more than once. For example, a film used to illustrate a point in a news programme shown on only one occasion can be charged a one-use rate, but a documentary programme which will have repeat showings requires continuing-use rates. Continuing-use rate is more economic than having to renegotiate additional usage and pay for another one-use rate. Continuing-use rates are not double one-use; they are more likely to be a 50 per cent increase. There are several variations of this type of usage and a television company for example may acquire film for 4, 8, 12 'flashes' or usages for continuing-use as well as one-use.

The distribution of the film has to be taken into account. If it is to be shown to a restricted 'national' audience the producer expects to pay at a lower rate than a film which may have a wide international distribution. Distribution charges are usually scaled for usage within a country with additional charges for world distribution, or world distribution excluding the United States, or

United States distribution and 'national' distribution only. The United States, which provides a large audience for television, merits special consideration and rates.

Distribution cannot always be calculated at the time of making the film and these rates may have to be negotiated and charged at some time in the future when the market becomes apparent. The distribution rates should, however, be made clear to all customers and the producer of the film will be responsible for notifying the supplier of any changes in distribution in order that charges can be made.

The size of the audience is closely allied to the distribution of a film, and should be taken into account in determining royalty payments where a programme is not put out on a national television network, but to a comparatively small local station. One way of calculating the audience potential on a network is by the number of television sets capable of receiving that network. Obviously a small television station cannot pay the same rate as a large national network and allowances should be made for these differences in audience size. One film company has a sliding scale of charges based on the number of television sets in a television station's area ranging from stations with under 250,000 sets to those over 5,000,000.

Newsfilm libraries connected with agencies may have an additional factor to take into account, that of whether a customer is a subscriber to the agency service or not. Subscribers to the service normally pay lower royalty rates than outside customers, and some pay a lump sum a year in lieu of royalties and are charged only processing costs.

The librarian has to be aware of all these customers and the contracts with them which lay down special conditions and rates of payment.

REVISION OF ROYALTY CHARGES

With so many factors to be taken into account the scales of charges are now becoming too complex and the work in applying them burdensome. A revision of scales is indicated for simplification. Some firms are already revising and reducing the number of points on the scale of royalty charges to only two or three possibilities; for commercial, television and educational use. In addition to this type of user, the extent of distribution will have to be allowed for, i.e. whether worldwide or restricted. Educational rates in particular will have to be reconsidered. It has been assumed to date that educational distribution was limited and non-commercial, and the educational rates were therefore low. However the higher education institutions are beginning to market their films to other interested bodies. They may do this for reasons of cost, i.e. covering their overheads, convenience (closed-circuit television use), or as part of their educational function. The Open University, for example, is in a position to sell whole courses or individual films to any potential buyer.

It is often difficult and seldom foolproof to charge a restricted distribution rate initially and then charge for wider distribution at a later date. For this reason some companies prefer the customer to pay for all rights at the first use. This prevents extra contractual work; only one contract need be drawn up. It saves paper work and extra accounting work in keeping track of the future use of film and ensuring payments are made. On the other hand it is uneconomic for the customer if he is not in a position to judge the future market of the film. The market may not arise for several years or it may not arise at all. In the latter case the customer has cleared the material and been put to greater expense than necessary, or than he could afford.

SEARCH FEES

Other charges the library makes to recover overheads are search and handling fees. Handling fees include viewing charges for the use of library machines and staff time to run the film. Users should not run library film, but have to pay directly or indirectly for the use of library staff time — directly as a handling charge or indirectly in higher search fees for the larger jobs. Despite improvements in the indexing and shotlisting of film, television and film producers still find it necessary to view a great deal of film in order to select a few pieces. A search fee does not cover the cost of many of these viewings as it does not apply to circumstances where the research is done by the production assistant rather than the library staff. Handling or viewing fees are charged to deal with the situation instead.

Search fees are chargeable whether the search is successful or not. They can be charged on the basis of each item retrieved, or a minimum charge can be made for any search increasing according to the numbers of items retrieved after the set minimum. Search fees are becoming a problem. Television companies have research workers on the staff but many still expect the library staff to do the work. The fees should be put on to a sliding scale according to how much research and handling the library staff are involved in, with an initial charge based on the amount of time library staff are required to spend on any one job.

13

COPYRIGHT

I N DISTRIBUTION libraries the agreement between the library and the company covers rights to exhibit the material for a set period only and then the rights in the film revert to the production company. But the copyright or rather the rights granted are only for public exhibition and do not include the selling of the film for reuse as a general rule.

Hire and educational libraries have to ensure that the material is not shown to fee-paying audiences and is used only for educational situations. These libraries normally have no rights in the film they hold and are restricted in the use they can make of the film.

Archives acquire film, but may not take over many of the rights in the material. The copyright normally remains with the owner of the film and is not transferred to the archive. The archive therefore gains the rights to exhibit or make the film available for exhibition or study and may also acquire the right to sell parts of the film with the proviso that the owner of copyright is compensated each time the material is used. The onus of contacting the copyright owner is normally on the user and often the archive will not release prints until permission is given and the material cleared for a particular purpose.

RESTRICTIONS ON USAGE

As a general rule copyright of film is vested in either the original company which produced or shot and edited the film, or in another company which subsequently acquired the collection. Except in the case of the National Film Archive, where the main purpose of the library is different, there is little point in acquiring and preserving film to which the library has no claim. A commercial film library that is unable to sell film under its own copyright, or liable to prosecution for violation of copyright is not an economic concern. Film libraries can act as agents for other companies, but a large proportion of the collection should belong to the library. Clearance of copyright where material is provided by a source other than the library's own company has normally been obtained by that company for its own production.

The company has to clear rights for its own productions and for the material to be stored and preserved in the library for distribution to library users. If this clause is not agreeable to the owner of the film, the library should refuse to handle the film and return it to the owners. The copyright has to be cleared with the owner each time the library is asked to supply and the additional work involved would override any benefit from having the film in the library. This is one reason why the BBC film library retains only BBC copyright material and buys only transmission rights on external material, not handling rights.

Some restrictions on the reuse of the film can be monitored by the library without too many difficulties. The distribution of a film can be restricted to countries other than the supplier. For example, a firm in the United Kingdom can act as agent for American film in Europe, but have no rights to sell the film to other American customers. Additionally the length of a news story which can be shown at any one time can be restricted. This applies especially to current agreements on the amount of a sports event which can be shown in a newsfilm. If the film is important enough to be kept, such restrictions can be enforced. The difference here between book and film libraries is notable in this connection. Book libraries retain stock in which they hold no copyright and lend this stock without having to clear copyright under the conditions of the Copyright Act 1956. But film libraries who sell stock material are normally required to own copyright in a large proportion of their material and can redistribute this film as they please.

HOW RIGHTS ARE OBTAINED

Transfer of rights. Apart from the copyright vested in the production company, copyright can be obtained by a transfer of rights from one company to another. There are several other ways of achieving rights to sell film even though copyright is not vested in the selling company.

When collections change hands, they are bought up by a new company which signs a contract with the previous owners concerning the transfer of rights to the film. The contracts become statements of copyright and often they are the only statements of original copyright the purchasing company has. As the industry grows and collections change hands, records are lost or destroyed, previous agreements are forgotten, and if several copies of the same film also come to light the copyright problems become complex. Old agreements with various suppliers or agents usually remain in the hands of the seller. Much of their content is not relevant to the present transfer. The new contract should list any restrictions, and any adequate written records concerning the film should also be transferred. An accessions list which names the sources of material is especially useful. Unfortunately these records are often either incomplete, or have been destroyed. In these cases considerable research is necessary to establish copyright and ownership. This research is in itself extremely difficult and time consuming. Early records of film sources are not easy to find and are not necessarily reliable when discovered. A film may have been released on a production company's stock, with titles which state the production company, and yet have used material from another company. Unless this is categorically stated in an accessions record, backed up with a clear statement in the contract of the rights held in such material, the company holding a copy of the film finds it difficult to assert copyright.

Distribution and usage agreements. Agreements between companies on distribution and usage of film frequently occurred in the early days of film and this adds to the difficulties. One company may have had a cameraman in a particular place, and other companies requested facilities and access to this film. This could have been granted on a temporary or more permanent basis. If several companies were involved in these agreements tracing the sources of the original material becomes difficult.

In making up a story, a production company may have used material from several sources in addition to its own, based on such agreements. The film company makes up an item using the best of all available material, and it may or may not use other material in preference to its own. In these cases it is virtually impossible to trace the various sources, and check where each shot in the finished film has come from. Even if accessions records are available the record shows only that a piece of film on subject A came in from three sources but the proportions of film used from the three sources in the final version cannot be estimated from the accessions record. Copyright on an item can be claimed by an outside company only if the coverage was exclusive to that company and no other film was intercut with it. This particular problem is most likely to arise with newsfilm material.

Rota service. The use of the 'rota service' for news material poses an additional problem. The material is shot by one or more cameramen and then 'pooled'. The story goes out in edited form from an official source and the original cameramen and their companies have no claim to exclusive copyright. This happens today with some news events, particularly those concerning the Royal family in England. Access to shoot the film can be restricted for security reasons, or because of the restricted space available for camera teams to work. Library usage of the film in most cases is not further restricted, except in so far that the material is not exclusive to that particular library, and only duplicate film is available for printing, not the original negative. The restrictions concern the quality of the film the library is able to provide.

The rota system was used for information film particularly during World War II, material being supplied from the Army Film Unit, and the Central Office of Information. Arguments as to rights in this film are still current. Often pool material was supplied to the newsreel companies who already had film of their own and used it in conjunction with the pool material. The newsreel companies therefore claim non-exclusive rights in these films.

A great deal of film became 'spoils of war' and is in dispute. This captured newsreel material was brought out of Germany and Italy by the conquering powers. Some of it was released on the rota system basis, but much of it remained in the hands of the War Office and has not been distributed or shown. The argument has now been revived however by a German film company, who are claiming exclusive rights to much of this film.

Multiple copies. Non-exclusive rights may be claimed in the case of multiple copies. Several copies of a film are frequently in circulation, the original negative in one collection with show prints scattered in several other areas. Prints or duplicates of the original negative may have been supplied uncut to several companies and each receiving company has cut a different showing copy for its own distribution. Even if the original uncut material is also available for study, it may prove impossible to show that a cut print came from this negative and no other. This situation does not arise with feature and documentary films where the copyright owner has rights over all negatives and prints of the material concerned.

ENFORCEMENT OF RIGHTS

Unauthorised use of film material, its showing and distribution have all to be prevented under the copyright agreement.

Considering the number of film companies and television stations throughout the world, the enforcement of copyright is difficult. A library can however keep a degree of control over the distribution of its film by using the contract to lay down how, when and where the library material may be used. The customer acquires non-exclusive rights in material, either for one usage, a set number of usages, or continuing usage in the one programme, or film, but he does not acquire rights to use this film in other productions, without a reapplication to the owner, nor does he acquire the right to supply this film to other companies either from his own library, or his own production. In the latter case an application to the owning company and the payment of the appropriate royalties are necessary before a sale or supply can be effected. The contract should make it quite clear that the copyright of the library film remains vested in the owning company.

There are two clear reasons for not violating copyright:

1. Possible legal action with, in the past, substantial legal damages does mean that people are very careful about pirating or using copyright material.

2. Once a company has had legal action taken against it for copyright violation, it is generally 'blacklisted' by other companies and is unable to carry on business with external suppliers.

A good or substantial company cannot afford to take such risks and should adhere to copyright agreements. It is in all interests to recognise copyright restrictions wherever they are known. Of course there are occasions when copyright is inadvertently infringed, but these instances can usually be settled on payment of royalties and signing new agreements. Deliberate infringements are taken more seriously. Ignorance of the law is no excuse. All users of copyright material should be made aware of the law and the consequences of its violation.

The librarian has to be on the alert for false claims to copyright. When a false claim is made it may establish a precedent, and all claims should be backed up by evidence. The librarian is entitled to require such evidence to be produced before he can be convinced that the claim is genuine.

MATERIAL NOT LIBRARY COPYRIGHT

Most film libraries probably have some material to which they do not hold rights. The material may be the copyright of an external owner or production company, non-exclusive or be subject to restrictions of supply, or it may require special clearance before use. Copyright and usage restrictions should ideally appear on all records relating to the film so that no matter how one approaches the film, whether by the catalogue card, shotlist or accessions list there is no possibility of supplying the film without being aware of the restrictions. On the accessions register or production sheet the source can be indicated and the name of the distributor. On the shotlist the distributor can be given and any restrictions on the usage of the film. The catalogue cards should carry the name of the copyright holder or distributor if different from the library. It is not advisable to detail the restriction on the catalogue cards because it can cause confusion if the restriction is later altered. The cards will all have to be changed to the new restriction, a process which takes a considerable time. It is better to make the distributor or source of the film clear on the card and have a separate list of sources together with the usage restrictions in force for reference. Constant users of the catalogue soon learn the restrictions which apply to each source, and the occasional user can be informed by the librarians.

The source of the film can be included on current catalogue cards and other records as the film is processed and released. With older material the position is more difficult. Old records may be incomplete or ambiguous and have to be interpreted and carried through the amended records. Again a separate list of restrictions should be available. If an accessions register exists, all restrictions should be transferred to the one record, so that when a film is researched a quick check with the film library number on the accessions register will show if the material can be used and how. This is particularly necessary if the catalogue cards are not amended all at once, but done as the collection is used.

CONTRACTS BETWEEN OWNER AND PURCHASER

Large scale — complete collections. Contracts have to be drawn up between the seller and purchaser of complete collections of film or the production company and distributor. All conditions of supply and the copyright position have to be written in to the contract. It must, for instance, be made clear whether the buyer is acquiring exclusive copyright on the material or is to act as an agent for the copyright owner and therefore has to refer to the owner for copyright clearance.

Any special previous agreements with other sources are notified to the purchaser in the agreement. These contracts will not normally be drawn up by the parties concerned but handled by their legal advisers.

Library and purchaser. These contracts are generally drawn up within the library in a standard form and approved after taking legal advice, but the library has control over the clauses within the contracts.

Contractual agreements should be made between the library and the customer as soon as possible. The contract exists to protect the rights of both parties and the sooner these rights are itemised and agreed to the more effective they become. A customer should be left in no doubt as to what he may or may not do with the film he has obtained. The customer should be informed, for instance, that the copyright of the library film and the original material remain vested in the owner, and if the owner is not the library the customer will be required to seek clearance from the owner before using the film, or being supplied with it.

CONTRACTUAL DETAILS

The contract should contain the following clauses to cover the rights and permissions of the customer:

Deposits and charges. The customer is informed of any charges incurred by him on entry into the agreement. A deposit may be required before any business is transacted and the contract drawn up. In this case the contract indicates that such deposits have been paid. Deposits are especially necessary with new or unknown companies. The film industry is notoriously unstable; small companies may only exist for a short time before disappearing or going into liquidation. In such cases the film library may not be able to recover charges for film and services unless a deposit has been paid before any transaction has taken place or film supplied. Some good faith is necessary in dealing with customers, but film making is a commercial undertaking and safeguards are all the more necessary. Deposits to be paid by a customer can be calculated on the amount of material to be supplied, that is the processing charge. This at least ensures that even if the proposed film is not made the library has adequate payment for the material processed.

If a deposit has not been taken before the agreement is signed a clause in the agreement may stipulate the immediate payment of a search fee. This is usually counted as part payment of the royalty charges in the final bill. On the other hand if a deposit has already been paid the search fee may be waived and the deposit count as payment. Finally both charges may be made at the discretion of the library concerned.

Royalty. The agreement should include definitions of the type of film production and the corresponding royalty charges. A sub-clause is needed to indicate that if a film charged at one rate becomes chargeable at another rate the library is notified and the customer charged accordingly. For example, a film initially contemplated as a short film may become a feature as production progresses, or a film screened under non-theatrical conditions may subsequently be shown at theatrical rates. The type of distribution acquired is also mentioned in these clauses, that is whether the rights are world wide or more restricted, for one use or continuing use.

Stock supplied. Another clause informs the customer of the material he is to be supplied with, i.e. a print or duplicating negative and the conditions of supply. For example, he may be allowed to take several prints from the duplicating material for use in his production, but it should be made clear that this covers only the one production and that these prints cannot be used for other purposes.

Destruction or return. The customer should be informed about the destruction or return of any unused library material. The producer of the film is normally supplied with a larger amount of footage than he uses in the final production. Although the customer has paid processing costs for the unused material he has no rights in it once the final version of his production has been made up. He must therefore destroy or return it to ensure that it is not used in another production, for which he has not compensated the owner of the film. The normal procedure is to return all unused material to the library, but where the customer is known to the library and there is no cause to question his integrity a 'certificate of destruction' might well suffice. If the unused material is not returned or a certificate of destruction sent, all the material can be charged at royalty rate as if used in the final production. It may even be found necessary to include a clause in the agreement permitting the company to examine a copy of the final production to enable the footage used to be checked.

The preceding clauses all deal with the rights of the customer. The library or owner of the film will need to insert other clauses to indicate its own rights in the film.

Footage used. The owner of the film is to be informed as soon as practicable of the amount of library material which has been used in the final production so that the owner can claim royalty charges on his material.

Usage restrictions. Before the library releases material to a producer it takes into account any restrictions on its own copyright and usage of the library film. For example, some films can only be used for television, other events are restricted in the number of times they may be shown or the length of film which can be exhibited at any one showing. The library adheres to these restrictions and releases the film only on firm understandings as to its use.

Indemnity clause. The film producer may run into trouble of his own on showing the final production. An indemnity clause is needed in a contract to cover this possibility, and the producer will indemnify the owner for allocations, costs and claims arising out of a breach of contract or use or exhibition of the film supplied by the owner.

The contract will have to be signed by representatives of both parties concerned.

Other contracts are required between libraries which hire film and their borrowers. This is usually a general agreement which the borrower enters into before acquiring his first film for viewing and then the conditions of the agreements continue for all transactions between the library and the particular user. These agreements usually stipulate the period of hire, the type of audience, and if this audience is to be restricted in any way, e.g. a medical audience; and the care and transporting of film. There is a clause to indicate that all such film is for public or private exhibition, with or without fees and that no prints or sections may be copied, cut, or sold by the borrower.

INVESTIGATING NEW CUSTOMERS

Before a contract is entered into for the sale of film the librarian has to consider the status and integrity of the company making the request for film and issue the contract after certain payments are made or at his discretion. Where the integrity of the production company is in no doubt and the owners have had considerable dealings with the company, material can be released and the company will pay all charges when invoiced for them. Where the company or individual is unknown to the film library several checks are possible to establish status. A formal request on the company's headed paper can be required and a check can be made with other film libraries or trade references can be asked for. If the replies are favourable, deposits for search fees, minimum royalties and processing charges together with the signed agreement can be obtained before any footage is released. When the final production is completed the customer makes a declaration of footage used and the charges are adjusted and made to the company.

More rigid rules may have to be applied to foreign companies than those within a country. There is less direct contact between a foreign company and the owner, and it is more difficult to obtain information on the progress of a production and the status of a production company. When dealing with unknown foreign companies and after status has been reasonably established it is often wise to insist that a percentage of the royalty on all material supplied be deposited to the film library's account. It is much more difficult to obtain redress from a foreign company in international law than a home based company where legal interpretation should be better understood.

PROGRESS OF PRODUCTION

Once an agreement has been entered into it is advisable for the library to keep in touch with the progress of the production. This can be done within a country by reference to trade magazines or television broadsheets. Some film and television companies send in declaration returns automatically, but other companies are very lax and reminders have to be sent until satisfactory returns are made. Libraries have to keep a record of these reminders and all outstanding returns. A standard form can be used for all reminders, or more than one form according to the number of reminders sent.

RECORDING CONTRACTS AND SALES

When a sales enquiry is first made to the library an enquiry form is made out. Details include the company making the enquiry, the contact and telephone number, the name of the proposed production and the company's project or order number, particulars of the enquiry and the type of film required. This form is passed on to the research staff who add the production numbers of material required. The film in then retrieved, viewed if necessary and printed. The requisition or enquiry form can be used to make out more formal request and supply forms. Requisition forms which receive unfavourable replies are retained for a short period and then destroyed.

The library schedule or job schedule is compiled from information given by the original enquiry form, the laboratory order form, despatch label and list of prices and royalties to be paid by the customer. Details are made out and duplicate copies of the schedule are sent for accounting procedures. Also a contract is made out between the library and the customer for the production concerned. Once the contract is signed a copy is retained by the customer and the other by the library.

The library schedules and contracts have to be filed and controlled and need their own separate system of records. The library schedule which includes all these other records in the same file can be given a running number for easy reference, sufficiently different from the production numbers when possible to avoid confusion. In this case a further index has to be maintained as a key to the schedules filed. This could be in the form of a visible index filed under customer, which would provide quick reference to production, amount of footage supplied and used, royalty and search fee incurred and a reference to the library schedule number where more complete detail can be obtained. This index could also be signalled to indicate outstanding accounts and serve as a guide to send out requests for payment or declarations of footage used, and reminders to customers.

While even a large library may have a maximum of only 500 customers there are difficulties in keeping accessible, quick reference records. The amount of paperwork connected with one job is bulky. There are original requests, viewing schedules, lists of material ordered, laboratory printing orders, contracts and correspondence. Any one of these items may be necessary to solve a particular problem and to transfer all records to one may not be feasible. Therefore all the forms have to be kept together.

Users may telephone requests or make written application to hire film. Normally, written application or confirmation is required in the case of all film. The borrower gives details of film required and cites dates on which viewings are needed. Sometimes alternative dates are required and all the information is included on the enquiry form. Film location numbers are added to the booking form and despatch dates are added to allow time for film to reach the customer for the booking date. A borrower from a large hire library is usually allocated a membership number which has to be quoted on all bookings. Film number, borrower's number and date of despatch or viewing are all entered in some form of register, visible index, or data processing unit. This system is devised so that all film to be despatched on a certain day is brought to the notice of the despatch clerk or film preparation assistants and also that a film booked out is not booked out again for a period after the booking date to allow time for return.

Invoices for hire fees can be sent out with the film or despatched on the same day, or may be despatched on the return of the film to the library. If the latter is the case the hiring library examines the film for damage before sending out the invoice, so that any additional charges for extra viewings or damage can be levied. One large hire library in London uses data processing methods for all film movements and produces a daily print out of all available film, together with film or accounts due to be despatched, recall of overdue film, or reminders of unpaid accounts. The size of the hire library in this case makes this method of holding information viable, but other smaller libraries can use less sophisticated automated and manual retrieval systems as effectively.

14

FUTURE DEVELOPMENTS

DEVELOPMENTS that could occur in the film industry and film librarianship in the foreseeable future can be divided into three fields for convenience:
1. Developments in the material handled, including tele-recording, videotape and EVR.
2. Developments in the techniques for handling the material.
3. Developments in the dissemination of information, standardisation and co-operation.

DEVELOPMENTS IN FILM MATERIAL

Film is only one of the materials used for recording pictures or visual images and sound. Not only does film record pictures, it can also be used to 'transmit' visual images, either by projection on to a screen over short distances or, by the intervention of television equipment, over considerable distances. Other media used for recording and transmitting visual images include the television techniques of telerecording, telecine, videotape and videodisc. Another material currently being developed is EVR, electronic video recording which is in essence a combination of optical film images and videotape recording.

Film libraries, as the name implies, currently use film for recording and storing the visual image. Film can be 35mm, 16mm, 8mm or super 8mm, it may further be packaged in a cartridge or put into an endless loop and packaged in a cassette. The most common gauge for feature film and much of the stock material designed for use in features is 35mm; 16mm is used for newsfilm and television and many educational film libraries as well as the distribution hire libraries. Wider use is being made of 8mm film for educational purposes, especially in cassette form. Prior to television, newsreels formed the visual record of news, and these newsreels were shown on cinema screens in the standard 35mm gauge which gave the necessary quality for the projected image. Today's newsfilm cameramen have, however, to be mobile and preferably unobtrusive and a 35mm camera besides being heavy and cumbersome is a prominent object.

In many film libraries there is a considerable stock of 35mm film which has to be taken into account in any handling procedures and processing for reuse. The problem with 35mm film is bulk rather than difficulty in handling; more space has to be allowed for it and special viewing machines provided. If the film is old it may also be on nitrate stock and this does require specialised handling and storage. If there is a lot of nitrate film, special vaults have to be used, but with small amounts it is generally more economic to dupe the film on to safety stock. Despite the amount of space which 35mm takes up, a library with a large collection does not find it economic, feasible or even desirable to transfer 35mm to the 16mm in wide use today. Television can cope with 35mm film easily enough and other users of film often require the wider gauge for quality reasons. In the future because much of the nitrate stock in existence is now reaching the limits of its life, it will gradually disappear and with it the necessity for closed vault storage and the more stringent fire regulations. (Fifty years has been estimated as the average storage life of nitrate stock and after this period it is likely to deteriorate rapidly. Deterioration of nitrate film is irreversible and inevitable and when it begins to go the film has to be duped on to safety stock).

Television does not use 8mm film for reasons of quality. There is at present therefore, no need for the newsfilm and television libraries to store and handle 8mm. A possible use of 8mm film is for duplicate copies of film which can be used as viewing prints. It does not take up as much room as 16mm or 35mm, is cheaper to produce and can be made into a cassette. Nevertheless, 8mm viewing copies present certain basic problems. Handling the narrow gauge in very short clips is difficult, but it may be possible to join several films together in a larger reel. There are administrative difficulties, too, for example in deciding which films to join together and also in ensuring that references are made back to the original films. The advantages are that less storage space is required and less handling of original film material, which can be reserved for processing usable prints.

Colour film is now standard in television and this has made a considerable difference to many film libraries in the past few years. Up to the introduction of colour television, film was shot and stored in black and white, and film libraries were designed and operated to cope with monochrome film. Colour film alters the economics of film library work because expenses and consequent

charges are much higher. Colour film is fragile and even more
easily damaged than black and white. Ideal storage conditions are
different and more space may be required for separating negatives.
Handling procedures are altered, for example more viewing prints
have to be provided in order to preserve the original film. Colour
film has therefore strained the economics of film libraries and
developments in the next few years will concentrate on coming to
terms with this expense. Improvements in colour stock, greater
stability, better tolerance of changes in temperature and storage
conditions will be provided. A method of making cheap viewing
prints will be devised to help preserve the original.

Telerecordings. Newsfilm libraries in particular have considerable
stocks of telerecordings and satellite recordings. Here the material
used to record the image is conventional film, but the source of
the image is the cathode ray tube of the television set. The image
on the television set may be from a videotape or from film, and is
recorded by taking the signal from a television screen and
converting it into film in a special camera. Telerecordings are used
for speed at present. Rather than shoot film, wait for the
developing and printing of the stock and then ship the film to
users and rerun the film in a telecine or television studio, the
direct television transmission is filmed and rerun when required.
The speed of telerecording transmission becomes even more
obvious in the use of satellites to 'bounce' the image across greater
distances than the normal television transmission. Film can be
'bounced' to the UK from Japan either direct or in a series of
'jumps' : Tokyo – San Francisco – New York to London (or
Goonhilly). Developments in the number of satellites or their
potential coverage will improve the speed of news transmission.

Advances in the transmission of news do not necessarily provide
advantages in a suitable medium for long retention of the visual
images for future reuse. Telerecordings do not give such a good
quality image as film. Present policy is to use the telerecordings
for immediate transmission but to replace them with film for
future reuse. This allows time for the film to be shipped from
source to user and to be incorporated into the system, by cutting
to match the telerecorded story which was used in transmission.
Thus, speed of transmission is obtained, but the material is stored
in the better quality form. The additional work thrown on the
library is better than retaining second class quality material for
future use. In practice it is found that the poor quality material is
avoided for reuse and the material is less stable for lengthy storage.

VIDEO RECORDING METHODS

Video recording is another method of recording images picked up by a television camera. In this respect it is closely related to telerecording, but in that it records images it is also related to direct filming. Both videotape recording (VTR) and filming use cameras and recording materials. The recording materials are acetate film for film and telerecording and a magnetic tape for videotape. In a film camera the optical image is focused directly on to film inside the camera, and this film then has to be removed from the camera and developed in a laboratory. In telerecording film is exposed to the 'optical' image from a cathode ray tube. But in videotape recording the camera and the magnetic tape recording medium are remote. The camera used in a television camera and the signal is sent to another remote unit where the tape is recorded. Video cameras need a power supply both to operate and to pass the signal back to the recording unit. This is the major disadvantage of videotape in outside broadcast work and newsfilm, although the lack of mobile power supplies for the video units is gradually being overcome. Cameras are becoming smaller and lighter and the restrictions imposed by the necessity for a link between power and recording unit on the one hand and cameramen and camera on the other are being reduced. Previously a video cameraman remote from the recording unit had to carry a heavy pack with batteries for transmission and this reduced mobility and could have proved dangerous to a cameraman in difficult situations.

The main advantages of videotape as a recording medium for television are not necessarily advantages when the requirements and purpose of newsfilm libraries are considered. Videotape can be replayed instantly without having to go through the developing stages of film and the tapes themselves can be reused several times over by wiping and re-recording. The facility of instant replay gives videotape considerable advantages over conventional film for news events. Television news is constantly looking for new methods and developments which will reduce the time lag between the actual event and the screening of a visual record of that event, and videotape has considerable potential in this field. But other factors make videotape the wrong medium to select for permanent or long-term preservation.

Videotape is not regarded as a technically sound or economic way of preserving visual material. Technically it is a fragile material, and unstable in that being a magnetic recording medium it is subject to accidental wiping and loss of the record. It is also bulky to maintain videotape in good quality for transmission. Transmission tapes are 2in wide, although copy tapes can be made in 1in and ½in widths, and the 2in transmission tapes take up a large amount of valuable storage space. Videotape is also a very expensive method of storing images. In order to use videotape recording effectively and make it economically viable the tape should be reused as often as possible and as a transitional step from recording to permanent preservation. Long events can be recorded in their entirety on to available tapes. Once the event is concluded the tape can be replayed and the highlights 'edited' and recorded on to another medium if necessary. The tape can then be wiped and reused for another purpose. (This is an advantage in long drawn out events such as sporting fixtures). If this was done with film, however, all the unused film would have to be destroyed and this would make the process expensive.

Editing videotape. It is essential to edit film and this is a highly skilled task; a film editor takes a camera record of a programme or event and removes poor quality film, dull patches, highlights the main areas of interest and may have to reorganise the camera record into the logical sequence. In doing this job the editor may remove only a few frames of the film or may extract whole sequences. Videotape editing is a different skill. Editing techniques are now highly advanced, usually electronic, and no longer involve cutting the tape, but the crisp techniques used for film work are still not adequately accommodated in videotape.

Videotape is more suited to forms of visual record other than short clips such as news events or stockshots. It is much more suitable for longer sequences of broadcast television such as whole programmes, drama or certain documentary programmes which are not required for retention beyond a short period.

Another disadvantage of videotape is evident when it is necessary to transport a programme from one country or area to another. If videotape has to be physically transported from one place to another there are problems of weight, bulk and dangers of destruction of the record on the tape either from distortion or accidental wiping. Videotape cannot be transported in the ordinary way that film can be. However, visual images can be transmitted from one area to another without the need to transport film or tape. Images are transmitted electronically using conventional transmitters or 'bounced' across greater distances using satellites. With improvements in methods of transmission the disadvantages are being reduced although it is still costly to transmit video over considerable distances.

Videotape standards are variable and this incompatibility adds one further difficulty to the transportation of videotape from one place to another. Film and telerecordings have the merit of being recorded on a universal medium. Most television stations have basic conversion units to transfer the film to the line standard in use but the transfer of videotape to a usable standard is not widely used. Telecine translates film into television; that is it converts the optical image on standard film into electrical television signals which can be transmitted on a television screen.

It does not appear therefore that videotape will displace film as a medium for recording visual images. Whenever a video record is selected for retention it is now transferred to film for safekeeping and preservation. Videotape could be used for viewing copies if necessary but the procedures in film libraries would have to be altered quite markedly to suit the other medium — e.g. viewing copies on videotape would be joined in long reels as it is not feasible to have short pieces of video as in film. Also the viewing machines for video recording are expensive.

ELECTRONIC VIDEO RECORDING (EVR)

This is a new type of recording medium which combines some of the advantages of film, cassette loading and television transmission. Two picture tracks of 30 minutes running time are loaded into a cassette which is then locked into a player attached by coaxial cable to one or more television sets. There is considerable flexibility and control of the viewing, unlike videotape. The image can be held on a still frame, whereas once the videotape stops running the image breaks up. The image can also be inched forward or reversed when necessary, a facility not available with videotape. Despite its advantages over videotape, EVR has other inherent disadvantages. The user cannot record his own material but has to accept the packages recorded by the distributor or manufacturer. This makes it less applicable to the educational field than videotape or, even better, videocassette recording which can be recorded by the user. EVR is a useful end product, a finished programme rather than the parts which make up a documentary such as short film or news clips. EVR is not useful as an original recording medium, but it has advantages over videotape in distribution and flexible viewing. The videocassette, that is a ½in tape enclosed in a protective cassette for recording and replay, is the most likely improvement to appear in the next few years. The user can record off air using a conventional television monitor and replay the material through the same monitor at will. There are many problems of copyright to be worked out before the system can operate smoothly, but it is now possible and within economic reach for many people to employ a videocassette recorder, and this is especially relevant to the educational library.

DEVELOPMENTS IN HANDLING TECHNIQUES

The techniques and procedures in a film library alter as the nature of the material alters, but basic film handling techniques continue to be required and the staff who work in these libraries need training in these techniques. Film has certain inherent disadvantages, but while some of these disadvantages do not necessarily apply to library work, e.g. the speed of transferring the event or information to the television screen or user, others do apply and help to determine many of the policies adopted by film libraries, e.g. the amount of space which has to be provided for film storage and the necessity for show or viewing copies of some sort to prevent the destruction of original film.

Despite its disadvantages film is still the best medium in which to preserve and store visual records. Film is less expensive and more stable to preserve than videotape. Videotape is economic only if wiped and reused several times and should not be tied up in storage for too long a period. Film in normal circumstances gives a better quality image than telerecording. The storage potential of film will be improved by the gradual elimination of nitrate stock over the next few years, and this elimination will also result in different methods of storage being widely adopted. Open racking will gradually replace all the old closed vault systems necessitated by nitrate film allowing greater utilisation of the space available to a film library. Incidental improvements will also be discovered in the materials for storing the film, e.g. the use of plastic 'cans' which are rustproof, watertight and airtight and not subject to attack by acids.

The results of research into suitable methods of storage and preservation will have an influence on systems and procedures in use in film libraries. This applies particularly to colour film. Colour storage conditions could be revised in the light of research and practical application. The use of colour film is now well established in television, but there is still some uncertainty about the best conditions for storage and preservation. Separation negatives preserve the colour but require assembly and printing before use or viewing and take up extra space. The ideal temperature for storing colour film often cannot be observed in film libraries because of the delay in making film available while it is warmed through after cold storage. Future developments in colour film may lead to an alteration of the types of colour stock used and the new stock may be less sensitive to normal storage conditions and have a potentially longer storage life than that in current use. The major consideration in the use of colour at the present time is the cost, which is at least double that of black and white. The cost of the original stock is higher, printing and storage costs are also high and there is an extra space problem with colour. Viewing copies in both colour and for black and white are costly to make and maintain.

There may in the future be differences in the material stored and used but these differences are likely to be in addition to the material already stored. For example, show copies may not be retained on film or they may be retained on narrow gauge film in order to save space. This is one of the major considerations for film libraries of all types to concern themselves with: the development and provision of a cheaper method of making show copies. When a method is found it may well alter or influence the administration of a film library. Videotape or a magnetic or video based record may be used instead of film or copies may be made on a narrow gauge film or electronic video recording. In either case additional machines and handling facilities will be needed to cope with the viewing copies as well as the library originals from which the printing will be done.

The present methods of viewing film may be developed and altered. At present a user has to narrow his viewing requirements down to essential items, because of the restricted viewing time available in the libraries, possible damage to original film by constant viewing, and shortage of space for viewing. He is unable to 'browse' among film images. This trend may alter with the provision of cheap viewing copies and closed circuit television facilities or computer-type display may be provided between library and user to allow for wider viewing of film material. This will provide additional facilities for 'pure' viewing as opposed to the type of viewing necessary today, that is viewing with selection for a particular programme or film in mind. Several viewing screens could be controlled from a central area in such cases and vidicon facilities could be used to assist this purpose. The viewing areas need not be manned by a member of the library staff, but several viewing areas could be serviced by a single member of staff at one time.

There is a minor point of planning and developments in this area to be considered here. With developments in certain areas of library work less space may be needed in the future for the storage of film and also of the documents which go with film; but to balance this more space will be needed for the accommodation of staff to exploit the collections effectively. There will probably be a different allocation of the space available, but this does not mean that less space is needed for the library.

The high costs of film and its storage as well as the lack of space for storage mean that selection is a very important part of the work of a film library. On the other hand this does not mean that when space and economic problems are solved or relieved selection can be omitted and all film retained. The users will continue to have problems of selection from all this information and the constant weeding of a collection will remain an important aid for the user to ensure that the best quality material is available in sufficient amount for him to be selective and still acquire the material he requires rapidly, but not enough to overwhelm the user by trying to present all the material available without any preselection on grounds of poor quality or repetitiveness.

Finally in considering film handling techniques, laboratory printing facilities can be mentioned. Printing techniques will obviously develop, and in any individual film library this will result in a speedier and more varied type of service as a wider selection of processing machines is installed.

Staffing. Another development in the handling techniques, although not directly related, is that of the staffing of film libraries. There is considerable room for improvement in both the calibre of staff and commensurate remuneration. The film technicians' unions may well have to extend or alter their rules and agreements to cover the non-technical, professional staff such as the shotlisters, cataloguers and information retrieval staff. Many of these staff members have to belong to the unions because they need to handle film, but the rules and conditions of service are being distorted or stretched to accommodate them at present whereas new rules should be devised to take account of these additional jobs.

More facilities and opportunities are needed for the junior members of a film library staff to have training in film methods used within a particular library and also those used in other organisations. Training is needed for both the technical staff in a library and for those members of staff carrying out tasks normally classed as librarianship, i.e. cataloguing, classification and retrieval. These members of staff need specialist training to encourage them to apply general principles of librarianship to the particular medium of film as well as basic technical training in the handling of film.

DEVELOPMENTS IN DISSEMINATION OF INFORMATION

Film libraries form a relatively small and new branch of the profession of librarianship. All are concerned with the same basic material, film and its handling, although they have different functions and are widely scattered throughout the world. As any one user of film could need access to several different film libraries for his raw material, information about available film needs to be organised.

There are two main points on which research is needed: the dissemination or circulation of information within an organisation, that is how the information is stored and presented to the user; and the wider dissemination of information to outside users in the form of lists of catalogues of material available.

Information distribution within an organisation could be improved as methods of mechanised storage and retrieval of information progress. For example the use of unitised microfilm and mechanised retrieval systems will assist in solving some storage problems. Microfilm will be useful in this especially if the microfilm system is used with some form of punched card technique to reduce the bulk of material to be stored and speed the retrieval of information. With advances in electronic transmission of film across the world, filmed information may be used on the same circuits. As film is transmitted, so shotlists and film lists may come to be transmitted between organisations as frequently as telex messages are. In the larger film organisations, as electronic transmission systems are installed, uses will be found in connection with the library film of these organisations. Experiments could be made initially on closed circuit transmission of information from one department to another. Shotlists and catalogue information could be fed into a system which would allow the information to be read elsewhere in the organisation, e.g. the projection theatre as and when library film is needed. Progress could then be made to transmitting information of this sort from the library to its main users, especially the television outlets, before going on to transmit information to overseas customers. These reader transmitters situated in the library and reader receivers at the other end of the connection would eliminate much tedious copying and heavy paperwork from the library's daily routine.

Computers and photographic techniques can be used to produce catalogues and lists more rapidly and with less time and labour expended in collation and editing. Developments in computer print-out possibilities will also be of use to central information services when costs are brought to a more realistic level. These central services will cover several organisations rather than be concerned with any one library. The nature of enquiries and the need for immediate access in many film libraries operate against the present benefits of computer retrieval of information in the more specialised agencies.

It is also necessary to bring the information about film and its availability to the notice of the new type of user as well as to the more expected users in television. Education is making an increasing use of film, not only in schools broadcasting, and people working in the education field need the opportunity to obtain information about film and other audio visual aids. In attempting to do this and make the service viable costs will have to be brought down for the educational market. This will assist and encourage central agencies to find the quickest and most economical methods, in terms of time and money, of collecting and distributing information about film.

These are possibilities for the future, but much has been done in the past or is being done at present to facilitate or augment the distribution of information. Film libraries quickly realised that no one library could necessarily meet all the needs of a customer. Many groups of libraries have interested themselves in these problems and some successful schemes are already in use.

In 1956 Aslib set up a Film Production Librarians' group to bring together as many film librarians in the UK as possible for discussion and mutual benefit. Two particularly useful documents were produced including a *Directory of Film and Television Production Libraries* published in 1959, with a second edition in 1963. This gave a brief résumé of film libraries, the type of stock available, subject matter held and period covered, and acted as a guide to the whereabouts of film in the UK. A film directory to be produced by the Aslib Audio Visual Group will have a subject index with a list of possible sources added to each heading. An alphabetical list of sources of film and their addresses will also be included. *The World Directory of Stockshot and Film Production Libraries,* published in 1969 under the auspices of Unesco, attempts the same information as the 1959 Aslib list on an international basis but with only a moderate success.

None of these publications attempt to include all the films produced by the organisations listed, only a general subject guide. This is probably of more use to the individual researcher who can discover a library which covers the subjects and period he requires and then approach that library for the complete catalogue of holdings. Catalogues of holdings differ from one library to another in completeness or availability. The National Film Archive has a series of catalogues covering different periods and types of film. One stockshot library in the UK issues a list of subjects covered but leaves details out. The distribution libraries of course issue catalogues of film available, but many film libraries do not have any printed catalogues. Newsfilm libraries rarely publish catalogues of holdings. The catalogues are too large and constantly being added to, so that no catalogue can ever be up to date or sufficiently accurate.

Other attempts to disseminate information on a national scale have taken the form of catalogues of film, whether general lists of film available, or more specialised lists of specific collections, or for particular users.

The British National Film Catalogue lists all film currently available in the UK. Based on the Universal Decimal classification it includes documentary and other non-fiction films, giving a complete list of credits and other information about the film such as gauge, colour, distributor, etc. This is an attempt to do for film what the BNB does for books. BNFC is published quarterly with annual cumulations and is retrospective to 1963. Fiction film has recently been withdrawn from the catalogue because it is already more fully covered by the *Monthly Film Bulletin* of the British Film Institute and it was felt that the BNFC listing contributed nothing further on fiction features. It has also eliminated newsreels because these are becoming more ephemeral with the growth of television.

The British Industrial and Scientific Film Association also holds card catalogues of information on documentary film before 1963 but has not yet published any of this material. This is one of the major gaps in information about film. The published catalogues do not go back far enough for the average enquirer. The British Universities Film Council have also published a film catalogue. New editions will be published irregularly although information about new film is available to membership of the Council. This catalogue represents a selective list of material drawn from other sources, and evaluated by university teachers for use in universities. For unpublished material the HELPIS catalogue published by the National Council for Educational Technology provides a useful source. Helpis (Higher Education Learning Programmes Information Service) deals with the material currently being produced in British institutions for higher education. It covers other materials as well as film, videotape, tape slide, etc.

None of these catalogues cover newsfilm. The most apparent barrier to an index of newsfilm is the amount. Newsfilm items are short but numerous and a listing of them would be bulky and not very informative. An attempt is being made at the Slade Film School to establish a centralised bank of information on the whereabouts of film, including newsfilm, for the benefit of historians, organised on a subject basis. This is to be used by university and other research workers and will provide them with a guide to the various collections, and their coverage. It is not intended as a union catalogue of film, rather a guide to sources showing the strengths and weaknesses of the collections.

Under the auspices of Unesco, conferences have been called to try and establish a system to provide descriptive data on film, information about availability and an evaluation of this information. Unesco are also exploring the possibilities of using computers or mechanised methods of retrieval to compile a union catalogue of film. The discussions involved are useful and fruitful to the members concerned, but it is felt that national houses will have to be put in order before vast international schemes can be attempted.

Finally the Library of Congress is exploring the possibilities of disseminating information about film on an international level through national cataloguing schemes such as BNB and the new MARC — BNB systems.

Co-operation between film libraries is more advanced than between the organisations which own film libraries. Relations between firms in television and newsfilm are highly competitive. Competition helps to keep the standards of service to the customer high, but customers should also have a wide choice of available material. Personal contact between librarians apart from airing their problems and reducing them to common factors helps to disseminate information on an informal basis.

DEVELOPMENTS IN STANDARDISATION

Standardisation is necessary in several areas of film librarianship, for example classification schemes, cataloguing rules for form of entry as well as descriptive rules, royalty and other charges, staffing requirements and training.

The standardisation of procedures for handling the contents and economics of film libraries is important as well as the cataloguing and classification of collections. More research is needed into codes of practice. Film in general has been served reasonably well with regard to cataloguing codes, but not all types of film were covered. For instance newsfilm is hardly touched upon in the general film cataloguing codes. Even the current work on non-book media cataloguing rules will not solve all the film librarian's problems. These rules will be aimed primarily at the collections which contain several media and as such will not be particularly specific to film and its problems.

The standardisation of descriptive cataloguing requires particular attention. This refers to the physical description of the film itself rather than its subject content. Rules and codes of practice for descriptive cataloguing could be carried over to help standardise the production of shotlists. While standardisation is not particularly necessary in the form of shotlist (that is whether a précis, or running shotlist is used or a list of shots), the descriptive details included in the shotlist should be standard so that they are easily understood by any user. Each organisation will retain the type of shotlist which is most suited to its work, those who have quick reference indexes may use separate full shotlists, but other film libraries may not have separate shotlists but include a précis of the film content on the catalogue card itself.

In spite of differences in functions and aims all types of library have to maintain indexes and catalogues to reveal the material available. Until some standardisation is achieved efficient methods of dissemination will be impaired.

Standardised cataloguing procedures are necessary for centralised indexes as well as individual collections, to prevent duplication of effort by the original cataloguer and the central indexer. Much useful work has already been done to provide cataloguing codes based on the National Film Archive's *Rules for use in the Cataloguing Department of the NFA,* fifth edition 1960. The Aslib FPL group realised that these rules, although primarily designed for a national archive collection, could be adapted and expanded to cater for most film libraries. The Aslib *Film Cataloguing Rules* were published in 1963 and are used extensively.

Unesco have also published international rules for the cataloguing of educational, scientific and cultural films to try to standardise procedures on an international basis.

Much additional work still remains to be done to provide a standard, widely-accepted set of cataloguing rules for film librarianship. Once standards have been agreed to it will make the work of preparing entries for published catalogues easier and encourage more co-operation in schemes for circulating information about available film.

Standardised procedures in classification have proved more difficult to formulate and as a result there are numerous schemes in existence, both notational and using subject headings. Different types of film have again complicated the issues and no classification scheme has been formulated yet. Several small schemes are in operation but none has been adopted by several film libraries. Many of these schemes are adaptations from UDC, e.g. RAE Farnborough, NFA, BNFC, BUFC. The National Film Archive have also devised a scheme for the classification of book materials on film adapted from the 791.4 number in UDC. There is scope for research into and development of a suitable classification scheme and also a list of subject headings or thesaurus for use with computers.

Standardisation of procedures for handling the film library's contents would also have value. Although there is considerable room for specialised techniques and procedures in film libraries it would aid both staffing and staff training programmes if there was greater uniformity in the more basic techniques. Staff trained in one organisation would be able to transfer to others without the lengthy period of training which is necessary at the moment. The National Council for Educational Technology is currently co-operating with the Aslib Audio-Visual Group, the Library Association and the Association of British Library Schools to try to find some way of introducing more consideration of and training for audio visual librarianship into the schools and colleges.

A manual of film library technique would be a valuable contribution to the scant literature on standards and techniques in the film libraries. Although libraries are so widely different in content and aims that no two appear alike, basic procedures are not radically different in these libraries. A manual would form a reference tool for film libraries and help prevent the continued use of unsuccessful methods.

One other area which could be rationalised and standardised is that of charges for supply of material to the customer. New scales of charges need to be drawn up and agreed by all supplying organisations. It is more a question of simplifying the complex scales in existence rather than altering the scales. At present a customer is not able to anticipate the likely costs of usage, viewing, processing and royalty payments because all suppliers have their own scales which do not coincide. Some material is still not being used as widely as it could be because of the high cost of viewing or printing, or the uncertainty in the customer's mind as to the costs involved. With simplified scales the customer would be able to plan programmes or film in the knowledge that no matter where his material was located he could obtain it at certain standard fees according to the intended use of the material.

DEVELOPMENTS IN NATIONAL AND INTERNATIONAL CO-OPERATION

Co-operative effort has already taken place on the national level with Aslib Film Librarians' Group. From 1963 to 1969 the Aslib group went through an unproductive period, partly as a result of apathy and partly from a lack of funds, owing to the small number of participating members. However, in 1969 the group was expanded into the Aslib Audio-Visual group which intends to include film users as well as film producers in addition to other librarians concerned with the audio visual media in general and it is hoped that interest will grow again and the group become both viable and active in promoting research in several of the areas mentioned.

On the international level there are organisations such as FIAF (the International Federation of Film Archives), Unesco and the International Film and Television Council (IFTC) working to try to combine efforts from several national sources as well as to investigate standards of procedure and codes of practice which might be applicable internationally.

FIAF was formed early in the history of film libraries and deals with questions of collection, preservation, classification and circulation of film to members. It has tried to standardise certain procedures in film archives and these can be adopted by other types of film library.

Much co-operation has already been achieved on the international level with FIAF and Unesco, but on the national level much is still waiting to be done or attempted. One of the main difficulties in the way of national organisation concerns the newsfilm libraries. Newsfilm library intake far exceeds that of others in number of titles taken. The footage may not be greater but the number of individual pieces of film is. Any union catalogue attempting to include all these titles would be swamped by newsfilm. Special schemes may have to be used to separate the short but numerous newsfilm from the longer less numerous features and documentaries.

Within special types of film library, more concrete forms of co-operation could be set up. Many television stations throughout the world are establishing libraries to cope with their own transmissions and provide a basic service of film to their own producers. The organisation in these libraries is often minimal, owing to lack of expertise and information. Established film librarians may be approached for assistance and advice, but no organised co-operation is in force. These embryonic libraries of today will grow rapidly and could with proper care and organisation become the major film libraries of tomorrow. Television stations should be made aware of the necessity for properly organised libraries run by suitably trained librarians. The seconding of experienced film librarians to developing areas could be one solution, either through the broadcasting or television unions, or through international bodies such as Unesco or the library associations. An advisory bureau could be set up to cope with the queries connected with organising film. These bureaus could in turn form the basis for international guides to the content of various collections by members and others.

Standardisation of cataloguing procedures is gradually being worked out, but the greatest need is for organised information about film available. M. Ledoux, in a Unesco Report on mass communication, outlined possible ways of achieving this information, some of which have been put into practice. His ideas for a national filmography have been achieved to some extent in the BNFC. He advocates building schemes of selective international cataloguing on the basis of national centres, i.e. selective subject catalogues which include summaries of film, data regarding availability and conditions for purchase or rental.

Much work remains to be done in organising and disseminating information about film and it will have to be done soon before the amount of material makes solution of the problem prohibitively expensive of time and resources.

CONCLUSION

Although film libraries are all concerned with the same basic material, there are special problems involved in the organisation of different types of film collection and the planning and running of the types of library which sell film make them sufficiently different to warrant separate consideration. Such libraries as newsfilm and stockshot libraries need this separate consideration.

The use and reuse of this film is different to other types of film. It is normally shown in short illustrative clips. There are places for example where a newsfilm camera is not or cannot go; it is not present at many decision-making committee meetings, in cabinet discussions, in union-management negotiations, and all that can be done in such cases is to question one or two members of the meeting and base the film of the event on their reports. In reuse newsfilm and stockshot material is used in short clips which are then compiled into longer sequences to show special events or illustrate a particular point of view. Handling the film for this type of usage has to be considered separately. This film is stored in short sequences which illustrate one point or event or aspect of an event. Film viewing sessions are a series of short clips rather than longer sessions devoted to one film, as in a documentary film library.

Cataloguing and classification of newsfilm and stockshots are also different to other film, and also to each other. Classification becomes a question of detailed indexing and cataloguing is aimed at locating one short sequence among many hundreds of thousands of pieces. Storage, location numbering and methods of referring to the film by number rather than title or director are all direct results of the peculiarities of the material being handled.

Selection becomes of importance in helping to control the collection and to aid the task of the researcher in finding the piece of film he requires without too much viewing of duplicates or repetitive types of sequence. Selection has a twofold function:

1. To assist the library to control its collection and not waste storage space and staff time in processing and retrieving useless pieces of film.
2. To assist the user by a policy of controlled pre-selection, endeavouring to keep those items which will be required for use and not losing them in a plethora of worthless material.

Other aspects of work in such libraries have been discussed which are similar to the type of work carried out in many other film libraries. In the storage and preservation of film, for example, it is the material which must be considered, rather than the type of information on that material. Basic considerations of the type of film, whether nitrate or acetate, and therefore the type of storage facilities required, preservation policies and the provision of show or viewing copies are common to all types of film library.

Film is easily damaged and constant viewing subjects it to a certain amount of damage. Additionally, film is not as easy or as quick to refer to as literature because the material has to be laced up on to a special projection or viewing machine. Therefore in any film library some other intermediate reference to the contents of a film is often required. This may take the form of a shotlist and in addition there will be other documentation about the film which has to be stored and made available for quick reference. Shotlisting of short pieces of information film is similar in many respects to shotlisting of other types of film and the problems attendant on the filing, control and accessibility of documentation are similar to any other film library and indeed to libraries which deal with print material.

Staffing in film libraries requires both technical staff to handle the film and staff to cope with the more conventional library skills of cataloguing and information retrieval. However, each type of staff needs training to acquire some of the skills of the other so that cataloguers and shotlisters are able to handle film and film handling staff can master the indexes and retrieve necessary information from them. An interest in and basic knowledge of film techniques, history of film, current affairs and modern history is a useful attribute to look for in any prospective film librarian.

Layout and planning of all film libraries is similar, the ideal being that the film is adjacent to the work area for speed of handling and supply, and the indexes and documentation are at a central point where they are easily accessible to all members of library staff.

The economics of film libraries are different to many other libraries in that the film library is in a position to acquire revenue rather than being run on a grant from some parent organisation or outside source, e.g. a government department or local authority. Scales of charges have to be drawn up and royalty charges administered by some senior member of the library staff. This adds extra administrative tasks to the normal library functions but it is common to most film libraries. Copyright problems are prominent in all types of film library whether they are problems of ensuring copyright on material produced by a parent organisation and administered by the library, or problems of observing the rights in material belonging to others.

Many film libraries at present work independently of others and there are few co-operative efforts. The amount and nature of some special types of film does work against successful co-operation, but efforts to indicate sources of material rather than indicating the exact material held are now being made and should provide more useful information and lead to a wider use of this film in several areas of television and education. Additional research is necessary to locate the stores of, as yet untapped, film, index the material for easy retrieval and disseminate the information gained to enable more widespread usage of the film.

BIBLIOGRAPHY

ANGLO AMERICAN CATALOGUING RULES, British Text. Library Association, 1967.

ANGLO AMERICAN CATALOGUING RULES. Film cataloguing at the Library of Congress *in Library Resources and Technical Services*, Vol. 13, no. 1, Winter 1969.

ASLIB Film Production Librarians Group. Film Cataloguing Rules, 1963.

ASLIB Film Production Librarians Group. The Directory of Film Production Libraries, 1959; The Directory of Film and TV Production Libraries. 2nd ed. 1963.

BAECHLIN, Peter *and* MULLER STRAUSS, Maurice. Newsreels across the World. Unesco 1952.

BLAIR, Patricia. Treatment, storage and handling of Motion Picture film. *Library Journal*, vol. 71. no. 5, Mar. 1st 1946.

BOARDMAN, Thomas H. A new style in audiovisual cataloguing. *Educational Screen and Audiovisual Guide*, vol. 39, no. 3, March 1960, p. 126–7.

BRADLEY, John G. A National film library : the problem of selection. *Journal of the Society of Motion Picture Engineers*, vol. 47, no. 1, July 1946, p. 63–72.

BRADLEY, John G. Specifications of motion picture film for permanent records. *Journal of the Society of Motion Picture Engineers*, vol. 48, no. 2, February 1947, p. 167–170.

BRITISH FILM INSTITUTE. Rules for use in the Cataloguing Department of the National Film Archive. 5th ed. London, BFI, 1960.

BRITISH STANDARDS INSTITUTION. B.S.1749 : 1969. Specification for alphabetical arrangement and the filing order of numerals and symbols.

BROWN, Harold Godard. Problems of storing film for archive purposes. *British Kinematography,* vol. 20, no. 5, May 1952, p. 150—162.

CARD, James. Film archives. *Image,* vol. 7, no. 6, June 1958, p. 137—41.

CATALOGUING OF FILMS AND FILMSTRIPS : UNESCO PROPOSALS. *Unesco Bulletin for Libraries,* vol. 8, nos. 5—6, May—June 1955, p. 98—101.

CHAPLIN, A. H. Names of Persons, National Usage for entry in Catalogues. IFLA, 1967.

CHIBNALL, Bernard. The National Film Library and its Cataloguing rules. *The Journal of Documentation,* vol. 11, no. 2, June 1955, p. 79—82.

CHIBNALL, Bernard. Shell Film Unit stock shot Library. *Aslib Proceedings,* vol. 5, no. 2, May 1952, p. 59—68.

CLARKE, Virginia. Non-book Library materials, 1953.

COBLANS, Herbert. Use of Mechanised methods in documentation work. Aslib, 1966.

COLLISON, R. L., *editor.* Libraries for Television. *Library World,* vol. 67, no. 781, July 1965, p. 3—7.

COLLISON, R. L. Filing and Indexing : Part 2. *Office Magazine,* vol. 10, no. 110, Feb. 1963, p. 101—103.

COLLISON, R. L. Filing and Indexing : Part 3. *Office Magazine,* vol. 10, no. 111, Mar. 1953, p. 184—186.

CUTTER, C. A. Rules for a Dictionary Catalogue, 4th ed. 1904. U.S. Bureau of Education.

DAVIS, Ewart. Problems of the Television film library. *British Kinematography,* vol. 33, no. 6, December 1958, p. 166—174.

DAY, Dorothy L. Films in the Library. *Library Trends,* vol. 4, no. 2, October 1955, p. 174—181.

DEAN, Colin. Celluloid Circus : a film about a film library. Report of Proceedings of the 21st Conference, 1946, Aslib.

DEMING, Barbara. The Library of Congress film project : exposition of a method. *The Library of Congress quarterly journal of current acquisitions,* vol. 2, no. 1, November 1944, p. 3—36.

EASTMAN KODAK CO. Industrial Motion pictures, 1957.

EFFINGER, Carl. The Filing and Cataloguing of motion picture film. *Journal of the Society of Motion Picture Engineers,* vol. 46, no. 2, February 1946, p. 103—110.

ELTON, *Sir* Arthur. The film as source material for history. *Aslib proceedings,* vol. 7, no. 4, November 1955, p. 2—7—39.

ENCYCLOPAEDIA BRITANNICA FILMS, INC. How to run a film library.

EVERSON, William K. Stockshots : potentially of great creative importance, they now bolster inferior films. *Films in Review,* vol. 4, no. 1, January 1953, p. 15–20.

FANG, I. E. Television news, 1968.

FILM CENTRE INTERNATIONAL LTD. Film Centre Production library practice : Parts 1, 2 and 3, 1963.

FILM LIBRARY OF BELGIUM, THE. *Unesco Bulletin for Libraries,* vol. 6, no. 8–9, Aug.–Sept. 1952, p. 106.

FOCAL ENCYCLOPEDIA of Film and Television Techniques. Focal Press, 1969.

FORREST ALTER et al. eds. Sixty Years of 16mm film, 1923–1983, 1954.

FOSKETT, D. J. Classification and Indexing in the social sciences, 1963.

FOTHERGILL, Richard. A challenge for Librarians? Report of the joint NCET/ASLIB Audio Visual Group Conference on multi-media resource organisation in higher education, held in Hull in December 1970. NCET Working Paper 4, 1971.

GALVIN, Hoyt R., *and* SCRANTON, Jenne T. Organisation of a Library film service. *Unesco Bulletin for Libraries,* vol. 11, nos. 11–12, Nov.–Dec. 1957, p. 267–270.

GILBERT, L. *and* WRIGHT, J. Non-book materials : their bibliographic control. NCET Working Paper 6, 1971.

GOSHKIN, Ida. The Why and How of Film Circuits. *American Library Association Bulletin,* vol. 55, no. 6, June 1961, p. 545–8.

GRAHAM, Ian *and* CROWTHER, Geoffrey. Cataloguing and classification of cine film at the Royal Aircraft Establishment, Farnborough. London, Ministry of Supply, 1959. Unclassified. (Technical memorandum, no. 1, instruction 291).

G.B. Department of Education and Science. Report of a committee to consider the need for a National Film School, 1967.

GRENFELL, David. The documentation services of the National Film Archive. *London Librarian,* vol. 7, no. 5, May 1961, p. 67–76.

GRENFELL, David. Standardisation in Film cataloguing. *Journal of Documentation,* vol. 15, no. 2, June 1959, p. 81–92.

GUSS, Carolyn. Evaluation and Selection. (In Sixty years of 16mm film, 1923–1983, ed. by Forrest Alter et al. 1954).

HENSEL, Evelyn. Treatment of Non-book materials. Library Trends, vol. 2, no. 2, October 1953, p. 187–198.

HUMPHREY, Lewis H. Stock film cataloguing *in Journal of the Society of Motion Picture and Television Engineers,* vol. 64, no. 9, September 1955, p. 494–6.

INTERNATIONAL FEDERATION OF FILM ARCHIVES, Preservation Committee. *Film Preservation.* NFA, 1965.

INTERNATIONAL FEDERATION OF FILM ARCHIVES. *Unesco Bulletin for Libraries,* vol. 9, no. 7, July 1955, p. 139.

KETCHUM, Elizabeth. Stockshot library of the National Film Board, Ottawa. Canadian Library Association Toronto chapter bulletin, vol. 16, no. 5, May 1956, p. 4–5.

KIMBER, R. T. Automation in Libraries. Pergamon Press, 1968. International series of Monographs in Library and Information Science, vol. 10.

KUJOTH, J. S., *Editor.* Readings in non-book Librarianship. Scarecrow Press, 1968.

KULA, Sam. Bibliography of Film Librarianship. Bibliography submitted in part requirement for University of London Diploma in Librarianship, May 1962.

LEAPER, William J. Copyright and performing rights, 1957.

LEDOUX, Jacques. Study and establishment of National centres for cataloguing of films and television programmes. Unesco. Reports and papers on Mass Communication, no. 40, 1963.

LEVITAN, E. L. An alphabetical guide to motion picture, television and videotape production. McGraw-Hill, 1970.

LINDGREN, E. H. Preservation of cinematographic film in the National Film Archive *in Journal of the Society of Motion Picture and Television Engineers,* 78, Oct. 1969.

MITCHELL, George. The Library of Congress : its little known film collection contains some of the cinema's greatest treasures. *Films in Review,* vol. 4, no. 8, October 1953, p. 416– 421.

MORSCH, Lucile M. Cataloguing, p. 193–201. (In Sixty years of 16mm film, 1923–1983, ed. by Forrest Alter et al. 1954).

POLITICAL AND ECONOMIC PLANNING TRUST. The British Film Industry; a report on its history and present organisation with special reference to the economic problems of British feature film production, May 1952. Supplements.

REPORT OF A CONFERENCE ON INTERNATIONAL STANDARDS FOR FILM CATALOGUING. Library of Congress Information Bulletin, vol. 12, no. 13, March 1953, p. 14. Announcement.

REUTERS LIBRARY. Reuters Library Drill Book, June 1967.

RIDDLE, J. et al. Non-book materials : the organisation of integrated collections. Prelim. ed. Canadian Library Association, 1970.

SHARP, J. R. Cataloguing and Indexing *in* W. Ashworth. Handbook of Special Librarianship, 1962.

SHARP, J. R. Information Retrieval *in* W. Ashworth. Handbook of Special Librarianship, 1967.

SPOTTISWOODE, RAYMOND. Film and its techniques, 1963.

STEELE, Robert. The cataloguing and classification of cinema literature, 1967.

STONE, C. Walter. Planning for media within university buildings *in Library Trends,* vol. 18, no. 2, Oct. 1969.

STONE, Dorothy T. The first film library : a collector's hobby, it became a necessary part of early motion picture production. *Films in Review,* vol. 2, no. 7, Aug.–Sept. 1951, p. 29–35.

UNESCO. Department of Mass Communication. International rules for the cataloguing of educational, scientific and cultural films. Preliminary edition, 1956.

UNESCO. Reports and Papers on Mass Communication, no. 35, 1962, p. 66. World Film Directory.

UNITED STATES. Library of Congress, Descriptive Cataloguing Division. Rules for descriptive cataloguing ·for the Library of Congress : motion pictures and filmstrips. 2nd preliminary edition. Washington. The Library, 1953.

WHATMORE, Geoffrey. News Information, 1964.

WORLD DIRECTORY of Stockshot and Film Production Libraries. International Film and Television Council, 1969.

YOUNG, Colin. An American film institute : a proposal. *Film Quarterly,* vol. 14, no. 4, Summer 1961, p. 37–50.

INDEX

Abbreviations, 80, 86, 134
Accessioning, 55, 109, 238
Accession numbers, 114, 115—17
Acetate film, 51, 178, 181, 190
Acquisition, 24
Acquisition number, 55
Added entries, 133, 143, 145, 170
Administrative staff, 193, 206, 215
Advertising, 17
Air conditioning, 179, 183, 213, 226
Alphabetical indexes, 159, 165
Alphebetico classed indexing, 166, 168—174
Analytical entries, 28, 128
Angle shots, 81
Anglo American Cataloguing Rules, 110, 144—5
Aperture cards, 97, 98
Archives, 41, 46, 118, 177, 197, 236
Association of Broadcasting Staffs, 205
ACTT (Association of Cinema and Television Technicians), 205, 206, 208
ASLIB (Association of Special Libraries and Information Bureaux), 208, 258
ASLIB Audio Visual Group, 258, 262
ASLIB Film Production Librarians Cataloguing Rules, 141—44, 262, 263
Association of British Library Schools, 262
Audio visual librarianship, 209
Assembling, 23
Authority file, 146
Automation, 64

Back projection, 17
Bobbins, 58, 61, 63, 185

Breakdown: film, 70
British Film Institute, 20, 25
British Industrial and Scientific Film Association, 102, 259
British National Film Catalogue, 102, 259, 264
British Universities Film Council, 102, 259
Brittle film, 187

Can numbers, 58, 92, 116
Cans, 59, 61, 120—4
Card catalogues, 131
Catalogues, 102, 113, 139, 154—5
Cataloguing see also Indexing, 74, 106—48, 149—50, 261, 264, 265
Cataloguing codes, 132—45
Cataloguing staff, 113, 200, 206, 209, 216, 266
Catchwords, 170
Classification schemes, 149
Central Film Library, 102
Cinematheque Francaise, 21
Classification schemes, 149, 163—5, 262
Classification index, 165
Classified indexing, 163, 166
Clerical staff, 194
Collation, see also Physical format, 111, 135, 142
Colour film, 35, 52, 59, 71, 178, 181, 186, 191, 229, 249, 254—5
Combining records, 99, 118
Commentaries, 28, 86, 90, 112
Compilation films, 79
Complete film, 35
Contact printing, 8
Continuing selection, 44
Continuing use, 233
Continuous printer, 68
Contracts, 238, 241—6

Copyright, 22, 26, 41, 230, 236—41, 266
Cores, 58
Cost, 42
Country of origin, 106, 121, 155
Credits, 77—8, 110, 122—3, 135, 140, 154
Current selection, 44
Cuts, *see* Offcuts
Cutting copy, 54

Daily storage, 93, 95
Damage, 207
Date index, 38, 107, 122, 155
Date of event, 108, 122
Date of transmission, 55, 95, 102, 114, 116, 117, 122, 156
Descriptive cataloguing, 110, 114, 119, 139, 140, 261
Destruction of stock, 243
Dialogue, 83
Dictionary indexing, 168
Directors, 107
Distribution agreements, 238
Distribution charges, 233
Distribution libraries, 20, 21, 29, 41, 46, 53, 60, 66, 70, 71, 115, 154, 188, 191, 197, 213, 220, 224, 236, 246, 259
Distributors, 112, 121
Documentary film, 14, 17, 23, 36, 107
Documentary film libraries, 23, 153
Duplicate negatives, 68, 177, 190
Duplicating film, 71
Duplication; selection, 34
Duration, 79

Edited film, 54
Edge numbers, *see* Key numbers
Education and use of film, 17, 125, 258
Education libraries, 29, 41, 51, 154, 213, 224, 236
Educational Foundation for Visual Aids, 102
Electronic video recording, 253
Emulsion, 182, 186
Enquiry records, 72
Enquiry staff, 29, 195, 198, 217
Establishing shots, 81
Evaluations, 125, 139, 140

Examination, 62, 70—1
Expenses, 224

Faking, 15
Feature films, 14, 17, 23—4, 107, 110
Feature libraries, 23—4, 37, 50, 54, 66, 91—2, 115, 118, 153, 198
Filing : documentation, 90, 119, 134, 156, 159, 160, 161, 165, 173
Filing cabinets, 219
Filing clerks, 194
Filing guides, 94, 131, 166
Film cement, 60
Film inspection machines, 21, 26
Film movement, 46, 63—4, 72, 90, 100
Film numbers, 55, 56, 70, 77, 115—7, 124
Film preparation, 63, 67
Filmostat, 187
Fine grain positives, 34, 68
Footage, 76, 78, 233, 243
Foreign names, 158
Furniture, office, 221, 226

Gauge, 50, 123
General view, 80
Government film libraries, 24
Government research film libraries, 13, 25

Headings : cataloguing, 106—10, 114
HELPIS, 259
Hire charges, 227
Hire libraries   *see*   Distribution libraries
     Educational libraries
History : film libraries, 20
Horizontal storage, 180
Humidity, 177, 182, 183

Imperial War Museum, 20
Imprint, 111, 136, 137, 140
Income, 224, 226—7
Indemnity clauses, 244
Indexing, 18, 23, 24, 25, 28, 49, 62, 73
Indexing systems, 152
Information retrieval, 29, 92, 149, 257
Initials (filing), 172
Inner London Education Authority, 102

International Federation of Film Archives, 21, 26, 181, 263
International Film and Television Council, 263
International Television Council, 208
In-training, 208
Irreparable damage, 33, 186
Issue number, 55, 116
Itemised storage, 91–2

Joiners, 60
Junking, 31

Key numbers, 70, 124, 143, 229
Kodak Museum of Photography, 21

Laboratory costs, 25, 228, 230, 242
Laboratory order forms, 67
Laboratory printing, 65, 68–70, 228, 256
Lateral filing systems, 94, 219
Leader film, 58, 61, 185
Length, 27, 36, 123
Library Association, 262
Library of Congress, 260
Library of Congress Cataloguing Rules, 137–9
Library schedules (sales), 245–6
Location index, 38, 107, 121, 150, 156, 160
Location numbers, 92, 109, 114, 116
Long view, 80

Magnetic sound, 69, 179
Maintenance costs, 25
Matching key numbers, 70
Mechanised retrieval, 88, 91, 129, 130, 174–6
Medium view, 80
Microfiche, 97
Microfilm, 88, 93, 96–7, 218, 257
Microfilm equipment, 98–9
Mobile storage, 95
Monochrome film, 35, 52, 59
Multiple copies, 239
Multiple entry, 128
Museum of Modern Art, 21
Music, 83

Name indexes, 157, 161
National archives, 20, 25, 43, 192
National Council for Educational Technology, 259, 262

National Association of Technical and Kinematograph Engineers, 205
National Film Archive, 21, 107, 181, 192, 236, 259
National Film Archive Cataloguing Rules, 135, 261
Negative film, 35, 53, 59, 68, 179, 190
Newsfilm, 16, 17, 18, 27, 28, 54, 86, 107, 109, 120, 133, 136, 142–3, 207
Newsfilm libraries, 20, 26–7, 37–8, 45, 47, 51, 53, 74, 92, 107, 110, 115, 118, 121, 124, 133, 153, 155, 191, 197, 198, 203, 213, 224, 227, 234, 250, 263, 265
Newspapers, 101, 103
Newsreel, 27, 55, 79, 86, 99, 116
Newsreel libraries, 26–7
Nitrate film, 51, 61, 178, 179, 181, 186, 190, 249, 254
Notes : cataloguing, 124, 136, 138, 140

Objective description, 82
Offcuts, 48, 54, 57
One-use, 233
Open entry, 139
Open racking, 180, 254
Optical printer, 69
Optical sound, 69
Overhead expenses, 224–6

Perfect copies, 112
Perforations, 182, 187, 188
Periodicals, 102
Personalities, 82
Personality index, 41, 107, 150, 151, 156–9
Photocopying, 95–6, 219
Photographs, 17, 104
Physical format, 85, 111, 123, 137, 140, 142, 145
Physical properties of film, 18, 117
Planning, 211–23, 266
Plastic bags, 60, 184
Plastic cans, 184, 254
Positive film, 34–5, 53, 59, 68, 179, 190
Precis shotlist, 88, 120
Preplanning, 211
Preservation, 71, 177, 186–92, 265
Press cuttings, 92, 103

Press tapes, 103
Processing charges, 227, 28, 262, 266
Producers, 106
Production credits, 77, 122—3, 153, 154
Production libraries, 20, 60
Production numbers *see* Film numbers
Production records, 55, 58, 59, 90, 99, 100
Production statement, 121, 142
Projection prints, 177
Projection speed, 123
Projectors, 66, 69
Propaganda film, 15

Qualifications (staffing), 204
Quality : selection, 32

Racking, 183
Recruitment of staff, 193
Reference material, 90, 100—5
Refile, 72
Relevance : selection, 36—41
Reparable damage, 190
Research film, 15
Research libraries, 13
Reshooting material, 16
Restoration : film, 186
Retrospective selection, 45, 46
Reuse of film, 13, 14
Reversal printing, 69
Review copies, 53
Rota service, 238—9
Royalties, 227, 230, 234, 243, 262, 266
Running time *see* Duration
Rushes, 54
Rust, 184

Salaries, 203—5, 225
Satellite recordings, 33
Scratch prints, 66, 229
Scratches : damage, 190
Scribing film 56, 70
Search fees, 227, 255
Secondary sources, 74, 111—2, 113
Sections, 65, 117, 29
See also references, 160, 161, 162, 172
See references, 134, 159, 162, 172
Selection, 26, 28, 31—49, 265

Selection : stockshots, 49
Selection staff, 95, 197, 217
Separation negatives, 178, 181, 191, 254
Separation of stock, 135, 178
Sequence listing, 83
Sequence lists, 73
Sheaf catalogues, 129
Shift working, 205
Shipping, 70
Shooting ratios, 36, 45, 48
Shot description, 81—2
Shotlisters, 113, 266
Shotlisting, 73—89, 100, 265
Shotlists, 73, 84—7, 90, 91, 93—4, 97, 100, 106, 113, 114, 120, 219, 261
Show copies, 22, 24, 52, 53, 191, 255
Shrinkage, 187
Site, 213, 214—5, 226
Slides, 104
Sound, 50, 52, 83—6, 138, 143, 179, 190, 229
Source material on film, 16
Space, 31, 218, 254
Spare prints, 54, 57—8
Splicers *see* Joiners
Spools, 58, 61, 184, 185
Staff manual, 148
Staff training, 207, 208—10, 256
Staffing, 193—210, 261, 266
Standardisation, 14, 87, 109, 131—2
Step printing, 69 26, 28, 31—49, 265
Stills, 104
Stockshot film libraries, 124, 151, 197, 227, 259, 264
Stockshot selection, 36, 217
Stockshots, 18, 23, 24, 30, 36, 38, 48, 49, 107, 115, 133, 143
Storage : documentation, 100—3, 218
Storage : film, 51, 52, 71, 177—85, 188, 212, 219, 226, 254, 265
Storage of film : permanent, 56 : temporary, 58
Stretch printing, 71
Sub-standard film, 249
Subject headings, 169—70, 171
Subject indexing, 39, 107, 114, 121, 150, 153, 154—5, 162, 172—3
Summaries, 124, 136, 138
Supplied title, 120

Technical staff, 195, 215
Telerecordings, 33, 123, 250
Television, 27, 50
Television and reuse of film, 17
Television libraries, 29, 43—4, 45, 93, 116, 198, 213, 224, 263
Temperature, 177, 181
Thesaurus, 165
Titles, 60, 75, 107, 108, 109, 113, 119, 133, 135, 137, 140, 141, 145, 154
Tracings, 124
Tracking shots, 81
Transcripts, 83, 84
Type of shot, 79

Ultracleaning, 186
Unedited film, 44, 54, 115, 179
Unesco, 260, 261, 263
Unesco Cataloguing Rules, 139—41
Unions, 205
Unit entry, 127—8

Universal Decimal Classification, 166
Usage restrictions, 42, 237, 244
Users guide, 147
Users, film, 231—3

Vault staff, 195—7
Vaults, 51, 178—80, 213, 254
Ventilation, 183
Vertical storage, 180
Videotape recordings, 29, 30, 33, 51, 249, 254
Viewing : staff, 65, 74, 75, 113
: users, 64, 65, 217, 220, 255
Viewing machines, 65—6, 75—6, 216, 220
Visible indexes, 129

Waste bins, 60
Winding benches, 62, 215, 226

Xerography, 96

Zoom shots, 81